ONE FOR THE BOOKS

ONE
FOR THE
BOOKS

Joe
Queenan

VIKING

VIKING

Published by the Penguin Group

Penguin Group (USA) Inc., 375 Hudson Street,
New York, New York 10014, U.S.A.
Penguin Group (Canada), 90 Eglinton Avenue East, Suite 700, Toronto,
Ontario, Canada M4P 2Y3 (a division of Pearson Penguin Canada Inc.)
Penguin Books Ltd, 80 Strand, London WC2R 0RL, England
Penguin Ireland, 25 St Stephen's Green, Dublin 2, Ireland
(a division of Penguin Books Ltd)
Penguin Group (Australia), 707 Collins St., Melbourne,
Victoria 3008, Australia (a division of Pearson Australia Group Pty Ltd)
Penguin Books India Pvt Ltd, 11 Community Centre,
Panchsheel Park, New Delhi–110 017, India
Penguin Group (NZ), 67 Apollo Drive, Rosedale, Auckland 0632,
New Zealand (a division of Pearson New Zealand Ltd)
Penguin Books, Rosebank Office Park, 181 Jan Smuts Avenue,
Parktown North 2193, South Africa
Penguin China, B7 Jaiming Center, 27 East Third Ring Road North,
Chaoyang District, Beijing 100020, China

Penguin Books Ltd, Registered Offices: 80 Strand, London WC2R 0RL, England

First published in 2012 by Viking Penguin, a member of Penguin Group (USA) Inc.

1   3   5   7   9   10   8   6   4   2

LIBRARY OF CONGRESS CATALOGING IN PUBLICATION DATA
Queenan, Joe.
One for the books / Joe Queenan
p. cm
ISBN 978-0-670-02582-4
1. Queenan, Joe—Books and reading. 2. Books and reading—United
States. 3. Books and reading—Psychological aspects. I Title.
Z1003.2.Q44 2012
028'.9—dc23
2012015087

Printed in the United States of America
Set in Caslon 540 LT Std
Designed by Francesca Belanger

To Skip McGovern, Lover of Books

Contents

CHAPTER ONE

Great Expectations

The average American reads four books a year, and the average American finds this more than sufficient. Men who run for high office often deem such a vertiginous quota needlessly rigorous, which is why they are sometimes a bit hazy on what Darwin actually said about finch beaks and can never remember which was Troilus and which was Cressida. I am up to speed on both. Yet I find this no cause for celebration, much less preening. For though I read at least a hundred books a year, and often twice that number, I always end up on New Year's Eve feeling that I have accomplished nothing.

I read books—mostly fiction—for at least two hours a day, but I also spend two hours a day reading newspapers and magazines, gathering material for my work, which largely consists of ridiculing nincompoops and scoundrels. I read books in all the obvious places—in my house and my office, on trains and buses and planes, in public parks and private gardens—but I have also read them at plays and concerts and prizefights, and not only during the intermissions. I have read books while waiting for friends to get sprung from the drunk tank, while waiting to have my meniscus repaired, while waiting for people to emerge from comas, while waiting for the Iceman to cometh. On more than one occasion I have buried my face in a book to take my mind off the lowlifes at the other end of the subway car in which I was inexplicably traveling at midnight, alone. I always carry a book I can page through while in line at the supermarket or during jury selection or at wakes of people I barely know and do not much care for. I read anywhere and everywhere, except in the bathroom, as I find this unspeakably vulgar and disrespectful to the person whose work one is reading, unless one is reading someone appalling.

I am enthralled by the concept of stolen kisses. In high school I used to prop up a copy of *Dr. No* or *The Spy Who Loved Me* against the back of the rhino-shaped youth who sat directly in front of me and delight in James Bond's spine-tingling adventures while the teacher was rattling on about the ablative case or the genetic fallacy or photosynthesis. During my summer vacations in college, I worked the graveyard shift in a bubble-gum factory, where I would volunteer to climb up into an overhead funnel and scour it, which the older, fatter, full-time employees were loath to do. Some of them feared heights; all of them feared ladders. Once ensconced in my stainless-steel crow's nest—whose filth or cleanliness no one down below was in any position to verify—I would stir up a bit of a ruckus every so often, creating the impression that I was getting on with the housecleaning job, and then settle in amidst the sugar and the debris and read F. Scott Fitzgerald all night.

In my twenties, when I used to load trucks at the A&P warehouse in a mirthless Philadelphia suburb, I would read during my breaks in the dead of night, a practice that was dimly viewed by the Teamsters I worked with. Just to be on the safe side, I never read Russians, existentialists, poetry, or books like *Lettres de Madame de Sévigné* in their presence, as they would have cut me to ribbons. During antiwar protests in the nation's capital back in the Days of Rage, I would read officially sanctioned, counterculturally appropriate materials like *Steppenwolf* and *Journey to the East* and *Siddhartha* to take my mind off Pete Seeger's banjo playing. I once read *Tortilla Flats* from cover to cover during a Jerry Garcia solo on "Truckin'" at Philadelphia's Spectrum; by the time he'd wrapped things up, I could have read *As I Lay Dying*. Often I have slipped away from picnics and birthday parties and children's soccer games and awards ceremonies to squeeze in a bit of reading while concealed in a copse, a garage, a thicket, or a deserted gazebo. For me, books have always been a safety valve, and in some cases—when a book materializes out of nowhere in a situation where it is least expected—a *deus ex machina*. Books are a way of saying: This room seems to have more than its fair share of bozos in it. Edith Wharton may be dead, but she's still better company than these palookas.

I have never squandered an opportunity to read. There are only twenty-four hours in the day, seven of which are spent sleeping, and in my view at least four of the remaining seventeen must be devoted to reading. Of course, four hours a day does not provide me with nearly enough time to satisfy my appetites. A friend once told me that the real message Bram Stoker sought to convey in *Dracula* is that a human being needs to live hundreds and hundreds of years to get all his reading done; that Count Dracula, misunderstood bookworm, was draining blood from the porcelain-like necks of ten thousand hapless virgins not because he was the apotheosis of evil but because it was the only way he could live long enough to polish off his reading list. But I have no way of knowing if this is true, as I have not yet found time in my life to read *Dracula*.

If it were possible, I would read books eight to ten hours a day, every day of the year. Perhaps more. There is nothing I would rather do than read books. This is the way I have felt since I started borrowing books from a roving Quaker City bookmobile at the tender age of seven. In the words of François Rabelais: *I was born this way.* And I know why I read so obsessively: I read because I want to be somewhere else. Yes, this is a reasonably satisfactory world that we are living in, this society in particular, but the world conjured up by books is a better one. This is especially true if you are poor or missing vital appendages. I was stranded in a housing project with substandard parents at the time I started reading as if there were no tomorrow, and I am convinced that this desire to escape from reality—on a daily, even an hourly, basis—is the main reason people read books. Intelligent people, that is. This is a category that would include people like my father, a Brand X prole who got started on the road to perdition early by dropping out of high school in ninth grade, thereby condemning himself to a lifetime of inane, soul-destroying jobs, but who was rarely seen without a book in his hands. He used books the same way he used alcohol: to pretend that he was not here, and if he was here, that he was happy for a change. I think this compulsion is fairly common. No matter what they profess to believe, no matter what they may tell themselves, most book lovers do not read primarily to obtain information or to while away the time or to better themselves or even, in the words of C. S. Lewis, to know that they are not alone. They read to escape to a more exciting, more rewarding world. A world where they do not hate their jobs, their spouses, their governments, their lives.

I have read somewhere between six thousand and seven thousand books in my life. I have not kept a running tally, but this seems like a reasonable ballpark figure. That number includes numerous books I have read more than once, like *Sentimental Education* and *Gulliver's Travels* and *A Tree Grows in Brooklyn*, and books I have read more than twice, like *The Iliad* and *Great Expec-*

tations and *The Sun Also Rises* and *Northanger Abbey.* (No, I cannot explain that one.) The list also includes a substantial amount of trash: mysteries, westerns, vacuous cut-and-paste jobs about pop stars, and unusual items my older sister Ree gives me every year at Christmas, titles like *Heinrich Himmler: The Sinister Life of the Head of the SS and Gestapo* and *The Butcher of Lyon: The Story of Infamous Nazi Klaus Barbie* and *Leni: The Life and Work of Leni Riefenstahl.* As a child, I once remarked to her that I didn't much care for the Thousand-Year Reich, and by the looks of things she took that comment to heart. Seven thousand books is a lot of reading, but the mysteries, the beach reading, and the out-and-out trash really puff up the numbers. And in any case it is nowhere near a record. Winston Churchill supposedly read a book every day of his life, even while he was saving Western Civilization from the Nazis. This is an amazing achievement, because by many accounts Churchill spent the Second World War completely hammered.

I did not start driving until the age of fifty-one. I am not sure why. I have never fully understood this biographical lacuna, but there it is. I suspect that the major reason I never bothered to learn was that I was too busy reading, and driving a car would do irremediable damage to a lifestyle I had come to enjoy. All those hours spent on buses, trains, trolleys, subways, jitneys, and even funiculars over the years add up; if a person spends just ten hours a week in his car—a lowball estimate, particularly in Texas or Montana or the Sudan—that works out to ten hours a week he could have spent reading, say, two books, or one hundred books a year, or six to seven thousand books over the course of a lifetime. It is probably no accident that William Shakespeare, Geoffrey Chaucer, Ralph Waldo Emerson, and Sappho all flourished in a pre-automotive age. And yes, I read less now that I drive more.

All my comments refer to the physical act of reading. I do not listen to audiobooks, for the same reason that I do not listen to baked ziti; it lacks the personal touch. Also, the person reading the book—usually a bit of a show-off—interpolates himself between me and the author, the same way gabby docents disrupt the emotional interplay between art lovers and Piero della Francesca. Moreover, audiobooks are usually condensations, and if I am truly interested in what I am reading, I want to read every word, even the ones that are not especially riveting.

I do not speed-read books; it seems to defeat the purpose of the exercise, which is for the experience to be leisurely and pleasant. When I was thirteen years old, I happened upon a mechanical device in the school library that could be wound up and set at various speeds, powering a small ruler that would slide down the page, like the iron door in the Temple of Doom, gradually obscuring one line after another, forcing the user to read faster. It was effective, I suppose, but maddening. It was the sort of thing that time-and-motion experts developed back in the Sixties. Speed-reading was all the rage when I was young; everyone was trying to master the skill. It would lead, we were ceaselessly assured by blithering ding-dongs who were not in a position to know, to fame and fortune. I never acquired that skill. I do not fast-forward through movies or meals, and I have rarely fast-forwarded through sex, just that one time in Morocco, so why should I fast-forward through books? The only books I might even consider speed-reading are bad books. But I am less and less likely to read bad books these days, only when I am paid to write about them, or when they are spectacularly bad, like when a solicitous hairstylist hands me her jailbird boyfriend's coming-of-age novel that turns out to be a contemporary retelling of *The Epic of Gilgamesh* set in Fort Wayne, Indiana. And even then I do not speed-read these books. I read them faster than I would read *The Charterhouse of Parma* or *The Idiot*, but I still read every word. This in itself may explain why I did not get further in life.

On average, I get through 150 books a year, not including titles I review for magazines and newspapers. I read less and less non-fiction these days, limiting myself to classics like *The Guns of August* and *Darwin, Marx, Wagner* and *The History of Western Philosophy* and *The Lives of the Twelve Caesars*, none of which I am opening for the first time. I never read books about current affairs. I almost never read biographies or memoirs, except if they involve madcap African explorers, George Armstrong Custer, or Klaus Kinski. I avoid inspirational and self-actualization books; if I wanted to read a self-improvement manual, I would try the Bible.

Unless paid, I never read books by or about businessmen or politicians, nor should anyone else. These books are interchangeably awful. The authors use the same ghostwriters and the same book doctors, and even the ones who purport to have written their own books somehow manage to develop a bilious, bromide-laden prose style they learned by reading knockoffs their colleagues paid industrious hacks to assemble for them. These books all sound exactly the same: inspiring, sincere, lethal. Reviewing them is like reviewing brake fluid: They get the job done, but who cares?

About half of the books I read are already on hand in my house or office; the remainder I check out of the library, receive as gifts, or purchase on my own account. I used to buy at least fifty books a year, but I stopped doing that a few years ago after I made a decision to read or reread every book I owned, and as there were still perhaps 250 unread books in my collection, plus another 200 or so that I wanted to reread, this would not leave much time to process new acquisitions. All told, three years' work would be called for here, and any new material would slow down production. So these days I buy no more than twenty books a year, almost always impulse purchases made at airports and train stations when I want to knock off something reasonably light and reasonably short. Often I select a title that was insanely popular a few years earlier: *Bel Canto, The Lovely Bones, Girl with a Pearl Earring.* Here I am referring to the types of books that thirtyish women devour at private swim clubs, often to the dismay of their drowning children. These women adhere to one inflexible cultural dictum: They read these books in the calendar year that they dominate the best-seller list, but if they have not finished them by the time the clock strikes midnight on December 31, they trash-can them. They then move on to the next fiendishly topical novel, one that frequently involves exotic brands of suburban-based autism or the improbable adventures of plucky ethnics. I once made plans to write a magazine article entitled "Last Man to Read *Corelli's Mandolin* Standing," but no one was willing to pay me for it.

I never read This Year's Book at the time everyone else is reading it; I like to wait a few years for the dust to clear. I usually get around to *Midnight in the Garden of Good and Evil* or *The Shipping News* or *Life of Pi* eventually, just as I usually get around to finding out what all that fuss was about string theory or Björk or the Falklands War. As a rule, these books are good without being great, and in a shockingly large number of cases they have been made into inept or laughable movies that unfairly detract from their hard-earned luster—*Atonement* being an obvious example. Ian McEwan, in my opinion, makes superb airborne reading. Just the best. Jonathan Franzen, by contrast, reads better on trains. I have never found anyone who is fun to read on a bus. Certainly not Marcel Proust.

. . . . .

Until recently, I was not aware of how completely books dominate my physical existence. Only when I started cataloguing my possessions did I realize that there are books in every room in my house, save for the bathrooms, and books in all three rooms in my office suite. My obliviousness to this fact has an obvious explanation: I am of Irish descent, and to the Irish, books are as natural and inevitable a feature of the landscape as sand is to Tuaregs. Because of this, we forget how out of place books look in the contemporary American household. Books no longer fit in with the décor; Inuit knickknacks make a bolder statement. When the English stormed the Emerald Isle under Cromwell in the seventeenth century, they took everything that was worth taking and burned everything else. Thereafter, the Irish had no land, no money, no future. That left them with words, and words became books, and books, ingeniously coupled with music and alcohol, enabled the Irish to transcend reality. This was my experience as a child. I grew up poor, and lots of times we had no food. Lots of times we had no heat. Lots of times we had no television. But we always had books. And books put an end to our misfortune.

Books are in my line of vision at all hours of the day and night. When you walk into my house, the first thing you see is books, and this is equally true when you enter my office, where the vestibule, save for a filing cabinet and a couple of paintings, contains nothing but books. There is a bookshelf in each of the three bedrooms in my house, and two bookshelves occupy pride of place in the walk-in closet that abuts the master bedroom. There are books in the garage, in the basement, in the attic, in the Camry, and in the Sienna. There are books everywhere, and with few exceptions they are very good books.

There are two large bookcases in the Lilliputian dining room in our house, which contains a partial set of encyclopedias we used to pull down and consult at dinnertime when the children were small and wanted to know what prompted Lady Godiva to canter off on her famous ride—it had something to do with taxes—and why the Iroquois were so inhospitable to prisoners. It was a set we had salvaged from the trash, and was missing six volumes, and only went up to the letter "t," but that was fine, because it forced the kids to work around the missing letters and be creative. Entries beginning with "z" did sometimes stump them. My wife recently said that with the children gone, we could finally get rid of those cumbersome objects, but I said no. Because of those books, my children grew up to be bright and inquisitive, while a lot of their peers grew up to be clowns. Social scientists, often based in Sweden, have conducted research among twins separated at birth and adopted siblings who have been reunited after many years of separation, and will tell you that surrounding your children with books will have no quantifiable effect on the molding of their personalities. Nature trumps nurture at every turn, they maintain. But, as is so often the case with social scientists, particularly the ones based in Sweden, they are wrong.

All told, I own 1,374 books, 400 of which are in my office. There are roughly 700 novels or collections of short stories or plays or books of poetry; the remainder deal with history, art, and music. My wife owns a couple hundred books, my children roughly the same number, left behind after they moved away. There are also about 72 coffee-table books or picture books, with titles like *The Sex Life of Flowers* and *Felix: The Twisted Tale of the World's Most Famous Cat.* This is a lot of books by the standards of the average person, but it is not a lot by the standards of true bibliophiles. Still, the average American visiting our house would find himself with enough reading material to get him through the next three hundred years, though it is unlikely that the average American would ever get around to reading Flaubert's unfinished novel, *Bouvard et Pécuchet*. I also own about 100 reference books, dictionaries, travel guides, and grammars, and perhaps 30 books I keep around as a joke. These include *Hoosier Home Remedies*, *The X-Rated Bible*, *Shakespeare's Bawdy*, *How to Start Your Own Country*, *Computer Gardening Made Simple*, *The Legal Whorehouse Owner's Handbook*, *Becoming a Jamaican*, and *Show Me the Good Parts: The Reader's Guide to Sex in Literature*. Several of these items are self-published. Most of them, in fact. They are silly books that arrived in the mail at various places I worked, and I will never read them, because they were never meant to be read, but they amuse me, so I display them prominently on my shelves. I have owned *Hoosier Home Remedie*s, which was sent to me by Purdue University Press for reasons I have never been able to decipher, for twenty-seven years. It would be pointless to get rid of it now.

There is also a small group of books I have held on to because they are so moronic or despicable that they could be of use in the future, were I ever called to testify before a federal tribunal investigating bad taste in American culture in the late twentieth century. These are stored in a metal case that I keep under lock and key in a hallway closet just outside my office, because I fear that they may emit thermonuclear radiation and contaminate the rest of the collection. They include Pat Robertson's demented early-Nineties screed *The New World Order*, in which the loopy televangelist theorizes that a number of Carter administration personnel decisions may have been influenced, at least indirectly, by minions of Satan. Also decomposing in that hallway septic tank is Geraldo Rivera's iniquitous autobiography, *Exposing Myself*. For many years I used to see Kurt Vonnegut shambling around the streets of Turtle Bay, on the East Side of New York, always with a disconsolate expression on his face. I could never figure out why he looked so miserable; he was, after all, one of America's most successful and admired novelists. Then one day, while reading *Exposing Myself*, I found out that Vonnegut had briefly been Geraldo's father-in-law. No worse fate has ever befallen any man.

I own several hundred hardbacks, some of them quite old, but most of my books are trade paperbacks. Today's trade paperbacks are packaged in a visually seductive fashion that tricks the reader into believing that the words within will be as enthralling as the artwork without. Usually, this is not the case; it is easier to paint a pretty picture or take an eye-catching photograph than it is to write a beautiful book. Picasso produced hundreds of great paintings; Ralph Ellison wrote one great novel. Art is hard, but literature is murder. Paulo Coelho's *By the River Piedra I Sat Down and Wept* and *Veronika Decides to Die* are elegantly packaged, but in each case, the cover has written a check that the book cannot possibly cash. By contrast, the original Scribner's cover of *The Great Gatsby* is, at least in my view, gaudy, confusing, and ugly. Yet the book itself is without equal.

With few exceptions, I write my name, the date of the purchase, and the city where the book was purchased on the inside flap of my books. If I have not written my name inside, it is because I have already decided that the book is not worth keeping. I do not write the name of the store. I suppose this is because writing "*Librairie du Vieux Quartier*" or "Prairie Lights" or "Tattered Cover" inside a book would forever conjure up joyful memories, whereas writing "Borders" would forever conjure up nothing. That said, I have bought an awful lot of books at Borders.

I do not collect first editions, and old books hold no great attraction for me. There is a copy of Gibbon's *The History of the De-*

cline and Fall of the Roman Empire in my library that has been sitting there for thirty-six years, since my wife gave it to me, shortly after we married. It was published in Halifax, West Yorkshire, in 1854 by Milner and Sowerby, and belonged to her grandfather, and has been quietly disintegrating for more than a century. It is brown and gold and hideous. The pages are covered with liver spots. It has a pungent smell, and when you pick it up, the binding starts to fall apart in your hands. For all I know, the book may be crawling with Late Victorian larvae. It is such a physically repellent object that when I set out to take a serious run at Gibbon's classic a few years ago, I purchased the three-volume Modern Library edition first. This way I could blithely underline interesting passages without fear of mutilating an irreplaceable heirloom, without having to worry about centuries-old insects wriggling out of the binding and infesting my well-appointed suburban home. As with Macaulay's multivolume *History of England*, I keep the books around as conversation pieces, though none of them have ever actually been the subject of any conversation, because I hide them away in the back room of my office and I never let anybody in there. I will never part with these treasures. It would be a crime to sell them or give them away or leave them behind. But I know that I will never read them.

I own no other books that match this description.

My books are organized not by subject matter but by texture and height. Hardbacks are shelved with hardbacks, trade paperbacks with trade paperbacks. Those sturdy little Bantam Classics—*Billy Budd, Heart of Darkness, Captains Courageous, Pudd'nhead Wilson*—are all bunched together. The only exceptions here are my 158 foreign-language books, most of them French, which are clustered together on their own shelves. The French sit next to the Spanish, which sit next to the Italian.

The Germans are quarantined off by themselves on another shelf. They get on the other books' nerves.

I sometimes read books that my friends have recommended, but I always buy my own copy. This is because I like to write in my books and fix the punctuation and make catty remarks like "Oh, really? Well, what about Mark Antony's surprise flanking action on the Plains of Philippi?" or "Just try saying that in the Bronx, Lizzie Bennet!" Flann O'Brien once devised a bespoke reading service that charged well-heeled illiterates a few pounds to "maul" their books and insert prescient comments in the margins to create the impression that they had read them. Things like "A point well taken!" and "Nonsense, nonsense!" and "Quite, but Bossuet in his *Discours sur l'histoire universelle* has already established the same point and given much more forceful explanations." That line of work would be right up my alley.

I also long ago developed the habit of underlining memorable passages in books and writing down any strange or unusual words on the inside flap of the back cover and then looking them up later. Words like "azoic" and "frottage" and "omphalos," odd, lapel-grabbing words that could never be used in mainstream journalism because they stop sentences dead in their tracks, as does any reference to Pär Lagerkvist. On occasion, I have even written notes to myself, or compiled to-do lists, or drawn up schedules, though usually I do this in poetry anthologies, where there is lots of white space. It is perhaps disrespectful to scrawl "Meet Annie LeCombe at Place Saint-Michel at 6:30" or "Learn German" or "Drastically reduce wine intake" in a book by Edna St. Vincent Millay, but years later, when I stumble upon these passages, I feel transported back in time to a safer, more congenial place. The past almost always seems cozier than the present, because you can no longer remember the fears and uncertainties that clouded your future at the time. And whatever the case, you were forty years younger. The unpleasant episodes in those long-vanished decades get edited out of our memories; we easily forget the war in Vietnam, the burning cities, the myriad assassinations, the women we used to date.

The delight I derive from writing in my books is one reason I do not own an e-book reader. To me books are talismans and *memento mori*, yes, but they are also toys. I like to play with my books, to mark them up, to give them a lived-in look. I like to stack them up on the shelf and move them about and rearrange them according to new parameters—height, color, thickness, provenance, publisher, author's nationality, subject matter, likelihood that I will ever read them. Then I put them back the way they were. I love to pull my books down off the shelf and read striking passages to baffled dimwits who have turned up at my house. From the moment I own a book, even before I open it to the first page, I feel that it has in some way changed my life. I treat my books the same way I treat my clothes or my shoes or my records: I use them. You cannot do any of this with a Kindle.

Though I write in books, I do not disfigure them by highlighting. I did this in college, but this deplorable cramming technique didn't work, primarily due to insufficient selectivity; if you start highlighting the memorable passages in *Macbeth*, you will end up highlighting everything. I do not write in books I borrow from the library, but I do jot down startling passages in a notebook. In *The Heart of the Matter*, Graham Greene writes: "In our hearts there is a ruthless dictator, ready to contemplate the misery of a thousand strangers if it will ensure the happiness of the few we love." In *The Picture of Dorian Gray*, Oscar Wilde writes: "There is always something ridiculous about the emotions of people whom one has ceased to love." In *Ordinary Love*, Jane Smiley writes: "I have given my children the two cruelest gifts I had to give, which are these, the experience of perfect family happiness, and the certain knowledge that it could not last."

Reading these passages has always made me want to commit them to paper, as if by doing so I could pay homage to the person who had written them. It is also, I believe, the best way to learn how to write, even if you end up being a terrible writer. Just as fledgling chess players memorize gambits they learned from Gary Kasparov and Bobby Fischer, young writers learn their craft by consciously or subconsciously imitating the rhythms and patterns of speech and turns of phrase of the writers they idolize. When I was growing up, most American sportswriters wrote prose that reflected the influence of Ernest Hemingway. Indeed, when the news of his suicide wafted in from Ketchum, Idaho, sportswriters everywhere were relieved that he was finally dead, because he did always on his typewriter the things they could only do sometimes. Aspiring human-interest columnists—invariably blowhards with "Mc" at the front of their names—learned to write by mimicking Jimmy Breslin. None of them ever learned anything from Faulkner.

I do not accept reading tips from strangers, especially from indecisive men whose shirt collars are a dramatically different color from the main portion of the garment. I am particularly averse to being lent or given books by people I may like personally but whose taste in literature I have reason to suspect, and perhaps even fear. I dread that awkward moment when a friend hands you the book that changed his or her life, and it is a book that you have despised since you were fourteen. People fixated on a particular book cannot get it through their heads that, no matter how much this book might mean to them, it is impossible to make someone else enjoy *A Fan's Notes* or *The Sot-Weed Factor* or *The Little Prince* or *Dune*, much less *One Thousand and One Places You Must Visit Before You Meet the Six People You Would Least Expect to Bump Into in Heaven*. Impossible. Not without assistance from the Stasi.

Close friends rarely lend me books, because they know I will not read them anytime soon. I have my own reading schedule, and as of this writing it has not included time for *Gravity's Rainbow* or *Pnin*. The only exceptions are books I have specifically asked to borrow: a well-regarded biography of Mark Twain, a book about the pivotal role Liverpool played in facilitating the Irish diaspora in the City of Brotherly Love. I borrow these books because I actually do intend to read them at the time, but once I get them home I experience an irresistible urge to start marking them up. Not wishing to insult my friends by failing to read a book I asked to borrow, but also not wishing to deface their property, I place them on the living room bookshelf, where they remain for years or, in some instances, decades. They sit there, right next to the first three volumes of Robert Caro's magnificent biography of Lyndon Baines Johnson and a paean to the underappreciated medieval rabble rouser Hereward the Wake and the collected essays of William Hazlitt, mesmerizing books I am planning to be mesmerized by just as soon as I have finished reading about Mark Twain and the Irish Quaker City diaspora.

I hate having books rammed down my throat. This may explain why I never liked school: I still cannot understand how one human being could ask another human being to read *Look Homeward, Angel* and then expect to remain on speaking terms. Saddling another person with a book he did not ask for has always struck me as a huge psychological imposition, like forcing someone to eat a chicken biryani without so much as inquiring whether they like cilantro. Giving a relative stranger a book is also a way of foisting an unsolicited values system on him. If you hand someone whose mother's maiden name was McNulty a book like *Angela's Ashes*, what you're really saying is "You're Irish; kiss me." I reject out of hand the obligation to read a book simply because I share some vague ethnic heritage with the author. Do you have to like Knut Hamsun just because you were born in Norway? Do you have to like Mario Vargas Llosa just because you grew up in Lima? Writers speak to us because they speak to us, not because of some farcical ethnic telepathy. Joseph Goebbels and Albert Einstein were both Germans; does that mean they should equally enjoy *Mein Kampf*? Perhaps this is not the example I was looking for. Here's a better one: One of my closest friends is a Mexican American photographer who grew up in a small town outside Fresno and now lives in Los Angeles. His favorite book is *Dubliners*.

When I do have books forced upon me, like Christmas puddings I will not eat or klezmer records I will not listen to, I stick them in a dark corner of one of my bookshelves, where they will rot forever. I have no qualms of conscience about doing so, because people who foist books upon other people don't really want them back. In most cases, they themselves have not read them, nor do they intend to. It has been scientifically proven by a research organization whose name currently escapes me that 87 percent of book buyers never get past the first two chapters of a magnificent but totally unreadable book like *A Brief History of Time* because books like this hurt their heads. In this 1991 best seller, Stephen Hawking suggests that the mere fact of having read his book "will increase the disorder of the universe by about twenty million million million million units—or about ten million million million times the increase in order in your brain." I, for one, would like to see his paperwork. The cheeky, irrepressible Hawking adds:

> We have no direct evidence as to whether the matter in other galaxies is made up of protons and neutrons or antiprotons and antineutrons, but it must be one or the other: there cannot be a mixture in a single galaxy because in that case we would again observe a lot of radiation from annihilations. We therefore believe that all galaxies are composed of quarks rather than antiquarks; it seems implausible that some galaxies should be matter and some antimatter.

This book sold eight billion copies. There are not eight thousand people on this planet who could understand that paragraph. There are not even eight hundred. There might be eight, but I am not one of them. People purchasing a book like this prop it up near the front door for a year or so, occasionally using it to make a postage stamp adhere more tightly or hurling it at a faithless spouse's skull, then hide it in the car trunk until they can off-load it on somebody who looks smart enough to read it. Lending books to other people is merely a shrewd form of housecleaning.

I enjoy discussing books, but I do not enjoy discussing them with the Great Unwashed. When book lovers have conversations with non–book lovers, it is the latter who set the conversational agenda. You can only discuss the books found in that microscopic subset that occurs at the intersection where your reading experiences overlap—*The Kite Runner, The Tipping Point*, or, in a worst-case scenario, *The Notebook*. Actually, the Bible is a worst-case scenario. I have spent countless hours over the years chatting with people about Anne Tyler, Tom Robbins, and David Lodge, all of them fine, accessible writers, none of them writers I especially enjoy.

Conversely, I have never discussed Juvenal's work with anyone. It's been years since anyone I know has mentioned John Donne in my presence. Decades go by without anyone breathing a word regarding Italo Svevo, Italo Calvino, or anybody else I admire named Italo. Among my favorite writers are Marcel Aymé, Ivan Doig, J. G. Farrell, Georges Bernanos, Thomas Berger, Junichiro Tanizaki, Robert Coover, and Jean Giono. I have never once been engaged in conversation about these writers. Perhaps I travel in the wrong crowds.

Book lovers are engaged with writers in a private communion that occurs in some vaporous cenacle of the mind. A friend once told me that he read Saul Bellow because Bellow seemed like the kind of guy who'd been around long enough that he might be able to teach you a thing or two. This is how I feel about my favorite writers. If you are an old man thinking of taking early retirement, you should read *King Lear* first. If you are a middle-aged man thinking of marrying a younger woman, consult Molière beforehand. If you are a young man and you think that love will last forever, you might want to take a gander at *Wuthering Heights* before making any long-range plans.

Book lovers feel that writers are speaking directly to them across the pages, perhaps even ministering to them, healing them. They sometimes forget that the writer is the one dispensing the Eucharist. People are always saying that the reason they like this or that writer is because the writer says in print exactly what the reader was thinking about a particular subject. In their view, the writer functions as some sort of psychic vessel, giving voice to the voiceless. I never feel this way. I feel that writers say things I would never have thought of saying, and in a way I would have never thought of saying them. I feel, as someone once said of America's finest poetess, that the only way to approach Emily

Dickinson is on your knees. Great writers say things that are so beautiful, the very act of repeating them makes life itself more beautiful. A city becomes a world when one loves one of its inhabitants, says Lawrence Durrell. People who believe in miracles, says Alice Munro, are never surprised when they happen. If we do meet again, then we'll smile indeed; if not, why then this parting was well made, says Shakespeare. Anyone who could mouth the words "You said exactly what I was thinking!" to writers such as this is a nitwit. There are lots of them about.

The confraternity of serious readers is united by a conviction that literature is an endless series of expeditions, some planned, some unplanned, all elating. None of us is doing this just to show off. Books do not always take us where we want to go, but they always take us places someone would want to go. Avid book readers are people who are at some level dissatisfied with reality. People in the nineteenth century fell in love with *Ivanhoe* and *Quentin Durward* because they disliked the age they were living through. Women in our own age read *Persuasion* and *Jane Eyre* and even *The Bridges of Madison County* because they imagine how much happier they would be if their husbands did not spend quite so much time at Myrtle Beach. Men devour *The Da Vinci Code* because they would like it if life were just a smidgen more complex, and if they were not married to someone obsessed with Pilates. Finding oneself at the epicenter of a global conspiracy involving both the Knights Templar *and* the Vatican would be a vast improvement over slaving away at the Bureau of Labor Statistics or being married to someone who is drowning in dunning notices from Williams-Sonoma.

Almost no one reads a book without some ulterior motive. Years ago, I started sending books to a woman in the Philippines named Evelyn. She is the lifelong pen pal of a close friend and operates some kind of store that periodically gets swept away by typhoons. She will read anything I send her: novels, biographies, sports books, magazines. Eighteen months after I send off the latest shipment, I receive an ecstatic letter announcing that the package has finally arrived, having languished for a year and a half somewhere until the thieves in the post office decided that it contained nothing of value and could thus be forwarded to its intended destination. My friend out in the Philippines, whom I have never met, reads books in part for pleasure, but she also reads them to help her forget that she operates a store that keeps getting washed away by typhoons. And that she lives in a world filled with illiterate thieves.

I have not always had a fetishistic relationship with my books. I have not always felt a need to possess them, to array them triumphantly on my shelves, to caress them, to revel in them. That came much later in life. When I was young, books were dull, bland, and generally quite ugly; they did not start to become attractive physical items until the 1980s. That is when I started collecting them in earnest. Or rather, that is when I started to amass them, as I do not consider myself a collector. Collectors obsess about first editions, and I do not. Collectors go to auctions, and I do not. Collectors feel emotionally transported if they can examine an original manuscript, and I do not. I do not care about autographed copies; I do not go scavenging for rarities, curiosities, out-of-print editions; I do not haunt antiquarian bookshops; and I do not trade anecdotes with wizened booksellers who once lit a Lucky Strike for Yevtushenko. I have never met an antiquarian bookseller who was not in some sense a priss or a fuddy-duddy or, in many instances, both. The most telling point is that I write in my books, which no collector would ever do. Even the most pristine, vintage edition of *Le père Goriot* would fetch a lot less on the market if it had wisecracks and asides scribbled everywhere. Unless, of course, the wisecracks were by Balzac.

I am not an autograph seeker. I have a few books in my library that have been signed by their authors, but with only a few exceptions these were gifts. I do not understand autograph seeking. I do not even understand the fascination with manuscripts. Once a neighbor showed me a folio copy of Shakespeare's plays that he had recently purchased. I didn't care. I tried to act as if I cared, but it was pretty obvious that I did not. Another time, while visiting the University of South Carolina, I was handed an original edited manuscript of one of F. Scott Fitzgerald's novels. It may have been *The Great Gatsby*; I honestly forget. The scholar displaying it was an expert on Fitzgerald's work. *The* expert. Clearly, he felt that he was treating me to a moment I would cherish forever, and I responded with commensurate enthusiasm. But the enthusiasm was faked. Seeing and even feeling the manuscript meant nothing to me. I had seen loads of manuscripts like this at the British Library and the Morgan Museum, and the only ones I remembered were Balzac's, because his manuscripts were a typesetter's nightmare. In the presence of such objects, I can never muster the emotions I am expected to muster. Perhaps this is because a manuscript or a musical score is a purely functional object, a set of symbols that convey ideas, while a painting is an object that in and of itself is beautiful. Or maybe it's because if I don't own a book, I don't care about it.

Still, that cannot explain everything. When I was assigned *The Great Gatsby* in high school, I surely must have read the famous passage:

They were careless people, Tom and Daisy—they smashed up things and creatures and then retreated back into their money or their vast carelessness, or whatever it was that kept them together, and let other people clean up the mess they had made . . .

This passage meant nothing to me at the time. But it would mean a lot to me years later, resonating with particular force after I had met people like Tom and Daisy Buchanan, those promiscuously generic prep-school types who are not overtly evil but who might as well be. Fitzgerald's words now grabbed me by the throat. He had written something about Americans that was so true it would be true forever. But seeing Fitzgerald's words in that manuscript in the archives at the University of South Carolina, whatever words they may have been, did not produce that same effect. It produced no effect at all.

With few exceptions, I do not possess the actual copies of the books that shaped my worldview as a young person. I lost them and bought new copies later. Most of those books—*Treasure Island, The Sea Wolf, Alice's Adventures in Wonderland*—were borrowed from libraries when I was young. So were a lot of ripping yarns set in Darkest Africa, where furloughed aristocrats impersonating gorillas were called upon to rescue smashing debutantes from Belgravia who had somehow fallen into the hands of stroppy cannibals. When we reconstruct our childhoods, we remember them as a series of cultural Himalayas, when in fact we spent most of our time cavorting in poorly lit ravines. I do have a vivid recollection of a child's edition of *The Iliad* that my father gave me when I was seven, complete with sepia-toned illustrations. I have always viewed *The Iliad* as the greatest book ever written, perhaps because the book was a gift from my father, but mostly because it is the greatest book ever written. It's helpful for small children if the first book that grabs their attention is also the first book that breaks their heart. It gets them in the mood for *Romeo and Juliet*, *Ethan Frome*, marriage, life. The great books of the world are like a gigantic warning from the Office of the Surgeon General: *Attention, readers: Even if you are a hugely successful, highly respected individual—a captain of industry, perhaps even a pillar of the community—this thing is going to end badly.* Yet much as I loved that sweet little book with its sepia-toned illustrations, I did not hang on to it. It disappeared from my life a long time ago, as did my father.

I regret that I no longer own the copies of *Madame Bovary, The Stranger, Native Son, The Loved One,* and *War and Peace* that I read in my teens and early twenties. I left some of these books at my parents' house, and they became casualties of war when my parents split up. They are long gone, and I do not know where they went. I do not even remember what they looked like. The books, that is. I wish I still had them, if only to go back and see which passages I underlined when I read them the first time around. To see if my perspective had changed. To see if they still took my breath away.

It is not surprising that so few books from my early life are still in my possession. I moved around a lot when I was young, and in the parlance of a dear friend, I adhered to the dictum "Travel right, but travel light." Basically, this meant to always ditch women before things got messy, but it worked well in other contexts, too. When I would light out for Texas or Paris or New York back in my twenties, I would always dump my belongings at my mother's house. She didn't care; the house was no more than a functional pigsty. But my mother also moved around a lot, and she subscribed to the same philosophy as my friend did, so most of my possessions from that era have vanished. She was definitely not the sentimental type; she did not go out of her way to hang on to baby pictures, so she certainly wasn't going to make any special effort to safeguard my copy of *La symphonie pastorale*.

Perhaps because so many books from my childhood disappeared, I have made a point of purchasing and clinging to those I have loved as an adult. I have kept every ticket to every concert I ever attended, and I have kept all of the books I truly worship since around the age of twenty-one. These are my *billets-doux*. Books as physical objects matter to me, because they evoke the past, because I find their presence emotionally enriching. A Métro ticket falls out of a book I bought forty years ago, and I am transported back to the Rue Saint-Jacques on September 12, 1972. A telephone message from a friend who died too young falls out of a copy of Henry Green's *Concluding*, and I find myself back in the Chateau Marmont on a balmy September day in 1995. A note I scribbled to myself in *Homage to Catalonia* in 1973 when I was in Granada reminds me to learn Spanish, which I have not yet done, and to go back to Granada. People who need to possess the physical copy of a book, and not merely an electronic version, are in some sense mystics. We believe that the objects themselves are sacred, not just the stories they tell. We believe that books possess the power to transubstantiate, to turn darkness into light, to make being out of nothingness. We do not want the experience of reading to be stripped of this transcendent component and become rote and mechanical. That would spoil everything.

I do not expect other people to lead their lives this way. They are free to download onto their e-readers books about strange worlds, strange planets, parallel universes where nine-eyed sea serpents pore over the Kabbala and blind marsupials join forces with deaf Valkyries to rescue high-strung albino virgins from the clutches of hermaphrodite centaurs. But by doing so, by refusing to patronize bookstores and libraries, by refusing to expose themselves to the music of chance, they have purged all the authentic, nonelectronic magic and mystery from their lives. They have rolled over and surrendered to the machines. This may be convenient, but that's all it is. All technology is corporate.

Certain things are perfect the way they are and need no improvement. The sky, the Pacific Ocean, procreation, and the *Goldberg Variations* all fit this bill, and so do books. Books are sublime, but books are also visceral. They are physically appealing, emotionally evocative objects that constitute a perfect delivery system. Electronic books are ideal for people who value the information contained in them, or who have vision problems, or who like to read on the subway, or who do not want other people to see how they are amusing themselves, or who have storage and clutter issues, but they are useless for people who are engaged in an intense, lifelong love affair with books. Books that we can touch; books that we can smell; books that we can depend on.

CHAPTER TWO

Face Without a Name, Bag Without a Number

I have not always had the best experiences in libraries. Some experiences have been good; some have verged on the criminal. One frosty morning in January 1988, I stopped by the New York Public Library's flagship Fifth Avenue branch to take in an exhibit entitled "William Wordsworth and the Age of English Romanticism." The exhibit included the original manuscripts of famous poems by Wordsworth, Coleridge, and other writers from the Romantic era, as well as drawings and paintings by their contemporaries Constable and Turner. I checked my shoulder bag at the coat-check counter, then ambled off to the exhibit hall. It was a splendid show. I spent about forty-five minutes inspecting the merchandise, then went back to the coatroom and handed my coat-check stub to the attendant.

"It's that gray canvas bag over there," I told her.

She took the stub but ignored what I'd just said, instead rummaging about disinterestedly in an overhead rack. A few seconds later she laid a white plastic bag on the table.

"That's not my bag," I said.

"You gave me this stub," she replied. "It matches with this bag."

"Then somebody put the wrong ticket on my bag," I explained. "My bag is that gray plastic one over there in the corner."

She was having none of it.

"Those bags have orange stubs; yours is pink," she said. She was getting a bit surly now. A line was forming behind me, so I figured I would raise my voice and try to gather some support from the hoi polloi, Jimmy Stewart style.

"No amount of conversation can turn this white plastic bag into my gray canvas bag," I said. *"I want my own bag."*

I got no support from the people behind me. I got the proverbial stony silence. In the eyes of those waiting for their own coats and bags, I was a nitpicker, a fussbudget, a jerk. The coat-check girl felt the same way.

"What are you waiting for?" she asked me.

"I'm waiting for you to give me my goddamn bag!" I said. "What do you think I'm waiting for?"

She stiffened. Our *tête-à-tête* was taking an ugly turn. In the parlance of the seasoned flunky, she had "a situation" on her hands here. She told me to step aside while she handled the other people in line. Then she reached for the phone.

"Security to the coatroom," she said.

Security soon arrived. Security was chunky, poorly dressed. Security was not happy to have been summoned. Security was dead serious.

"What's the problem here?" security demanded.

"She won't give me my bag," I said. "Someone mixed up the tickets. Look, I'm a writer—so all you have to do is look inside the bag and you'll find a bunch of stories I've written."

"Do you have any I.D.?" he asked. I did. When I had established my identity as Joseph M. Queenan, he circled behind the counter, eyeballed the controversial stub, and then looked directly at the vexatious white bag.

"This isn't your bag?" he asked.

"No. Mine is the gray one. It was a gift from the French government. Let's not go into the details. But if you look inside, you'll see a bunch of stories I wrote and this week's *New Republic*, open to a story about the underclass."

He walked over, grabbed my bag, opened it, ignored what I had just said about its other contents, and pulled out my checkbook.

"Is this your checkbook?"

"Yes."

"What bank?"

"Citibank."

"There's another name on it. Whose name?"

I told him the identity of the other person on the account. One Francesca Jane Spinner.

"Who's that?" he asked.

"My wife."

"Where's she?"

"At home with the kids."

"How do I know she's not upstairs?"

I wasn't sure what he was getting at here. Was he suggesting that somebody named Francesca Jane Spinner was the real owner of the disputed item, that she was upstairs visiting the Wordsworth exhibit, and that somehow I had learned the contents of her cheap-looking satchel, skulked off, tiptoed downstairs while she was not looking, and was now trying to spirit away her property without anyone being the wiser? Perhaps he believed that the bag contained the Hope Diamond or Sophocles' rough draft of *Oedipus at Colonus* or one of the few remaining copies of Hammurabi's Code.

"I don't bring my wife with me every time I go to the library," I told him. "We have a little arrangement. She does what she wants to do, and I do what I want to do. But we share the same checkbook."

He shook his head and turned away.

"You gotta call your wife," he said. "I'm not giving you the bag until I talk to her."

I went downstairs to a public phone booth and called Francesca. She wasn't in. This was in the days before cell phones, so there was no way to reach her directly. I was stuck. I would have to wait until she answered the phone to get my bag back. Typical. Every time I needed my wife to confirm her existence so I could retrieve my property from some overzealous coat-check personage, that was the day she decided to take the goddamn kids to the playground.

I went back upstairs.

"She's not in," I told the security guard.

"Can't give you the bag, then," he said.

"I want to talk to whoever's in charge."

"I'm in charge" was his response.

I thought about it for a second. Then I decided to go nuclear.

"Call the cops," I told him. "I'm not leaving till I get my bag. So call the cops."

Security did call the cops. Thirty minutes later, one of New York's Finest turned up. He was from central casting: medium height, mustached, Italian, world-weary, could have passed for Serpico. He also looked like a guy who didn't need any of this.

"What's the problem?" he asked.

"Somebody put the wrong stub on my bag, and now they won't let me have it back. It's that gray canvas bag with a maroon strap."

He walked over to my bag and opened it.

"Tell me what's inside," he said.

"The *Times*. An umbrella. A copy of *Commonweal*. A pair of gloves. They're gray."

He nodded.

"What else?"

I have to admit, I didn't see that one coming. I really thought the *Commonweal* remark would have closed the deal. The whole thing was like some insanely difficult entrance exam that the Amazing Kreskin had to pass in order to be admitted to the Harry Houdini School of Urban Prestidigitation. It was just a tad too comprehensive. But I wasn't giving an inch.

"A dental appliance in a green plastic case. Pea green. A white plastic Afro comb. This week's *New Republic*, open to a story by Robert Kuttner about the underclass . . ."

"Anything else?" he asked.

"Yes," I said. I realized now that even though I was six for six in the intra-library telepathic speculation department, they still didn't believe me. The more detailed and nuanced and precise my knowledge of the contents of the bag, the more obvious it seemed to them that this was all some kind of ingenious scam. But I had plenty more ammunition.

"A Tarrytown train schedule," I said. "From Grand Central Station. A Bic pen. Blue, if memory serves me well. In the side pocket with the zipper. A black folder with a dozen stories I've written. Look, if you just pull out the *Newsweek* story, it has my picture on it. The My Turn column, all the way up in the front. It's called 'Too Late to Say I'm Sorry.' It's about my alcoholic dad."

He transfixed me with his stare. *Yeah, right. You expect me to fall for the old headshot-in-*Newsweek *ploy? In a pig's eye, buster.*

So this is where things stood. At an impasse. A Mexican stand-off.

And then, from out of nowhere, salvation.

"Is this your checkbook?" he asked.

"Yes," I said.

"What are the names on it?"

"Joseph Martin Queenan and Francesca Jane Spinner. Citibank. 30 Wildey Street. Tarrytown, New York."

I paused. Then, for effect, I added: "And the zip code is one-zero-five-nine-one."

The cop turned to the security guard. His expression was a mixture of contempt and disgust.

"I think it's pretty obvious that it's his bag," he said. And he handed it over.

And so the Curious Case of the Face Without a Name, the Bag Without a Number was officially closed. In retrospect, the logic of the cop's interrogational style made itself clear to me. *Anyone* with reasonable prestidigitation skills could have guessed what was in somebody else's bag—even *Commonweal* and the white plastic Afro comb. That kind of stuff happened every day in the asphalt jungle. But not even the most resourceful plastic-bag heister could have pulled an obscure Westchester County zip code right out of thin air.

Later, in the safety of my home, I opened my bag and discovered that the *New Republic* piece had not been written by Robert Kuttner. It had been written by somebody else entirely. Whew—had I ever dodged a bullet on that one! A few weeks later, my account of this incident ran in *New York* magazine. Right after that I got a conciliatory note from New York Public Library president Vartan Gregorian apologizing for the rudeness and incompetence of his security personnel. He hoped I could find it in my heart to let this one pass. I could. He hoped that it would not poison the waters. It wouldn't. Just the same, I did not set foot inside that branch of the library for the next twenty years. I figured those two security guards were laying for me. And packing heavy.

I do not mean to suggest that my experiences at the 42nd Street library are typical of my dealings with these glorious institutions over the course of my life. And yet it is safe to say that after a promising start, libraries and I have not always seen eye to eye. When taking my first steps toward literacy, I lived in a neighborhood that had no public library. Luckily, the city of Philadelphia sent around a bookmobile that visited my street every week. It was, for all intents and purposes, a magic bus. Each Friday night I would borrow as many books as permitted, devour them, and come back the following week for more. They were mostly things like *The Call of the Wild*, *The Black Rose*, *A Journey to the Center of the Earth*, and *Swiss Family Robinson*, or books about chippy underdogs like Vercingetorix and the Count of Monte Cristo and Cochise. Simultaneously, I would read any palatable materials my sisters brought home, excluding obviously unsuitable items like *The Child's Mansfield Park* or *The Adventures of Trixie Belden*. Like many children growing up in crummy neighborhoods, I honestly believed that if I read enough books and learned the root causes of the War of the Austrian Succession and the location of the final resting place of the Persian tyrant Ahasuerus—sometimes known as Artaxerxes—I would one day come into possession of a demure but well-appointed three-bedroom Colonial, with two cars, two children, a white picket fence, and a spectacular river view. This is exactly what came to pass.

When I was eight years old, a brutal recession hit the nation, and my father lost his job. Shortly thereafter we were evicted from our house—a cute little redbrick affair—so we had to move to a housing project. The project was no picnic—the tenants, by and large, were not avid readers—but about a mile away there was a well-stocked public library. Unfortunately, the stately old stone building was at a considerable distance from our new home, and books were heavy, so I did not visit it anywhere near as often as I had visited the bookmobile.

Maybe another deterrent was at work here. The bookmobile had a driver and some sort of factotum in charge of checking out books and collecting fines. I recall nothing about this person's identity, physique, or gender, except that he or she must have been fairly inoffensive. The East Falls library, by contrast, was staffed by grumpy, autocratic, middle-aged women who seemed to dislike children. The crotchety librarian is a vicious stereotype, but like most vicious stereotypes, it is rooted in truth. You could sense the staff's animosity as soon as you walked in. *What, you again?* Maybe, sensing that we were from the housing project, they feared gunplay, though my sisters and I were fairly young for that sort of thing. Years later, when my children grew up directly across the street from the public library in Tarrytown, New York, they would form a strong bond with the patient, affectionate assistant children's librarian, Mrs. Firmin. A diminutive, theatrical Englishwoman who seemed to have matriculated from the Beatrix Potter Academy of Small-Town Librarian Charm, she would read them stories and sing songs and teach them crafts and play educational board games and host Saturday-afternoon get-togethers showcasing sporadically competent magicians and harmonica-brandishing folklorists and industrious clowns whose comedic reach too often exceeded their greasepainted grasp. The children reveled in these outings because, until the age of seven, children think that all adults know what they are doing, even the ones manhandling the harmonica.

I had no such formative experiences in East Falls: no magicians, no musicians, no clowns. The closest we ever got to edification or diversion or laughter was when my sisters and I sat through an interminable routine by a local TV personality named Chief Halftown. His act suffered from a dearth of variety, and he was a bit on the catatonic side. I long thought he was Polish, but learned years after the fact that he was a full-blood Seneca. His performance did little to elevate the reputation of Quaker City Native American television personalities.

There was another contrast between the bookmobile and the public library. The bookmobile had a finite number of books on hand, so you never felt intimidated or paralyzed by the possibilities presented to you. The public library, by contrast, had thousands of books bivouacked in rows that seemed to stretch forever. The presence of all those books that I would never have time to read discouraged and saddened me. But I also felt sorry for the authors. "No place affords a more striking conviction of the vanity of human hopes than a public library," wrote Samuel Johnson; "for who can see the wall crowded on every side by mighty volumes, the works of laborious meditations and accurate inquiry, now scarcely known but by the catalogue."

It also didn't help that so many of the books were atrocious. The problem in public libraries is that the wheat and the chaff are commingled. Especially today. Unlike museums, which conscientiously segregate the Bronzinos from the Bouguereaus, sticking the hideous paintings out in the stairwell, barely lit by forty-watt bulbs, where they can inflict no further damage on a society that has done nothing to merit such mistreatment, and where rodents or insects or mold might finally get to them, libraries jam everything together in one vast, alphabetically organized maw, with James Patterson sharing a shelf with Marcel Proust. Putting James Patterson next to Marcel Proust is like displaying Babe Ruth's uniform alongside Three Finger Brown's. It's as if the library expects some knucklehead, discovering that *Along Came a Spider* is currently out on loan, to declare, "Oh, well, I guess I'll just borrow *In the Shadow of Young Girls in Flower* instead."

But it's not just that libraries are filled with horrible books that I am never going to read. They are filled with books I have made a deliberate point of never reading. I am never going to read *Sister Carrie* or *An American Tragedy*. I tried Theodore Dreiser once, and I am not going back. James Gould Cozzens is out, as are John Galsworthy and Jean Rhys and any book connected in any way with the exploits of Studs Lonigan. I have read *The American, Washington Square, The Aspern Papers, Daisy Miller*, and *The Portrait of a Lady*, but I am not getting to *The Princess Casamassima* or *The Spoils of Poynton* in this or any other lifetime. I am not even sure I will get to *The Golden Bowl* or *The Wings of the Dove*. Still, the presence of these menacing titles on library bookshelves makes me nervous. It's as if they are stalking me, taunting me. *Think you're so smart, do you? Think you're so urbane and sophisticated? Well, we keep track of these sorts of things, and we know for a fact that you've never read* Go Down, Moses, The Birth of Tragedy, *or the* Collected Stories of V. S. Pritchett, *much less Madame de Lafayette's* La Princesse de Clèves *or* Freedomland. *You're not fooling anybody, pally. If you haven't read* Ulysses, *you're still a pathetic rube off the streets of Philadelphia. And you always will be.*

I am not afraid of these books. I do not fear their gibes and threats. What I do fear is that they may one day catch me in an unguarded moment and overpower me. Then, I will find myself bound, gagged, and bolted to the floor in the musty library reading room, and forced to suffer through the complete works of William Styron or, if my assailants are in a particularly sadistic mood that day, all four volumes of *Joseph and His Brothers*. How I will turn the pages, fettered like that, I have not yet determined. I am not being facetious when I say that some of those unread masterpieces may have it in for me. I honestly believe that they are preparing an ambush, with the seemingly harmless Gertrude Stein luring me into a box canyon where the murderous Alice B. Toklas can take my scalp. These books think that if they can catch me at just the right moment, I will break down and finally read *Middlemarch* from cover to cover in one sitting. Dream on, public libraries. Dream on.

After we moved to a new and better neighborhood when I was twelve, I stopped using libraries on a regular basis. By this point my older sister Ree was starting to buy paperbacks, and I was getting old enough to read my father's books. Many of these were *Reader's Digest* condensations of best sellers by Edwin O'Connor and A. J. Cronin and Morris West, solid middlebrow writers of a type that has largely ceased to exist. Around the age of thirteen I began buying books, in part because I liked the idea of seeing them up there on the shelf after I was done with them, but also because I was already getting into the habit of underlining things and writing in my books. So for most of my high school years, libraries got shunted to the side.

Things changed in college, where I spent sizable portions of my time in the tiny, fetid smoking room of the school library. I have no idea why; it was not a good place to study. It may have been in the desperate hope of meeting girls, though the haze in the room was so thick that I would not have been able to tell what they looked like had they even been there. The college I attended did not go co-ed until my senior year, and the girls from nearby all-girl colleges who liked to hang out in a smoke-filled room at an all-male Catholic college miles and miles from their campuses—not a physics major in the bunch—were not really the kinds of girls I wanted to meet. Or were they?

It is all a blur today.

During my summer vacations, I camped out at the central branch of the public library in downtown Logan Square, though mostly I passed my time listening to jazz. Charles Mingus, Ornette Coleman, and Sun Ra, an influential local screwball whose arrangements were heavily influenced by a visit to Saturn relatively early in his career, were right at the top of my playlist. It was here that I first heard the Duke Ellington–John Coltrane rendition of "In a Sentimental Mood," the most beautiful recording ever made. The library had a rooftop restaurant, with a terrace that looked out on the city's nonexistent skyline; the eatery always struck me as the quintessence of class and elegance, even though the food was barely edible. The restaurant was actually more like a cafeteria, but it was bathed in sunshine. Years later I came back and gave a speech on the top floor of that library. I talked about the many happy hours I had spent in that building, seeking asylum from my violent, alcoholic father, remarking that it was more than a repository of wisdom; it was a hideout. With a rooftop restaurant. It was my favorite place in the City of Brotherly Love. Even though my affection didn't have all that much to do with books. It was mostly about jazz.

There are only a few other experiences that stand out in my memory. In Jenkintown, a genteel Philadelphia suburb where I met my wife, I used to borrow lots of books from the local library. It was a classic nineteenth-century structure filled with busts and portraits; you got the feeling that William Dean Howells could stroll in at any minute, testily demanding when his reserved copy of *The Blithedale Romance* might be available. Like many classic nineteenth-century structures, it was actually built in the early

1900s, though the library itself was founded in the middle of Thomas Jefferson's first administration. Edith Prout, the cataloguer who worked there when I was twenty-three, is still there; it is the only job she has ever had. The name Prout is Cornish—her grandfather hails from Saint Tudy, as did Captain Bligh—though if it had just one more letter, it would be quite spectacularly French.

Only in libraries do people stay in the same place for so long; even churches and urban crime syndicates move the personnel around. I have always felt that there is something courageous about librarians. Because the staff is asked to man the same barricades in the same fortress for so many years—in Edith's case, forty-five—the library becomes a community touchstone, a faint beacon of light that survives calamity after calamity as the darkness of contemporary American culture threatens to extinguish it. Librarians are always there when you come back to visit, almost as if they were expecting you. I don't know how they feel about all this. Anytime I am in the general vicinity of Jenkintown, I stop by and have a nice little chitchat with Edith. She is still very wry, very censorious, very independent-minded, just as I remembered her from my youth, which was also her youth, and she always seems glad to see me. She still likes the fact that unusual people with unusual requests walk through the door every day, even though some of them have to be hustled right back out. The library owns one of my books, which is very civil of them, though Edith herself isn't all that taken with my work. Too cynical, she says. Too snarky. The librarian who did enjoy my writing, she notes, passed away a few years back. When Edith passes along information like this, I can never tell whether she is being informative or wry or censorious. Probably wry.

. . . . . .

I have spent almost half my life in the village of Tarrytown, thirteen miles north of the Bronx, and for ten of those twenty-nine years I lived with my wife and two children across the street from the Warner Library. The Warner Library is an imposing stone building with massive windows and high ceilings and comfy wing chairs and gargantuan heating bills. Construction started in 1928, and the library opened the following year. That was also the year it added an oculus. Nineteen twenty-nine was not a good year for libraries, much less oculuses. Outside the building stands a tree with a plaque bearing my children's names. My wife planted the tree when the children were small, out of gratitude to the angels of mercy who worked inside, because when my entitled, overstimulated kids were growing up, they literally lived in the library, thereby preventing my wife and many other mothers like her from going insane.

I have gone through periods when I use the Warner Library on a regular basis and periods when I do not step inside it for months. Many of my visits are to donate review copies that have come across my desk. They are usually about business or politics, often instant hagiographies written by dopes in the service of doofuses. These items are sometimes added to the permanent collection, but more often than not they are sold to raise money at the annual book sale. In donating titles like *Confessions of an Economic Hit Man* and *Shackleton's Way: Leadership Lessons from the Great Antarctic Explorer*, I have never been entirely convinced that I am doing anyone a favor. Least of all Shackleton.

On the bulletin board at the entrance to the building, there is always a list of language classes, investment seminars, films, concerts, and other upcoming events. Library events scare me, as they provide refuge for local historians, fabulists, tellers of tall tales, historical reenactors, and even dream weavers. Not to mention the single most feared creature on the planet: the self-published poet. Libraries, perhaps out of pity, schedule visits by local authors who reimagine *The Legend of Sleepy Hollow* set in contemporary times. The flyer announcing the reading says: "I don't think that Washington Irving, America's first great satirist, would mind that someone had decided to rouse him after so many years of placid entombment and allow him to experience the faded glory of the 1960s."

Yes, he would.

Because I soon became reasonably well-known in our town, a dim star in an otherwise dark galaxy, and was often seen in the downstairs children's library with my kids, the library director, Florence Kane, constantly tried to persuade me to give a talk there. She was the product of a bygone era, one of those blustery, larger-than-life invincible women who always seemed to be bustling about, in a way women of today never bustle. Though I liked her very much, I resisted her overtures, telling her that no one will come out to hear a local writer they can just as easily hear holding forth at the nearby diner unless the writer is Dr. Phil or Jane Austen. What's more, events where writers discuss their careers always attract amateurs, who think that successful writers are only successful because they got all the breaks or because their father was a famous writer. Only the second part is true.

The problem with living in a small town is that your neighbors will eventually wear you down. Mrs. Kane kept begging and begging and begging, saying how much it would mean to her personally if I would give an informative talk. So one spring I caved in and agreed to give a speech explaining how to become a freelance writer. The speech was not well received, because while there are rules about launching a writing career that must be strictly adhered to, the rules do not apply to freelance writers. Also, you have to be able to write. Nobody wanted to hear that. The speech was given the same night a public hearing about the fate of a concrete-crushing plant down by the river was held in the village hall. The debate pitted townies against newcomers and was pretty nasty. Trouble had been brewing for years; now had come the time for a reckoning. The village hall was adjacent to the library; several hundred people attended. Twelve people came to my reading, including a man from the Rotary Club who only popped by to ask if I would give a similar presentation at the club's get-together the following month. I would not, as I have long subscribed to the credo *Pro bono? No bono.* But a few years later, even he got the best of me.

Mrs. Kane was not in the audience the night of my talk; she had flown to Paris for the week. She later told me how sorry she was that she had missed my speech, but I think she made the right choice in flying to Paris. I told her that on the whole the outing had not been terribly successful and would not be repeated. But Mrs. Kane was a deceptively determined woman, and a few years later I agreed to appear on a panel with several other local writers. This time, among other things, we discussed the importance of finding an agent, doing so in a room full of aspiring writers who would never need an agent because their careers would never get beyond the aspirational stage. I think that may have been the night the Yankees won their first World Series in eighteen years.

I have given no other talks since then.

A few years ago, several people in my town asked if I would like to join a book discussion club. We would vote on a book, read it, convene at the library, discuss it, and then retire to a local brasserie for a few beers. I left town for about six weeks, disconnected my phone, stopped answering e-mails, and told people that I had a weird retinal pigmentation disease that made it impossible for me to read books. Especially books like *The Curious Incident of the Dog in the Night-Time.*

I have always had an aversion to book clubs. I have always had an aversion to people who belong to book clubs. I would rather have my eyelids gnawed on by famished gerbils than join a book club. Book clubs pivot on the erroneous, egotistical notion that the reader has something to add to the conversation. What might that be? A book is a series of arguments between the author and the reader, none of which the reader can possibly win. This is especially true if James Joyce is involved. The reading experiences that book club members share are not intimate; they are generic. Participants want to connect with other people who feel exactly the same way they do about a book. Book discussion clubs have almost nothing to do with reading. This may be why they so rarely choose good books. Participants are seeking unanimity, and good books do not invite unanimity. They invite discord, mayhem, knife fights, blood feuds. The people I know who attend book clubs are generally intelligent, but they are rarely what I would call interesting. They want something out of books that is not there.

One of the things about book clubs that I find extremely annoying is those "Questions for Discussion" that appear at the back of books. I first noticed this after reading Andreï Makine's novel *The Crime of Olga Arbyelina.* This is the hard-luck saga of a Russian émigré with a hemophiliac son who pops up in France after World War II, hoping to put her life back together. Rumored to be kin to the hapless royals who ran afoul of Lenin and the boys back in the old country, Olga endures a life of uninterrupted misery and heartbreak.

The novel's story line isn't all that hard to follow, so by the time I reached the end, I had a pretty clear idea that Olga hadn't gotten a fair shake in life. Be that as it may, I was startled when I turned to the back of the book and encountered eight questions prepared for book clubs that might be interested in discussing the novel further. Question No. 5 ran like this:

> Olga has been driven from her homeland by the Bolsheviks, raped by a soldier, abandoned by her husband, treated with indifference by her lover, drugged, sexually violated, and impregnated by her son. Does the novel lay the blame for Olga's fate on the shoulders of the men in her world? Would you?

At first, I thought this question might be a joke, an oversight that had somehow made its way into print. But then I paged through a pile of other novels containing similar supplementary materials. Now it became clear to me that impish, seemingly off-the-wall questions were a staple of the genre, deliberately designed to shake up the musty old world of literature and force readers to think "outside the box."

For example, one edition of *Anna Karenina* contains this question: "Can *Anna Karenina* be read as a cautionary tale, a warning against adultery?" *Well, I guess.* A follow-up question runs: "Would divorce and remarriage have helped Anna Karenina? If Anna had lived in our time, how might her story have been different?" To their credit, the folks preparing these questions made a habit of challenging readers' assumptions, scattering the cobwebs, going for the throat. For example, the person preparing the questions for *Ethan Frome*, the Edith Wharton novel that ends in a toboggan disaster, got right down to the nitty-gritty with this gem: "Is this novel just too grim to be enjoyed?"

Yes. It is. I have checked.

I soon found out that there are several Web sites that list proposed questions for book discussion groups and that a kind of down-home, no-holds-barred irreverence rules there as well. On BookSpot.com, readers who may not have grasped all the nuances of *The Diary of Anne Frank* are confronted by this no-frills brain-stumper: "Nazi leader Adolf Eichmann was asked how he could explain the killing of six million Jews. He answered, 'One hundred dead are a catastrophe, a million dead are a statistic.' Have we become more or less tolerant of murder since he made this observation?"

Every so often, a question seems to have been included merely to see if readers are still awake. Consider this one in the back of Susan Fraser King's *Lady Macbeth*: "Thorfin Sigurdsson, the Raven-Feeder, first steals Gruadh away from her father when she is thirteen years old. Why? When does she see Thorfin again? Does she learn to trust him?"

Admittedly, these matters are open to debate, as Raven-Feeders traditionally fall just below Gryphon Trainers in the hierarchy of Neo-Faux-Quasi-Hyborian Age trustworthiness. A more relevant question is: How did Thorfin the Raven-Feeder finagle his way into a book about the Macbeth family? Most of us who have more than a passing familiarity with the genre assume that characters like that are only supposed to turn up in books like *The Vexing of Wotan* or *How Green Was My Fjordling*. But that's the whole point of these questions: BookSpot zigs when we expect it to zag.

Since throwing curves is second nature to me, I decided to take a crack at writing my own unorthodox book-discussion materials and see if some publishing house might purchase my wares. Here are a few examples:

The Odyssey

1. After the fall of Troy, it takes Odysseus ten years to return home. *Ten years.* Since Troy was only a hop, skip, and a jump from Greece, do you think Penelope should have been more skeptical about her husband's explanation for the long delay (a cabal of one-eyed, man-eating giants; a troupe composed entirely of homicidal, aquatic chantoozies; a sorceress who can turn sailors into pigs)? Isn't the whole thing kind of sketchy?

2. In describing a woman who can effortlessly turn a man into a pig, is Homer criticizing men in general? Or only sailors? Or is he perhaps referring to a particular kind of female?

3. Do you personally know any women like that? Are any of them named Brandi?

4. What time does her shift end?

5. If it took Odysseus ten years to make a short trip across a body of water roughly the size of a plastic kiddie pool, why does everyone in the *Odyssey* keep insisting that he's so smart?

Moby-Dick

1. Things completely fall apart at the end of the novel as Captain Ahab starts totally obsessing about the white whale. Do you think Ahab should have taken a page out of *Jaws* and gotten himself a bigger boat?

2. Is the white whale a symbol for great white sharks?

Wuthering Heights

1. Did you see the movie based on this book? Didn't you think Laurence Olivier was too old to play the part? Boy, I

sure did. I never thought he was all that good-looking, did you?

2. If Heathcliff had fallen in love with somebody like Jane Eyre instead of Cathy, do you think his house would have burned down?

3. If Heathcliff were alive today, would he mention Cathy's death on his Facebook page and say that he was no longer in a relationship?

Remembrance of Things Past

1. This novel is four thousand pages long, yet nothing ever happens. Is Proust making some kind of veiled comment about French society?

2. Do you think this book would have been more interesting if Swann had been replaced by Thorfin Sigurdsson, the Raven-Feeder? In French, that would make Volume 1 of the series *Du côté de chez Sigurdsson*.

Frankly, I thought I was getting somewhere with my questions, going that extra yard to make them seem idiosyncratic and iconoclastic and thought-provoking. I was all set to move on to *A Passage to India* and *The Natural* and *The Three Musketeers* and maybe even *And Quiet Flows the Don*. Then I turned to the back pages of *The Strange Case of Dr. Jekyll and Mr. Hyde and Other Stories* and found this one:

What do you make of Hyde's appearance? (He is small and subtly deformed.) Do you think he should have been depicted as tall and hypermuscular, or obese and debauched, or pale and cadaverous? Why? Or why not? Is there a specific meaning in, or reason for, Hyde's appearance?

That's when I decided to bag the whole enterprise. I was a dwarf among giants. These guys were totally out of my league.

It is widely known that libraries exist in large part to divert and service cheapskates. Libraries provide cost-free reading material so that tightwads and misers can tell local writers that they borrowed their books and then expect them to be grateful. These villainous skinflints, who cannot bring themselves to spend fifteen bucks on a book written by somebody they have known for thirty years—a person who may have helped them land a job, a person who may have cheered wildly for the only base hit their spaz kid ever got in ten years of playing T-ball, a person who may have once given their ailing, epileptic grandmother a ride up the hill from the train station during a raging hailstorm—also labor under the misconception that writers value their input. We do not. Writers only care about money. Yes, we care about truth, justice, and the American way, but mostly we care about money. Penny-pinching sons of bitches and parsimonious scabs who borrow our books from the library do not put money in our pockets. They are like people who come to the church social and sample those delicious little sausage rolls that your wife stayed up all night preparing and then complain that they were too greasy. This may not be a perfect analogy, but it will do.

When I was young, I thought of the public library as a cultural powder magazine where I could requisition matériel that would help me obliterate my enemies and rise in social class. No more. Today I think of libraries as a great place to pick up reading material I would never dream of purchasing and might not even want to keep around the house. When a person borrows books from the library, there is no physical evidence of his appalling taste or deplorable penchant for slumming. The books that line my shelves at home—Shakespeare, Dickens, the Brontës—create at least a visual impression that I am a paragon of taste. The books I borrow from the library are often about bitter, hard-drinking coppers who've been divorced three times, whose children hate them, whose new girlfriend is a diseased slut, and who are trying to figure out why decapitated bodies keep popping up in a drainage ditch in that play area right behind the nursery school. A lot of these books are set in Scandinavia, a hotbed of angst, anomie, alcoholism, and decapitation.

Without question, libraries are a good place to launch offbeat reading enterprises. Once, when my children were small, I spent an entire year reading books I pulled off the shelf haphazardly, without even looking at their titles. Some were good; some were bad. The bad ones I disposed of quickly. There were a handful of great discoveries—*The Northern Lights* by Howard Norman, *So Long, See You Tomorrow* by William Maxwell, *A Month in the Country* by J. L. Carr, *The Siege of Krishnapur* by J. G. Farrell—and a lot of execrable women's fiction. It was an interesting experiment, but not one I would want to repeat.

Another time, I decided to spend a year reading a short book every day. When I embarked upon that adventure, there were some books that I already owned and a few that I bought, but the lion's share I borrowed. This meant that I was in the library all the time. But one afternoon, as I was wending my way through the stacks at the Warner Library looking for easy little numbers to knock off, I noticed that some of the books had been pulled out of their normal positions and laid on their sides. Included were four books by Nadine Gordimer, who won the Nobel Prize for literature in 1991, and several by Doris Lessing, who won the Nobel Prize in 2007, and a couple by Günter Grass, who won the Nobel Prize in 1999. There were also novels or collections of short stories by Thomas Hardy, Carlos Fuentes, Muriel Spark, John

O'Hara, Daphne DuMaurier, and, yes, even Charles Dickens. The illustrated version of *A Christmas Carol* was among them. It was a wonder to behold.

I continued my search, and in the next aisle, while perusing the "h's," I came upon Maureen Petry, who had replaced the now deceased Mrs. Kane as director of the Warner Library. We chatted for a few moments—her son Alex, whom I had known since he was quite small, was going out with an immensely likable young woman who worked at the jaunty suburbohemian coffee shop in my town—and then I asked Maureen why the books were perched at a funny angle. She explained that she was in the process of culling the stacks, setting aside any book that had not been borrowed for the past five years and then having a powwow with the staff to decide whether it should be kept, replaced with a new copy, or purged from the collection. She asked what I thought about this.

There was no point in asking my opinion, because I am Irish American and working class and the kind of Roman Catholic who has never forgiven the Church for ditching the Latin Mass and replacing it with the Guitar Mass back in the 1960s and am therefore opposed to change of any sort in any situation for any reason; so I would simply tell her to keep the Gordimers and dump the Picoults. But here we come face-to-face with the very notion of why a library exists and what community it serves. Most people read drivel. That is their prerogative. The case can be made that it is better to read drivel than to read nothing, on the theory that people will eventually tire of garbage and move on to something more meaty, like trash. I believe that this may sometimes occur with the young, but I doubt that it ever happens with adults. Adults do not suddenly tire of reading Nora Roberts and jump up and exclaim: "Screw this crap; by God, I'm going to give Marcus Aurelius a rip!" People read bad books because bad books serve their needs. Bad books are not good books written in a less literary style. Bad books are bad books. They have bad prose, bad ideas, bad characters, and bad themes. Bad books are written by people who would never even think of writing a good book. What would be the point? You'd only end up like Günter Grass or Nadine Gordimer or Doris Lessing, Nobel Prize winners whose masterpieces were now in the process of getting purged from the stacks of the local library. People who like bad books are not bad people, any more than are people who like bad food. They are simply people who like bad books. They are people on whom the gift of literacy may have been wasted.

When I realized what Maureen was up to, I started maniacally borrowing all the books that seemed in danger of being deep-sixed. I figured that if I checked out these books, it would enable them to survive until the next round of purges a few years down the line. I felt like the very last acquisitions director at the Library of Alexandria on December 22, A.D. 640, feverishly stuffing a few dozen plays by Euripides down his trousers twenty minutes before the Arabs showed up and set the whole place ablaze. The first time around, I borrowed three novels each by Fuentes and Gordimer and two by Mary McCarthy. Fuentes's *Aura*, just seventy-four pages long, was a tantalizing love story; *The Old Gringo* was slight but endearing; *Diana: The Goddess Who Hunts Alone*, a *roman à clef* about the unfortunate actress Jean Seberg, was incredibly sad, and began with the line "No bondage is worse than the hope of happiness." *The Late Bourgeois World* by Gordimer was also quite good, as was *The Conservationist*. I knocked off a few Iris Murdochs and Isaac Singers and John O'Haras, then moved on to *The Groves of Academe*, Mary McCarthy's McCarthy-era novel about a dithering, left-leaning professor at a small Keystone State college who loses his job. I had never read anything by McCarthy, perhaps because I loathed *The Group*, the 1966 motion picture based on her 1962 novel, but also because, while I often get around to reading books that close friends have recommended to me, not once in my life had anyone mentioned Mary McCarthy.

I began reading *The Groves of Academe* and immediately disliked it. McCarthy overwrote and was none too subtle. She reminded me of countless peevish jazz musicians I had heard over the years, ostentatious virtuosi whose dazzling technique ultimately led nowhere. But that wasn't the only problem. A bigger drawback was the physical object in my hands. It was orange, undistinguished, and unappealing, with no dust jacket. The pages had long ago acquired the hue of jaundice, and the book was covered with those brown liver spots that old books inevitably develop. The novel, published in 1951, made me feel that I was thrust back into the year 1951, a place I did not want to be. I was born in 1950 and I didn't want to be there, either.

Hardcover books of yesteryear often had an off-putting, ominous quality; it is entirely possible that their harsh, imperious covers were designed to intimidate the public. *This is serious material, chump; purchase it at your own risk.* It was a perverse and puzzling marketing strategy: *Hands off* Being and Nothingness, *Stretch; you'll find more what you're looking for over in the Zane Grey section.* It was as if publishers wanted to sell books exclusively to readers who would know what to do with them. This policy is now a thing of the past. When Howard Stern's autobiography was published, in 1993, I saw a man walking down Fifth Avenue who manifestly was not sure how one went about holding a book. Its inscrutable rectangularity perplexed him. He wasn't sure whether to stuff it under his arm or cradle it like a football. His maiden voyage on the sea of literacy had not prepared him for this daunting adventure; the book-maneuvering skills most of us acquire relatively early in life, via Richard Scarry or Judy Blume, were not available to him. There is no telling what happened when the poor man opened the book and found that it contained words.

Books did not need to be beautiful back in the Fifties, because nothing else was beautiful back then. Books were simply there; you read them because they were diverting or illuminating or in some way useful but not because the books themselves were aesthetically appealing. Books of the Thirties, Forties, and Fifties often had the texture of rhino hide. They seem to have been constructed with a dual purpose: as sources of unalloyed reading pleasure, yes, but also as emergency interrogation room devices policemen could smash down on criminals' heads to elicit confessions without leaving telltale scars. Work over a snitch with a copy of *Jude the Obscure* for a few minutes and you'd have Legs Diamond's whereabouts pinpointed by lunchtime.

Still, I kept borrowing these books no matter how ugly they were. It was like rescuing antisocial orphans from a fire: You didn't have to like the moody little tykes to want to save them. But eventually I got tired. It was too much work. And a lot of these books weren't so great-looking. Maybe the library should bundle them up and ship them to my friend out in the Philippines. The fact was, I could not save these books all by myself. Somebody else would have to help. And apparently, somebody did. When I last visited the library a few days ago, nine months after I became aware of the culling process that was under way, the books I had checked out by Carlos Fuentes, Nadine Gordimer, Muriel Spark, and John O'Hara were still there. Günter Grass, too. It was a small victory, but a victory all the same.

Not long ago I was invited to an awards ceremony hosted by the county library association. The organization honors anyone who is still breathing, provided they have recently written a book and live somewhere south of the Bear Mountain Bridge and north of the Bronx. I have attended it on two occasions because it helps support the county library system, a noble institution which does the work of the Lord. There is a luncheon and a ceremony, and each of the winners is asked to talk about his or her work for three to five minutes. The event would have been tolerable save for two things. The first was the smarmy Washington Irving impersonator, who was ostensibly hired to provide comic relief. In this neck of the woods, you cannot escape the parlous specter of Brom Bones, Ichabod Crane, Katrina Van Tassel, and Rip Van Winkle. Having seen many of these jokers in action—at Mount Vernon, at Colonial Williamsburg, at points west—I have come to believe that people who get dressed up in period costume, with three-cornered hats and high-buckle shoes, and who speak in archaic English, suffer from Reenactor's Autism, a malady that renders victims incapable of detecting otherwise unmistakable visual cues indicating that most of the people in the room would like to see them disemboweled.

The second drawback was the keynote speaker, one of those middle-aged dinks who wear blue jeans and sneakers to a formal event in the misguided belief that he will be mistaken for Johnny Depp. The man, a famous market researcher, held up a long-playing record and asked if anyone in the room knew what it was. Titter, titter; guffaw, guffaw. I'd heard this spiel before. *Listen up, librarians: Physical books are a thing of the past. Your delivery system is antiquated. Downloads are the wave of the future. Your business model doesn't work anymore. You should run your library more like a business. Businessmen, after all, have successful business models.*

Do they? Really? As in the AIG business model? Or the Bear Stearns business model? Or the Lehman Brothers business model or the WorldCom business model? Yes, by all means, let's get some of those "scary smart" masters of the universe who designed the Enron business model or the Pets.com business model in here to review our operating procedures. Libraries may not turn a huge profit, true. But no library system I know of has ever required a multitrillion-dollar bailout to keep the global economic system from collapsing. As Jim Harrison put it in *The Woman Lit by Fireflies*: "Businessmen would be utterly destroyed if they didn't think they were the most practical men on earth."

Shortly after this self-absorbed dunce finished pontificating, it was my turn to speak. I told the assembled librarians that while Attila the Hun would always be at the gates of Rome, I didn't see why it was necessary to invite him in as a keynote speaker. By discarding tradition, librarians were digging their own graves. In the new command model designed for libraries, at least as delineated by this techno-twit, librarians would have no reason to exist. Patrons would already know what they wanted and would merely come to the library to pick it up. Librarians would no longer be asked to advise and consult; they would merely be on hand to change printer cartridges. The element of serendipity, of taking a flier, of trying something different, of asking for suggestions, that has always made libraries so appealing would vanish, ceding pride of place to an unyielding, market-driven machine. Welcome to the Leviathan.

I think that such a rupture with the past would make the world a cheerless place. No more accidentally crossing paths with searing novels about gringo playboys who get on the wrong side of Pancho Villa. No more chance discoveries of books by gifted, if obscure, Finns, Peruvians, Cambodians, Belgians. No more stumbling upon Amish mysteries set in rural Ohio—which were there in the first place only because the longtime reference librarian got put in charge of ordering mysteries and took a shine to whodunits set in Ohio that featured the Amish. In short: no more surprises. One day I was wandering through the stacks at the Warner Library when I noticed a short novel called *Coda* in the recent-acquisitions section. It was a literary thriller by a French writer named René Belletto. I did not know him. The book had been translated by Alyson Waters and published by the University of Nebraska Press. I took it home and read it that afternoon. It was offbeat, strange. It was just what the doctor ordered. It was a perfect example of the way happenstance makes the world a thrilling place. Somehow this odd little book had made its way into my library. Even the head librarian did not know exactly why it had been acquired. Variety, perhaps. A change from the humdrum. Which is the way things should be. If you want organization and logic and efficiency, visit the cemetery. As one of my friends at the Warner Library expressed it to me, perhaps repeating something she had heard elsewhere: "A library is not a business. A library is a miracle."

In the *Your Business Model Is Broken, But I'm Here to Fix It* scenario, a book like *Coda* will never inveigle its way into my library. Neither will the book about Nikola Tesla's lifelong duel with Thomas Edison or the book about the man who wants to steal *Winged Victory* and return it to Greece or the book about the charismatic Turkish kleptomaniac. No one will order them; no one will borrow them; no one will read them; no one will even be aware of their existence. It will be like a J. G. Ballard novel in which randomness has been outlawed and happenstance is now a capital offense. I will never again simply stumble upon a book like *Coda* or *Light Years* or *The Fly-Truffler* or *Anil's Ghost*. I will never stumble upon a jewel like *Silk* or *The Snow Goose* or *Shadow Without a Name* or *Silence*. For that matter, I will never stumble upon a book by J. G. Ballard. I will never stumble upon anything.

CHAPTER THREE

Opening the Books

Somewhere along the line, I got into the habit of reading several books simultaneously. "Several" soon became "many," and "many" soon became "too many." A few of my female friends read one or two books at a time; my closest male friends insist that they are always reading at least one, though I believe this figure may embody the triumph of hope over truth. In my adult life I cannot remember a single time when I was reading fewer than fifteen books, though at certain points this figure has spiraled far higher. I am not talking about books I have delved into, perused, and set aside, like *Finnegans Wake* or *Middlemarch*, which I first took a crack at in 1978, or *The History of the Decline and Fall of the Roman Empire*, which I have been reading, on and off, since I was about twelve. That would get me up way over a hundred. No, I am talking about books I am actively reading, books that are right there on my nightstand and are not leaving there until I am done with them. Right now, the number is thirty-two.

Like any addiction, the habit of ceaselessly starting new books provides me with immense pleasure. Still, it is a monkey I sometimes wish I could get off my back, because I do not want to wait another twenty years to find out how *The Decline and Fall of the Roman Empire* turns out, and I would dearly love to know what Shelby Foote (*The Civil War*) thinks about the bizarre, stand-alone burial of Stonewall Jackson's arm. At my current glacial pace—I am now roughly a thousand pages into each—I will be a grandfather before I get to the sack of Constantinople and will be festering in my grave long before Pickett rolls the dice at Gettysburg.

There is no discernible rhyme or reason to my frantic reading pattern, except that the books are rarely less than good and are usually great. In the last couple of months I finished *The Man with the Wooden Hat* by Jane Gardam, *Driving on the Rim* by Thomas McGuane, *Train Dreams* by Denis Johnson, *Seven Loves* by Valerie Trueblood, *The Crazed* by Ha Jin, *An Accident in August* by Laurence Cosse, *The Waitress Was New* by Dominique Fabre, and *31 Hours* by Masha Hamilton. I also finished rereading *No Great Mischief* by Alistair MacLeod, *Blood Meridian* by Cormac McCarthy, *Meeting Evil* by Thomas Berger, *The Pornographer* by John McGahern, *The Samurai* by Shusaku Endo, and Elise Blackwell's haunting first novel, *Hunger*. It took between three and six weeks to finish each of these projects, with *The Waitress Was New* serving as a seventy-five-minute pit stop between a book about the destructive effects of PowerPoint that I was reviewing for *Barron's* and a radiant Phaidon picture book about Odilon Redon.

Simultaneously I was blasting away at short-story collections by William Trevor, Andre Dubus, James Salter, and Mavis Gallant; had battled about two hundred pages into Wilkie Collins's *The Woman in White*; and had reread the first half of *The Picture of Dorian Gray*, which I was treating myself to for perhaps the seventh time. I had also finished rereading William Kennedy's *Legs* and *Billy Phelan's Greatest Game* and had started his latest novel, *Chango's Beads and Two-Tone Shoes*, which I got as a Christmas present. I also cracked open Hans Fallada's recently translated *Every Man Dies Alone*, an even more unexpected Christmas present, and a truly unforgettable novel. That's without mentioning

The Discovery of France, a book I began in 2009, on another continent, and *A History of the Indians of the United States* by Angie Debo, which I started three years ago, got halfway through, and set aside. For reasons I myself do not understand, I am concurrently making my way through not one but three books about the Roman Empire, in addition to Edward Gibbon's classic, and three books by Paul Johnson: *Art*, *Modern Times*, and *A History of the American People*. When you add to all this such lighthearted fare as *A Conspiracy of Paper* by David Liss, *The Vault* by Ruth Rendell, and *Remembering Harry Kalas*, a collection of warm and often humorous reminiscences honoring the beloved, dearly departed Philadelphia Phillies announcer, it becomes clear that this is a serious problem. In fact, it is madness.

My addiction is so acute that I cannot even limit myself to reading one foreign-language book at any one time, as I am currently two-thirds of the way through *L'enfant et la rivière* by Henri Bosco, halfway through *Ondine* by Jean Giraudoux, and just about to finish *Mon ami Maigret* by Georges Simenon, which I am tackling for the second time even though it is not especially good. Other books I am working on in some desultory fashion include *Dear Departed* (the first installment of Marguerite Yourcenar's autobiography); *The Autobiography of Bertrand Russell*; and *Sodom and Gomorrah*, the fourth volume in Proust's *Remembrance of Things Past*, which I have just begun reading for a second time. At this rate I will never get back to *Ulysses*.

My reading habits are unusual, perhaps counterproductive. Sometimes I think that I am reluctant to finish books because I want to let the joy of reading them go on and on forever. Other times I believe that I get a particular kind of thrill out of starting books that I do not get from finishing them. Another possibility is that, at any given moment, I am distracted from the subject I am reading about—the life and times of Mata Hari—by a far more pressing concern—the neutral-zone trap employed with such great success by the New Jersey Devils.

Friends say that I suffer from a short attention span, an inability to stay focused, but I think exactly the opposite is true. If anything, I have too long an attention span, one that allows me to read dozens of books simultaneously without losing interest in any of them. Moreover, I have an excellent memory that permits me to suspend reading, pick up a book six months later, and not miss a beat. I did this with *The Magic Mountain*, *All the King's Men*, and *La Cousine Bette* and will almost certainly do it with *The Moonstone* and *Clarissa*, neither of which I intend to read at a single sitting. A chess player once told me that a good memory is a trick that creates a deceptive aura of intelligence around an otherwise humdrum intellect. This is certainly true in my case. As it was in his.

For a long time, I believed that I became addicted to starting books as a child, because books usually begin like a house on fire but then cool off around page seventy. Some cool off even earlier. *The Iliad* kicks off with Achilles' unexpected decision to go off and pout, denuding the narrative of its star performer, so it is understandable that a thrill-seeking kid might set it aside for a few days and instead give *Tarzan and the Jewels of Opar* a rip. This habit persisted later in life when I started to read truckloads of nonfiction as part of my work. Most books written by journalists open with two reasonably good chapters, followed by loads of padding, then regather a bit of momentum for the big roundup. This is because editors encourage writers to front-load the merchandise, jamming the best material into the first two chapters, the only ones that will ever get read. I was once told that readers of topical books regularly abandon them around page sixty, vowing to get back to them later. Well, I *do* get back to them later. I started *Lord Jim* in high school and finished it when I was fifty-two. Better late than never.

But more recently I have started to think that these habits formed when I was in my early twenties and employed by a New Jersey–based term-paper factory. The job itself, though sleazy, was a godsend. It turned me into a fast, efficient writer, because I had to conduct research quickly on a wide variety of topics and turn around the finished product in as little as twenty-four hours. I never made any real effort to dumb down the material I submitted, and have always believed it was apparent to the teachers who graded my term papers that they could not possibly have been written by the slothful cretins who handed them in. But whether they did or not made no difference to me. For the first time in my life I was being paid to write. That was all that mattered.

I was also being paid to read. On an average day I might delve into as many as fifteen books on topics as varied as the untimely death of Montezuma, puzzling elements in the late plays of Maxim Gorky, quirks in mid-century Bolivian agronomic policy, the rise of the bourgeoisie in eighteenth-century France, and the too-often-overlooked nautical imagery in *Hamlet*. I read hundreds and hundreds of books during the two years I worked for the term-paper factory, and this, I am sure, is where my literary *coitus interruptus* problem began. I was getting paid to write, but I was also getting paid to multitask. I have multitasked ever since.

A few summers back I tried an experiment: seeing how long I could go without starting a new book. With about thirty titles on the active list, I was hoping to slash the number to a manageable dozen by the middle of July, which I could do if I read at least three books a week and did not start any others in the meantime. Things started off just swell, as I finished off two mysteries by

Barbara Vine (Ruth Rendell under a *nom de plume*), Haruki Murakami's entrancing *Norwegian Wood*, and a genial Joanna Trollope novel called *The Men and the Girls*. But one afternoon my
resolve weakened, and I cracked open Penelope Fitzgerald's *The
Bookshop*, which I had already read six years earlier; Paul Fussell's
Wartime, a gift from one of my college English professors; Henning Mankell's unnerving *Before the Frost*; and a book about the
1954 French catastrophe at Dien Bien Phu, lent to me by a friend
who served in Vietnam. Here, in a nutshell, was the problem: No
matter how good the book I am currently reading—be it *The
Aeneid*, *War and Peace*, or *The Red and the Black*—I am always
ready to drop everything and crack open a forty-year-old book about
the 1954 Viet Cong triumph at Dien Bien Phu.

The same thing happened last winter, when I again tried to
shrink my pile of books to a manageable size. I eventually whit-
tled the number down to around fifteen, but then I got engrossed
in Peter Carey's *Parrot & Olivier in America* and Ron Rash's *Serena*
and Jim Thompson's *Pop. 1280*, and before you knew it the total
had shot right back up into the thirties, which is where it is now.
This is one large, determined monkey, and it is clinging quite te-
naciously to my back. I have a close friend who has a habit I do
not have: constantly purchasing books he suspects he will never
have a chance to read. There are books in my collection that I
may never get to—*History of the Franks* by Gregory of Tours, *Vessels of Rage, Engines of Power: The Secret History of Alcoholism* by
James Graham, *Memoirs of Napoleon Bonaparte* (which were not
even written by Napoleon Bonaparte)—but these are not books I
have acquired recently. I no longer purchase books in the expectation that I will read them sometime further down the road; I am
already sixty-one years old, and there's not all that much road left.
My friend, only one year younger, periodically goes on feverish

reading binges. He, too, is Irish American. When I visited him recently, he had a pile of books arrayed on the coffee table that he proudly, yet apprehensively, pointed out to me. They included *American Speeches*—one of which was John F. Kennedy's memorable 1961 Berlin Wall "I Am a Jelly Donut" peroration—as well as *Thucydides* by Donald Kagan, *Angels and Ages* by Adam Gopnik, *The Marketplace of Ideas* by Louis Menand, and *The Lie of the Land* by Fintan O'Toole.

"These books have to be read by the end of January," my friend told me. "That's the deadline; they *have* to be read."

It was January 15. I counted six books in the pile. Maybe seven.

That's a cakewalk. If I made a similar commitment to demolish my own pile of partially read books, it wouldn't take sixteen days. It would take sixteen months, and only if I did not start reading any new books in the meantime. When I look at that stack and try to imagine the order in which I might read them, I always arrive at the same conclusion: *Middlemarch* is the last book I will ever finish. I'm not going down without a fight. I have started it six times; I am now 312 pages into it; but it is much like the mandolin or snooker or tantric sex: something I would dearly love to master without ever believing for one second that I would actually enjoy the experience.

It is entirely possible that I regularly finish three novels and then start four others because I do not ever want to reach the point where I have nothing left to read but *Middlemarch*. *Middlemarch* is one of those books that I long ago enshrined at the very top of my desert-island reading list, that compendium of elusive, difficult, fundamentally unreadable books I have always wanted to finish or at least start, if I only had the time to do so. But I know that if I were shipwrecked and somehow managed to stay afloat by clutching the splintered, though jagged, remnants of the main-mast and started paddling through shark-infested waters toward a distant shore and then, just as I was dragging my battered, bruised, waterlogged body out of the surf, spotted a pile of desert-island reading books that included *Mrs. Dalloway*, *Finnegans Wake*, and *Middlemarch*, I'd turn around, plunge right back into the surf, and start paddling toward another island. I wouldn't care how big the sharks were.

I used to think that I kept stopping and starting books because I could never find the right one. Untrue. Virtually all the books I start *are* the right one. It's the fact that all these books are so good that makes me stop reading them, as I am in no hurry to finish; the bad ones I could whip through in a few hours. The problem is simple: There are just too many good books, and I would like to at least sample all of them. Reading is like visiting the Louvre: Just because you adore the Titians doesn't mean you won't be tempted by the Bellinis. Life doesn't work that way.

Starting books one after another makes me feel that a long-awaited voyage has already begun; that while it may take five years to finish Theodor Mommsen's *History of Rome* or Churchill's six-volume *History of the Second World War*, these are no longer dimly envisioned, unrealistic projects, like learning to play the accordion or competing in a vintage-hovercraft race, but in some sense they are already a part of my life. Other people say, "One of these days, I'm finally going to get to *Ulysses*." Well, I've already gotten to *Ulysses*. I've been getting to *Ulysses* for the past thirty years.

One day a few years back I visited the postage stamp–sized bookstore in Grand Central Station, where I bought Andrea Barrett's *The Voyage of the Narwhal*. Since I had only just started Tacitus's *The Annals of Imperial Rome* the night before and was still hammering away at Proust, Gibbon, George Eliot, and all the rest, this was hardly an essential purchase. But for whatever reason, I felt an overwhelming urge to take a stab at that book right away. Some people go into bookstores and are seduced by classics they absolutely must read; I go into bookstores and am seduced by classics I absolutely must start.

"I'm already reading twenty-five other books, so why am I buying this one?" I asked a friend who was standing there with me. "Do you think this is a disease?"

"Yes," interjected the cashier. "But it's a good disease to have."

Six years later, I still have not finished *The Voyage of the Narwhal*.

I am not the only person who has trouble getting across the finish line. Many writers suffer from the same affliction. In 1921 Robert Musil began writing a gigantic book called *The Man Without Qualities*. It was about an attempt by a small group of peppery, *fin de siècle* Viennese to make the twentieth century the Austrian Century. In a way, this came to pass: Adolf Hitler was Austrian, even though he got an awful lot of help from the Germans. But that was not the Austrian Century that Musil's protagonists had in mind.

Musil had poor writing habits. He dallied; he temporized. He lacked focus. By the time he died, in 1942, *The Man Without Qualities*, already 1,130 pages long, not counting 640 pages of outtakes, alternate versions, and supplementary materials, was still not finished. Yet even incomplete as it is, it is often singled out as one of the three greatest novels of the twentieth century, the others being *Ulysses* and *Remembrance of Things Past*. *Remembrance of Things Past* is now routinely referred to as *In Search of Lost Time*, as this is the literal translation of *À la recherche du temps perdu*. But *Remem-*

brance of Things Past is more poetic and beautiful, and because I started reading the book thirty-five years ago, when it was still called *Remembrance of Things Past*, it will always be *Remembrance of Things Past* to me. The past must be remembered as it occurred, not as it is subsequently reconfigured. When the great Henry Aaron was pummeling the Phillies back in the Fifties and Sixties, routinely belting line-drive home runs out of Connie Mack Stadium, he was always identified as Hank Aaron. In fact, he was always referred to as Hammerin' Hank Aaron. Years later, it came out that Aaron preferred the name Henry. While still in the minor leagues, his team had foisted a folksy, somewhat rube-like nickname upon him purely for promotional purposes. Be that as it may, he will always be Hank Aaron in my book. I don't care if he hated the name. Marcel Proust probably hated the title *Remembrance of Things Past*, too.

Musil spent the rest of his life writing and rewriting *The Man Without Qualities* without ever crossing the last "t" and dotting the last "i." This was a man who simply couldn't pull the trigger; enough was never enough. So when people say, "How could you get 1,047 pages into a book and then stop reading it?" I merely respond: "Well, Musil himself got 1,130 pages into a book and didn't finish writing it. So let he who is without sin cast the first stone."

These conversations, in fact, never occur. If this were a world where people asked probing questions about the work habits of Robert Musil, this would not be a world where people asked probing questions about the work habits of Stephenie Meyer. The only people I know who have even heard of Musil are those to whom I have given the book as a present, none of whom seem terribly pleased. *The Man Without Qualities*, for the record, is one of those novels about which you remember almost nothing after you have finished reading it, but do recall, quite vividly, that you enjoyed every second of the experience. Or in my case, it is one of those novels you cannot remember a thing about after you have *almost* finished reading it, but do recall, quite vividly, that you enjoyed every second of it at the time. It is a book that I shall *almost* finish reading for the rest of my life. I've got it all planned out.

I am not always in the mood to read the classics, especially if I am overworked or depressed or violently ill. Some of the classics are deadly. Some of the classics can make a sick person sicker. Who really enjoys Rudyard Kipling? Who still gets a kick out of Émile Zola? Does anyone actually like Ben Jonson? Yes, they are brilliant writers, but sometimes genius isn't enough. I have been reading fiction for half a century, yet have never worked myself into the proper frame of mind to go head-to-head with *The House of the Seven Gables*, and at this point there is no reason to believe I ever will. This is puzzling. In theory it should be possible to read every indisputably great book in a single lifetime. In fact, you should be able to do it in about five years. But I have not done it. In the case of *The House of the Seven Gables*, I know perfectly well why I have never read it—I hate people from Massachusetts, and I know the book is going to give me a headache—but I do not understand why I have never read books that I truly want to read, like *The Histories* by Herodotus or *The Divine Comedy* or *Faust*. Perhaps I am saving them for a rainy day. That must be it. Reading a great book late in life—as I did with *Jane Eyre* and *Don Quixote*—does not diminish the pleasure one takes from them; it may indeed enhance it. If I were asked to name the books I love most dearly, both of those would be right at the top of the list. Yet I did not read *Don Quixote* until I was fifty-one and *Jane Eyre* until I was fifty-three. Proving that a pleasure deferred is not a pleasure denied.

This delay in getting to the classics is a bit like what occurs with my DVD rentals. Even though the three films sitting on the coffee table are of the very highest quality, they are never the films I want to watch that evening. The films on the coffee table are a sensitive coming-of-age tale directed by Eric Rohmer, an obscure black-and-white Kurosawa film about a botched kidnapping, and a film about gritty miners in northern England so gosh-darned inspiring it makes you want to stand up and cheer. But the film I would really like to watch tonight is *Scarface*.

For most of my life, I found it very hard to not finish a book once I got a good way into it. On occasion I would ditch a book after a single chapter, which is what I did with *Nana* and *Auto-da-Fé*, but once I had made significant inroads into a book, I found it impossible to call off the dogs. I could stop only if I felt morally justified in doing so. I do remember not being able to finish *Elmer Gantry* and *Dodsworth* when I was in my teens, but I certainly recall the enormous feeling of accomplishment in high school when I finished *The Return of the Native* and *Far from the Madding Crowd*, both of which I hated. I felt much the same way about *Oliver Twist*, a problematic novel, because its central character is not in fact its central character but is in fact a hapless goofball floating around at the periphery of the narrative. There are a handful of novels that I was forced to read in high school, disliked immensely, and then went back and tried again years later, with completely different results. I did not enjoy *The Comedians* when I first read it as a high school assignment in 1967, shortly after it first came out, but when I reread it forty-four years later, it knocked my socks off. It was about an intense but doomed love affair—aren't they all?—and contained this line: "It sometimes seemed to me that we were less lovers than fellow-conspirators tied together in the commission of a crime." It was impossible not to be impressed by this sort of material, though why anyone would give a steamy novel about high-octane tropical infidelity to high school boys is beyond me. I had a similarly hard time getting through George Gissing's *New Grub Street* and Ford Madox Ford's *The Good Soldier* when I read them in my twenties, but have returned to each twice since and taken great delight in doing so, even though the prose never gets any less dense in either novel. *New Grub Street* falls into that special category of astounding books that absolutely never come up in conversation. It shares this distinction with the novels of Maurice Maeterlinck and Blaise Cendrars, the theater of Paul Claudel and Cyril Tourneur, the short fiction of Villiers de l'Isle-Adam, and the poetry of Galway Kinnell. I have never, ever been engaged in conversation about any of these authors, even when grilled by the most pedantic of exotics. Never. You can throw Alejo Carpentier, Juan Rulfo, and Robert Pinget right in there, too. And, just for good measure, Bohumil Hrabal.

I no longer feel obligated to see a book through to its end. These days, I can set down a book I do not immediately take a shine to without any hesitation whatever. And when I set such a book aside, I set it aside forever. Most recently this happened with *One Good Turn* by Kate Atkinson. What annoyed me here was that one hundred pages into the book the author was still introducing new characters and had still not made clear precisely what the book was about. It was as if she had assigned herself a daily word quota, and those first hundred pages were no more than a warm-up for the main event. It got on my nerves. I was visiting friends in the south of France at the time and found myself in that uncomfortable situation where it would be impossible to give up on a book they had enthusiastically recommended without feeling that I had insulted them. Nor could I lie about having read it from cover to cover, as they might quiz me, in the way that people who live in the south of France so often will. Somehow I had to cushion the blow by finding another book in their library that would give me pleasure.

After much thought, I ended up choosing *Anne of Green Gables*, which I had never even glanced at prior to that moment. It hooked me from the very first sentence. I know that it is not fair to judge Kate Atkinson by the standards of *Anne of Green Gables*, any more than it is fair to judge *Tuesdays with Morrie* by the standards of Boswell's *Life of Johnson*. But as a hugely successful author of commercial fiction, Kate Atkinson enjoyed a vast competitive advantage over L. M. Montgomery. Atkinson's book benefited from a particular kind of brand loyalty on the part of the reader that kept them plowing ahead for a hundred pages even though nothing much was happening, because they were confident that their patience and industry would eventually be rewarded. People were reading *this* Kate Atkinson book because they'd read lots of her other ones, and the books had always delivered. But when L. M. Montgomery sat down to write *Anne of Green Gables*, the novel that made her famous, she could not depend upon this sort of indulgence from her readers, because she had only just shown up. She was a nobody who had to seize readers by the throat from the very first sentence. Which she did. Again, to compare Kate Atkinson to L. M. Montgomery is not fair. But this is what happens as one approaches old age and its concomitant, death. Life becomes a zero-sum affair, where every second spent reading mediocre books is time that could be spent reading great ones.

That said, I have never been able to stop reading a highly respected book—a classic—without first establishing a rationale for doing so. I must have an excuse. The same dictum applies to a not-so-good book by a great writer, like Faulkner's *Pylon* or

Fitzgerald's *Pat Hobby Stories*. I cannot simply put them down. I cannot be cavalier about this. I must have just cause. It is as if I subscribe to the literary equivalent of *omertà*, the Mafia code dictating that one must never rat out a fellow gangster. One afternoon I brought home a copy of Yasunari Kawabata's novel *The Old Capital* that I found at the library. I have loved Kawabata since I was a sophomore in college when I read *The Master of Go*, *Thousand Cranes*, and *Snow Country*. I read these books because I felt that they would teleport me far away from joyless Philadelphia, which they did, but also because I thought news of my wide-ranging reading habits would impress girls, which it did not. I have since passed along this information to my son, who has, as of this writing, led a studiously Kawabata-free existence. *The Old Capital*, it turned out, was a bit on the dull side, and I had trouble getting into it. The introduction said that it was one of the books cited by the Nobel Committee when they gave Kawabata his well-deserved award in 1968, but I found it tough sledding. It didn't surprise me that Kawabata took the pipe not long after the book came out overseas; you could see that he was running on empty. Nevertheless, I had no choice but to finish it. Otherwise, I would have been guilty of monstrous ingratitude to the author. This was an obligation that was entirely beyond my control. It came from some other place.

In seeking an excuse to scuttle a famous work I have made serious inroads into, my experience with William Makepeace Thackeray is typical. I was halfway through his implacably precious *Vanity Fair* before I finally tossed in the sponge at age thirty-two. I hated it. Despised it. Yet because of the author's lofty stature, and because of the sacrosanct position his masterpiece occupies in the Western canon, for the next twenty-three years I felt guilty about setting the book aside. Then one day I was walking down the main street in Augusta, Georgia, when I happened upon a plaque noting that Thackeray had actually stood on that very spot during a sojourn in Dixie. The plaque contained a quote from Thackeray to the effect that Augusta was such a swell little town that even the slaves wore happy expressions on their faces. Well, *hasta la vista, Guillermo.* I discovered this plaque right about the time the lantern-jawed Reese Witherspoon was taking a stab at the role of Becky Sharp in the latest film version of *Vanity Fair*. It occurred to me that a person named Reese Witherspoon would inevitably turn into a fiercely annoying human being, because there was nowhere else to go with that name. The same, I assume, would be true of Becky Sharp. It also occurred to me that I had never read a single issue of the magazine *Vanity Fair*, in either its Tina Brown or its Graydon Carter manifestation. This almost morganatic combination of circumstances relieved me of any lingering guilt I may have felt about ditching Thackeray's 1848 classic. I have now turned my back on it forever. But such a fortuitous rescue from ethical bondage is rare indeed.

I once tried to devise a term to describe the euphoria a person feels when he approaches the end of a book he has not enjoyed reading. I think the term is in fact "euphoria," as the closest I ever got was *Buchendungfreudejoie*. Others share my inability to chuck away a book once they have slogged a good way into it. One of the best friends I have ever had says that when reading a book she dislikes but cannot quite bring herself to abandon, she is thrilled when she suddenly, unexpectedly stumbles upon a passage so awful or disgusting or immoral that it would make it a crime to continue holding the book in her hands.

"Thank you for just diving right off that pier" is what she silently murmurs to the author whenever this occurs. "Thank you."

. . . . . .

My life, such as it is, has been a series of crackpot escapades involving books. I ceaselessly engage in demanding, sometimes byzantine, stunts that for one reason or another never reach a satisfactory conclusion. For example, there is a part of me that wants to compile a list of books I have always wanted to read, stick to that list, and dash right across the finish line. But there is another part of me that resents it when Mister Gradgrind starts throwing his weight around, that finds the very idea of lists and schedules and objectives oppressive. This is the part of me that revels in the random and the unexpected, that delights in those moments when I find myself standing in Penn Station waiting to meet someone who can have a serious impact on my flagging career and suddenly experience an uncontrollable urge to slip into a bookstore, pick up a copy of Willa Cather's *O Pioneers!*, and disappear into the gloaming.

I think it is important to have goals in life, as long as you understand that achieving those goals will not make you happy. It is also important to reach that critical point in any cultural decathlon where you realize that the entire enterprise is stupid. When I was twenty-four, I spent a year reading most of the world's greatest books, ranging from Plato's *Republic* to *The Canterbury Tales* to *War and Peace*. I also started but never got around to finishing *Ulysses*; in fact, I never got close. A few years later, I started in on the Modern Library list of the greatest English-language novels of the twentieth century and made it all the way through *Zuleika Dobson* and *The Wapshot Chronicles* and *The Sheltering Sky* but still never got around to finishing *Ulysses*. After that, I began working my way through Anthony Burgess's list of the ninety-nine greatest English-language novels written between 1939 and 1983 and had no trouble whatsoever with *The Girls of Slender Means* and *The Unlimited Dream Company* and *The Victim* but eventually realized that even if I lived to be a hundred I would never get around to finishing *Titus Groan* or *Giles Goat-Boy*, much less *Ulysses*, which was not even on that list. I am beginning to suspect that deep down inside I do not really want to finish *Ulysses*. In all likelihood, it will be the second-to-last book I finish before the Grim Reaper darkens my doorstep. The last, of course, being *Middlemarch*.

I am incapable of reading a book without beforehand having some sort of long-range goal in mind—some reward, or at least some consolation prize, awaiting me at the end of the trail. This does not mean that I am unable to grab any old book off the shelf and enjoy it. It means that once I have done so, once I have taken a break from my latest grueling adventure, I jump right back onto the treadmill. My adult life has been one long process of reprioritizing, recontextualizing, and redeploying my resources. For example, I now find it extremely difficult to purge books from my collection. For me to not get around to reading a book is to admit that my acquiring the book in the first place was a mistake, a concession I am loath to make. My shelves today are filled with books whose purchase once seemed like a good idea but that I have never found the time or the inclination to read. Here I am including such obvious titles as *Orlando Furioso* and Rousseau's *Confessions, Volume II*, but also far less essential material like *The Dimwit's Dictionary* and *The Last Playboy: The High Life of Porfirio Rubirosa*, books written by Punch for the edification of Judy. In order to justify keeping so many books on hand, and so many peculiar books, I periodically engage in epic literary undertakings that in theory require their continued presence in my library. Here are a few projects I have undertaken over the years:

1. *Reading all the books in my collection.* Close, but no cigar.
2. *Re-rereading all the books in my collection that I had already read twice.* Been there, done that. Great fun. *Emma, At*

Swim-Two-Birds, The Big Sleep, and *Beau Geste* never fail to step up to the plate.

3. *Reading all the books that close friends have lent me.* Not happening.

4. *Rereading all the books I read in a particular year that I remember fondly.* Still working on that one.

5. *Spending a year reading nothing but short books.* My favorite year.

6. *Spending a year reading books I picked off library shelves with my eyes closed.* That got old quick.

7. *Spending a year reading books I had always suspected I would hate.* I tried this once, but got only as far as Frederick Exley's *A Fan's Notes* before bagging it. Books I did go the full fifteen rounds with include *Babbitt* (loved it), *Lolita* (bad timing: My daughter was fourteen), *The Mill on the Floss* (brutal), and *The Octopus* (no picnic). Books remaining on that list include *The Golden Bough, The Education of Henry Adams, The Collected Stories of Rabindranath Tagore*, and, of course, *Finnegans Wake.* To be perfectly honest, I'm glad that I stopped when I did.

8. *Devoting a year to reading books by authors who burned out early.* F. Scott Fitzgerald, Arthur Rimbaud, Ralph Ellison, Alfred Jarry, Harper Lee. God, was that depressing.

9. *Reading all the coffee-table books in my collection.* I was exactly two-thirds of the way through *Hoaxes, Humbugs and Spectacles: Astonishing Photographs of Smelt Wrestlers, Human Projectiles, Giant Hailstones, Contortionists, Elephant Impersonators, and Much, Much More!* when I decided that it was time to put this project in dry dock.

10. *Devoting a year to reading all the books in my library that I had started but not finished.* There are 138 books of this de-

scription in my home and office. One—José Ortega y Gasset's *The Revolt of the Masses*—I started reading in 1972 and set aside, figuring I would get back to it. I have still not gotten back to it.

11. *Devoting a year to reading all the books in my library that I had never even started.* There are actually only about fifteen of them, twenty max. The books include *The Rise and Fall of the Great Powers* by Paul Kennedy, *The Tree of Man* by Patrick White, *The Age of Jackson* by Arthur Schlesinger, *All That Is Solid Melts into Air* by Marshall Berman, and *Paroles* by Jacques Prévert. They are all books that I want to read. They are all books I am sure I will enjoy. The entire operation would probably take me no more than three months. The books are all sitting right there in the middle of my office. Why, then, can I not finish them? Or even start them? I have no idea.

12. *Spending a few years only reading books in foreign languages that are already in my library.* I have 158 such books, though several are in German, a language I do not read. This project has never achieved serious liftoff. The three experimental novels by Nathalie Sarraute and Alain Robbe-Grillet are probably not helping.

13. *Spending a year reading books by writers from Iceland.* Only funning.

Most of these projects got derailed quickly because they were tedious or inane, and I soon came to my senses. But even when I did not complete the self-imposed assignment—the literary equivalent of Hercules' scouring the Augean stables—I derived huge benefits from the experience. Here is a case in point: A couple of years ago, I decided that I would try to read a book every single day for the next year. As previously noted, Winston Churchill supposedly got through at least one book every day of his adult life, and I had always envied him. But I saw no way that I could equal his feat unless I stuck to reasonably short books. So one fall day, I began visiting my library and borrowing books that I could read in less than two hours. Three max. I also read thirty books that I already owned, a couple dozen sent to me by my publisher and by one extremely close friend, twenty-five that I borrowed from the Center for Fiction (a private library in midtown Manhattan that is not as well known as it should be), and a couple I found in the trash. They were almost all novels, novellas, or collections of short stories, because short fiction is easier to read than short nonfiction, unless Henry James or Thomas Mann is at the helm. Only a handful were less than 100 pages long; most logged in right around 150; only two or three ran longer than 200 pages.

What I liked most about this enterprise was its random quality. I would go to the library—often without my reading glasses—and select compact works of fiction that seemed like things I would enjoy. Often I was only guessing, as the jacket copy was in type too small to read. If I got home and discovered that I had checked out a bittersweet, life-affirming novel about a recently divorced woman who had moved to a small town in Maine or the Massif Central or the Mull of Kintyre and, after initially being shocked by the ham-fisted demeanor of the rough-hewn locals, was seduced by their canny charm, I took it straight back. I proceeded in this fashion, reading at least one book a day, for four months straight, keeping right on pace with my schedule. There were wonderful discoveries: *Far Bright Star*, a searing novel about the Mexican War of 1917, written by Robert Olmstead; *The Enigmatic Eye*, a collection of strange fables and stories by the Brazilian author Moacyr Scliar; *Tokyo Fiancée*, a short novel by Amélie

Nothomb about a Belgian woman giving French lessons in Japan whose incompetent student falls in love with her, and which contains the line "If someone mattered once, they will matter always," a sentiment I find profoundly inspiring and beautiful, even though it is almost certainly not true. And then, of course, there were all those zany mysteries set among the Buckeye State Amish.

This was a noble and invigorating project. I loved every second of it. But it fell apart when I flew to Sweden, got sick, got depressed, got a growth on my neck that began to turn septic, got a ticket to London, got taken to the cleaners by a Harley Street walk-in clinic, and got deflected from the trajectory of my enterprise, the way I always get deflected from the trajectory of my enterprise. For even though I always embark upon these forays with the best will in the world, determined to see them through to their conclusion, I always run out of gas or get distracted. The spirit, it would seem, is willing, but the flesh, it would seem, is weak. I'm not even all that sure about the spirit.

The long and the short of it is, I fell hopelessly behind and read but a paltry 250 books, nowhere near my original target. I might have pulled it off had I cheated by speed-reading or feasting on children's books. But this I would never do. Speed-reading is for slobs. And children's books are for children. In the end, it didn't matter, as no one was keeping score. The whole endeavor was like running a marathon just to see if I could do it and then realizing halfway through the race that marathons are idiotic. I did enjoy that interlude very much, however; it was exhilarating to start a day on page one of a book and polish off the very last word by midnight. In the course of the exercise, I read classics like Robert Nathan's *Portrait of Jenny* and Italo Calvino's *The Baron in the Trees* and Ambrose Bierce's *The Devil's Dictionary*. I read three mordant novels by Muriel Spark and a couple of quickies by Joyce Carol Oates, including *Black Water*, in which she imagines Chappaquiddick from the point of view of the drowning victim. I read three novels by Alberto Moravia, Paula Fox's harrowing memoir *Desperate Characters*, *A Woman of Means* by Peter Taylor, *The Chant of Jimmie Blacksmith* by Thomas Keneally, and collections of short stories by such famous writers as Lorrie Moore, Susan Minot, Reynolds Price, Patricia Highsmith, and Barry Hannah and by less-famous writers like Tim Parrish, Eva Figes, Mark Richard, Brad Watson, Christine Schutt, and John Biguenet. Parrish's *Red Stick Men* and Biguenet's *The Torturer's Apprentice* were particularly rewarding discoveries.

I also read Truman Capote's listless first novel, *Summer Crossing*; Tennessee Williams's bleak first novel, *The Roman Spring of Mrs. Stone*; and Wallace Stegner's remarkable debut effort, *Remembering Laughter*, which was part of a first-novel competition held by Little Brown in 1937. The book was seventy-two years old. The faded, aged cover announced: "This story, chosen from 1,340 manuscripts, is the first fruits of a successful search into the neglected realm of the short novel, in a contest intended to encourage the many writers who write at their best in this distinctive literary form." The cover was in fact one huge advertisement for the book and even mentioned the prize money right at the top: $2,500. I had never seen anything like it. It floored me. This was a book I found in my local library. Needless to say, no one had borrowed it in years. It was one of the books I rescued from the Great Warner Library Book Purge of 2011. It is still there.

I delved into famous authors I had never tried before, including Naguib Mahfouz (*Before the Throne*), Jamaica Kincaid (*Lucy*), and John Berger, whose poignant novel *From A to X* is a series of letters, presented out of order, that chronicle the love affair between a political prisoner in an African prison and the woman who dreams of his release. My adventure took me many places I never expected to go. Because I made my choices randomly, I ended up reading short novels by writers from Venezuela, China, Thailand, Norway, Sweden, Denmark, Japan, Argentina, Ethiopia, Chile, Belgium, and Israel. Among others. They dealt with everything from a Finnish woodcutter who stays behind when the Nazis close in on his village in 1941 to the plight of rambunctious Thai cross-dressers during religious-festival season. There was a novel whose main character was an English survivor of the Luftwaffe's bombing of Coventry, and a novel whose main character was a German survivor of the RAF's bombing of Hamburg. Several of the books were extraordinary: *Small Lives* by Pierre Michon, *The Maytrees* by Annie Dillard, *Running* by Jean Echenoz, *In the Company of Angels* by N. M. Kelby, *The Gangster We Are All Looking For* by Lê Thi Diem Thúy, *Grief* by Andrew Holleran. I loved these books. They were in my life for only a day—two days at most—but made those days seem incredibly special. Each day I looked forward to the vest-pocket treasure I would see off before midnight. Small books possess qualities that large books do not; large books are Cézannes; small books are Dufys. Small books make their own terms and succeed on them. Reading longer books, no matter how good they are, can be a chore. Reading *Nicholas Nickleby* is hard work. Reading *Adam Bede* is drudgery. Reading *The Jungle* is torture. Reading these 250 tiny volumes was never torture.

Not all of the books were equally memorable. *Red Dog*, Louis de Bernières's short book about the adventures of a perky Australian mutt, strove for a cuteness it did not ever attain. Banana Yoshimoto's uncompromisingly slight books were aimed at a demographic group I do not belong to. Gore Vidal's *Clouds and Eclipses*, his collected short stories, were cynical and cruel. Philip

Roth's *The Humbling* was dreadful. But it didn't matter, because reading a bad book by a good writer is compelling in a way that reading a good book by a mediocrity never is. It was like watching Willie Mays fall down in center field at the end of his career, when he played for the Mets. It was sad, but he was still Willie Mays.

Just because a book is short does not mean that it can be read quickly. Anita Brookner's elegant novels often run fewer than two hundred pages but take more than a day to devour, because they are languid and dispiriting and the narrative does not race along at locomotive speed. Brookner's novels are not on the cutting-edge stylistically, and they are not trendy. They are almost always about unhappy middle-aged women—you can almost discern the smell of camphor—and they are all pretty much the same. They are a bit like Chieftains records: Unless you're a hard-core fan, you probably don't need more than one of them in your collection. But there is something reassuring about maintaining a fierce allegiance to an author who keeps writing the same book over and over again, a writer who either isn't aware of this repetitive element in their work or who simply doesn't care. Thomas McGuane and John McGahern fit neatly into this class. They are like Haydn: They always rise to the occasion. They always rise to the same occasion, but they rise to the occasion all the same.

By the time that year was up, I had run through most of the short novels in my local library that were worth reading. This seemed like a good time to bring down the curtain. I now returned to weightier tomes like *Eugénie Grandet* and *The Woman in White*. These books would provide an entirely different kind of pleasure, because with them I knew that I would open a book safe in the knowledge that it would be my trusty companion for the next few days, perhaps the next few weeks, perhaps even the next few years. This is a joy whose appeal cannot be overestimated. When I was reading *Don Quixote* for the first time, a decade ago, I refused to come to the phone for the next six weeks. I did the same with *Jane Eyre*. I only wish there were more books like that. If there were, I would never come to the phone.

Small books are a genre unto themselves. When they are good, they are as long as they need to be and no more. Alan Bennett's *The Uncommon Reader* is a perfect example. It is a charming and witty novella in which Queen Elizabeth accidentally stumbles upon a bookmobile in the backyard of Buckingham Palace and suddenly develops a passion for literature. It includes a very funny passage where the queen leaves a book behind in her limo and the British secret service spirits it away, mistaking it for a bomb. When the queen returns, she finds out that the book has, in all likelihood, been hauled off into the woods and detonated.

"Exploded?" the queen says. "But it was Anita Brookner."

The Uncommon Reader was a clever idea for a book, and I had no trouble reading 120 pages on this subject. But I could not have read 220. Even 130 might have been a stretch. As Miles Davis once explained it: Genius is knowing what to leave out.

On page 21 of Bennett's novella, fairly early in a voyage of self-discovery that will ultimately lead the queen to Proust, there appears this passage: "What she was finding also was how one book led to another, doors kept opening wherever she turned, and the days weren't long enough for the reading she wanted to do."

My sentiments, exactly.

CHAPTER FOUR

Shelf Life

Legend has it that more homes were sold in the fall of 1982 than in any other comparable period in the history of the United States. That was the year the National Football League went out on strike for six weeks, and desperately unhappy men found themselves with nothing better to do on Sunday afternoons than go shopping for houses with their ecstatic wives, suddenly emancipated from the hegemony of the gridiron. This is what happened in my home. Having thrown in the towel on my youth and my dreams and reluctantly agreed to acquire a house, a garden, and children—almost simultaneously—I accompanied my wife on a short, fateful train trip up the Hudson from our Manhattan apartment to Dobbs Ferry. There we would begin our house-hunting expedition.

Dobbs Ferry was a harmless, well-meaning suburb about ten miles north of the Bronx. It was a community whose name evoked an aura of bucolic charm that the village itself could not quite muster. The real estate agent who greeted us, a furloughed historical preservationist, told us that even though house prices were relatively low, thanks to astronomical interest rates and the crushing recession the country was currently experiencing, we still could not afford to buy a house in culturally monochromatic Dobbs Ferry. But we could probably afford something in Tarrytown, a slightly less vivacious hamlet five miles farther north. House prices in Tarrytown were substantially lower than in nearby villages because the community was racially mixed, with 50-percent minority representation in the public schools. If we were really in the market for a bargain, she noted parenthetically, we could try Yonkers. At no point did we ever seriously consider moving to Yonkers. Particularly my wife, English born. One does not grow up in the verdant, pastoral Cotswolds and then move to Yonkers. It simply isn't done.

And so we set our sights on Tarrytown. Affordability was the dominant factor here, but several other elements made Tarrytown more appealing than adjacent villages like Elmsford, Valhalla, and North White Plains. For one, it did not have a preposterous name like Valhalla. Second, it had a boisterous, aromatic Italian deli, which made me feel like I was back in Philadelphia, where lively, aromatic Italian delis could be found everywhere. It also had a Woolworth's—complete with the archetypal lunch counter— which also evoked bygone Quaker City days. Still, for me, a life-long urbanite who had no desire to move to the suburbs in the first place, the worm that baited the hook was that Tarrytown had a cute little bookstore right in the middle of the village. Being cut off from art, music, and civilization in general is the thing city dwellers fear most when they move to the suburbs, because suburbs *are*, with few exceptions, cut off from art, music, and civilization. For me, the presence of a bookstore in what I initially feared might be, yea, the very valley of the shadow of death in some way eased the sting of jettisoning the city for the suburbs, cashiering my dreams, bidding *adieu* to my youth, just generally hanging up the urban six-guns. In some way.

We bought the third house the agent showed us—a dirt-cheap fixer-upper that had never been inhabited by anyone other than

Irish Americans going all the way back to the 1850s—and moved in the following May. The house was a wreck, but it was nicely situated—directly across the street from the public library and less than a hundred yards from a small but well-stocked supermarket. It was also just two doors up from the Shiloh Baptist Church, founded in 1883. The church had once been an opera house, and Euterpe, the goddess of music, had never left the building. If you didn't like gospel music, you were in the wrong neighborhood. We were instantly smitten by the village, though that may have been in part because our first child was born on Christmas morning, and we would have been smitten had we just pitched camp in the Black Hole of Calcutta. Our enchantment survived the disappearance of two of the attractions that had enticed us there in the first place. The Italian deli went out of business within a year of our arrival and was replaced by a heartless, inhospitable CVS, managed by a profoundly grumpy man who never smiled. (CVS, it was suggested by one local cutup, was an abbreviation for "Chuckles Very Sparingly.") The Woolworth's didn't last much longer; times had changed, but Woolworth's didn't change with them. When it did go under—largely because CVS had usurped most of its functions—a marginally upscale gourmet store took its place, so its disappearance was not a complete loss. Happily, unexpectedly, the bookstore hung on considerably longer than the fabulous deli or the fabled five-and-dime. And that helped make those first years in Tarrytown very special indeed.

The bookstore, flanked by a jeweler, an optometrist, and a bank, was a serviceable if pedestrian establishment initially called The Book Inn. But it came into its own when it was sold five years later and became Books & Things, a bad name for a good bookstore. The store was ferociously incongruous, a classy, sophisticated operation in a working-class town that generally lacked class and certainly lacked sophistication. People read in Tarry-town, but they didn't read much—mostly street signs and laundry instructions and cereal boxes and the fine print on the backs of unmerited parking tickets. Under the original management the store was good; under the new management it became excellent. It was run by an engaging, erudite, underpaid young man named Corey Friedlander. The store carried all the merchandise one might expect in a traditional small-town bookstore—mysteries, romances, self-help manuals, junk—but it also offered esoteric items like *The Temple of the Golden Pavilion* by Yukio Mishima and *How German Is It* by Walter Abish and *Utz* by Bruce Chatwin and *Anthills of the Savannah* by Chinua Achebe. The store tricked the community into being smarter and better informed than it would have been if left to its own devices. It belonged somewhere else, perhaps the East Village or Sedona or Avignon or Mars. The presence of these cosmopolitan titles in a suburban bookstore conferred upon the establishment an aura one would not have expected to find in a town whose streets were lined with hair salons and pizza joints and saloons. The store posited a village that did not in fact exist but soldiered on in the hopes that if everyone pulled together and was very, very discreet, the locals wouldn't notice. It was as if some puckish god had planted a pricey butcher shop in a town teeming with penniless vegetarians.

For a while the store did quite a handsome business. My patronage helped; between November 1982 and the day it closed in 1994, I bought more than two hundred books there, including titles by Charles Bukowski, Iris Murdoch, Paul Bowles, Julian Barnes, Robert Stone, Ryszard Kapuscinski, Penelope Lively, Richard Price, Thomas Bernhard, Ivan Doig, J. M. Coetzee, Eric Kraft, Margaret Drabble, Michael Frayn, Wright Morris, Charles Baxter, William Boyd, Donald Westlake, and Petronius. I bought

The Sun Also Rises and Sherwood Anderson's *Winesburg, Ohio* in that store the day we bought our house and have read and reread them many times since, because rereading these books takes me back to that precise moment, when the future seemed to stretch out endlessly in front of us and the future was both bright and beckoning.

I was very friendly with the staff, including a peppery senior who ran her own printing press on the side and the assistant manager, who lived across the river in Piermont, not far from the spot where British Major John André was hung by the neck until dead after being apprehended by stout local patriots while carrying a note hidden in his boot heel written by Benedict Arnold, offering to surrender West Point to the Redcoats. Why they were fussing about in André's boots is beyond me; by the looks of things, the stout patriots were nothing more than highwaymen. The arrest occurred in Tarrytown, or on its outskirts, and is the only thing the village is famous for.

I did a reading at the store after my first book was published, in 1992, and my daughter worked there on several Saturday afternoons, dressed up as one of the Berenstain Bears. It was boiling hot inside the costume, but she put on her game face and gutted it out. It was her first paying job. My children quickly got into the habit of believing that the most natural thing in the world was to visit a bookstore several times a week. Somehow or other I found my way into that shop practically every day for the next twelve years. It was the best thing about living in Tarrytown.

Books & Things was owned by a middle-aged couple who operated another, larger store about five miles north on the edge of Ossining, home to Sing Sing Prison. This is the institution where in 1899 the first woman was executed by electric chair, a device that owed its existence to Thomas Edison, whose casual, reflexive depravity is not as well known as it should be. The electric chair was nicknamed Old Sparky. The Books & Things flagship store, however, was not located in that part of Ossining; it sat about a mile away in a snooty, accessorial village called Briarcliff Manor, smack-dab in the middle of a busy strip mall that featured a supermarket, a bank, and several other statutorily unexciting enterprises of this general ilk.

The store had a devoted following, or so the owners believed. It, too, purveyed a classy line of goods. If you were in the market for the latest Chinua Achebe title, you'd come to the right place. But when the landlord who owned the building precipitously raised the rent, the owners decided to relocate to a much less well-traveled strip mall more than a mile away. They were certain that their clientele would follow them, and the more faithful ones did. But the owners had miscalculated here, significantly underestimating the enormous volume of casual, walk-in traffic they had enjoyed all those years because of their ideal location. The new store had virtually no walk-in trade. To get there, you had to go out of your way, and you had to travel by car. It was a perfectly fine location for a Japanese restaurant or a pet store or even an undertaker's, but it was a bad place to put a bookstore. Books & Things went belly-up within a year or so, taking its Tarrytown sibling down with it. The owners were probably bitter about what had befallen them; they had a right to feel betrayed. A few years later, when I read Penelope Fitzgerald's heartbreaking novel *The Bookshop*, I was transfixed by the final sentence describing the heroine's departure from the village of Hardborough: "As the train drew out of the station she sat with her head bowed in shame, because the town in which she had lived for nearly ten years had not wanted a bookshop." This is exactly how the owners must have felt. Books & Things had been their gift to the community. Two communities. And the communities did not want them.

It was a sad day when the Tarrytown branch of the bookstore closed, a modern suburban American tragedy, if such a thing is possible. I do not recall what happened that day, or what I felt, or when I last visited the store or what my final purchase was, just as I cannot recall what happened the day my mother died. Who would want to commit to memory the details of such an unpleasant event? And to what purpose? There was talk that the store would reopen under new management, but this was wishful thinking. In the end it was replaced by a tearoom. Given my druthers, I would have preferred something less pugnaciously twee, like a hardware store or a barbershop or a cut-rate taxidermist's or any other business that did not rely on Andrea Bocelli to generate an ambience of chintzy Neapolitan refinement. But a tearoom it was. Once the bookstore was gone, many people forgot that it had ever been there. I didn't. The closing of the bookshop was an event in my life that I would never forget. I had loved Tarrytown unconditionally for the first twelve years we lived there, and continued to enjoy many of its delights after that. But the town was never the same after the bookstore closed. Nor was I the only one who felt that way. Friends shared that opinion, dating the gradual but inexorable decline in the quality of life in the village from that moment. The town had lost something rare, precious, and beautiful, something enchanting that it could never replace. Its heart was still beating, but its heart was no longer beating fast.

That Tarrytown experience aside, I am not terribly sentimental about bookstores. I go to the bookstore for a specific purpose; I make my purchases quickly; I am in and I am out. If I visit a bookstore, it is either to buy something I need for my work, which will then immediately be discarded, or to buy a book I plan to read that very day, as I did recently when I picked up *The Tempest*, a book I had never even glanced at before. But it is almost never necessary for me to do this, because I already own most of the books I plan to read between now and my death.

I rarely visit bookstores simply to pass the time of day. I'd rather sit in the park or read a newspaper. I do not go on aspirational book-buying binges, lining my shelves with the complete correspondence between Walker Percy and Shelby Foote, a fearsome collection I will not read for years, if at all, and only after first finishing the complete works of Walker Percy and Shelby Foote. For similar reasons, I have never bought the Bhagavad-Gita or the Tibetan Book of the Dead or *The I Ching* or Oswald Spengler's *The Decline of the West*, because I have no intention of ever reading them and I am not going to pretend otherwise. When I was in college, in the late 1960s, it was fashionable for young people to cite passages from these works, particularly from *The Decline of the West*, as if the mere recitation of a few daft Teutonic theories would in and of itself hasten the West's decline. Since then, my college classmates have entered into an accelerated period of decline, as has Oswald Spengler's reputation. The West seems to be holding up just fine.

I do not make ceremonial purchases of books and then act as if acquiring them signals a sincere desire to read them. This is like buying pants one size too small in the hope that you will shed twenty pounds and one day fit into them. I have a pair of black jeans in my wardrobe that I bought when I was thirty-two years old and weighed 162 pounds. I used to think that the day would come when I would be able to wear them again. My weight has since soared as high as 227, though it is now down to around 195. In the fullness of time I might make it back down to 175, but I will never again hit 162. Thus, I will never fit into those jeans again. I merely keep them around as an objective correlative, as a physical symbol of *Paradise Lost*. Those jeans are like the proverbial snowfalls of yesteryear. *Où sont les neiges d'antan?* the poet asks. *Dans mon placard.*

The difference between those jeans and *Daniel Deronda* is that I still love those jeans and believe that if I could ever fit into them again, my life would improve markedly. I do not feel this way about *Daniel Deronda*. I will never love *Daniel Deronda*. And I will never believe that reading *Daniel Deronda* will dramatically improve my lot in life. Reading *Daniel Deronda* would have the same effect on my life as visiting Buenos Aires. It would not be uninteresting. It would not be unpleasurable. I would come back with a few good stories. But it would be a clear-cut case of fulfilling a lifelong dream I had never actually had.

More to the point, I have no desire to turn my books into little more than souvenirs, though one or two do fit into this category. I bought Colette's *L'ingénue libertine* when I was twenty-one years old and living in Paris. It was an eye-catching little Livre de Poche with a somewhat risqué illustration on the cover. It cost me ninety-five centimes, about eighteen cents at the time; the penciled-in price is just barely visible on the inside cover of the book. *L'ingénue libertine* is yet another link with a distant, fondly remembered past when I was beatifically happy and life's possibilities stretched before me. Now that I am sixty-one, though I am intermittently happy, life's possibilities no longer stretch in any specific direction, if at all. But every time I look at the cover of that book I think about the year I spent in Paris, before life took me into the back alley and roughed me up. So it's here for the duration. That said, I have no intention of ever reading *L'ingénue libertine*. I tried other books by Colette and never warmed up to them. It is a classic case of *Chacun à son gré*, as the French might put it. Colette is not *à mon gré*.

Although I purchase most of my books in bookstores, and rarely online, I have had very few bookstore experiences that stand out in any way. I would love to be able to say that there was a musty old shop I haunted as a youth—The Bookworm's Nook, let us say—where I curled up in a corner reading *The Master of Ballantrae* and *Kon-Tiki* beneath the beneficent gaze of some kindly old gent who had abandoned a promising career as a barrister to open a matchbook-sized bookstore that catered exclusively to the poor. But this was not the way things happened. There were no bookstores in the neighborhoods I grew up in. There were very few bookstores in *any* of the neighborhoods that ordinary Philadelphians grew up in during the 1950s, unless they happened to live all the way downtown, where ordinary Philadelphians tended not to go. To get to a bookstore, unless you lived in Center City, you had to travel miles and miles by foot or bus or trolley, and when you got there, nothing special awaited you. Certainly not any kindly old gents. What passed for bookstores in that era were mostly hole-in-the-wall operations staffed by oafs, curmudgeons, and lechers. There was always a section in the back dedicated to smut, a kind of literary *cordon pas tout à fait sanitaire*, but you were not allowed to go in there if you were under the age of eighteen. Still, some of us tried, desperate to get our hands on seedy paperbacks with names like *Part-Time Harlot, Full-Time Tramp*, and *Hell's Belles*. They were usually written by somebody named Ben Dover or Norman Conquest. Aside from that, these rattraps have left little imprint on my consciousness. My experiences with the bookmobile that visited our neighborhood every Friday when I was a kid had been epochal. My formative bookstore experiences were uninspiring. I remember just about none of them.

For this reason I have no precise recollection of the first book I ever bought or the bookstore I bought it in. It may have been an Agatha Christie mystery or an anthology of creepy stories "presented" by the famous director Alfred Hitchcock, who moonlighted as the host of a popular television series in the early 1960s, specializing in a choreographed weirdness that Americans for some reason found quite engaging. It was one of the strangest things about Americans of that era: They were not themselves droll; they did not go in much for drollness; but they were enthralled by the droll Alfred Hitchcock.

Whatever my first purchase was, it probably took place in a drugstore while I was waiting for the K bus to take me home from my Saturday job in a clothing store on the other side of town. Prior to this momentous purchase, I would buy a new comic book every Saturday night, sometimes *Batman*, sometimes *Justice League of America*, occasionally *Superman*, but quite often one of the beautiful issues of Classics Illustrated, which brought stories like *Les Misérables* and *Frankenstein* and even *Caesar's Gallic Wars* to life. I would have been around thirteen or fourteen years old when I started retreating from comics and buying books, though the details of these transactions escape me.

I do remember *some* of the books I bought as a teenager; I simply cannot recall the order in which I bought them. There weren't all that many, because I only pulled in six smackers a week working at the ramshackle clothing store and, like most of my peers, I would much rather spend my spare cash on records or movies or candy or girls than on books. My boss, a barrel-chested ex-Marine who devoured motivational guides like *How to Win Friends and Influence People*, frequently offered to lend me his reading material, but I preferred something less stultifyingly hortatory. One early purchase that does stand out was *The Cardinal*, a high-class potboiler by Henry Morton Robinson. I bought it at a drugstore in what was then a brand-new, state-of-the-art mall about two miles from my home. The mall no longer exists. This seminal purchase would have taken place around June 1964. I was getting ready to enter the seminary to become a Maryknoll missionary at the time and had hopes of one day rising to the lofty rank of cardinal, even though I was already falling in love with every third girl who crossed my path. The Maryknolls were always getting themselves hacked to pieces by godless communists or disgruntled fascists, which definitely took the bloom off the ecclesiastical rose, and as a result my career never achieved serious liftoff.

The Cardinal was published in 1950, the year I was born, and was loosely based on the life of Francis Cardinal Spellman, a New York City prelate about whom I knew nothing except that he was one tough customer. By the time I bought the book, my father had already taken me to see the motion picture based on the novel, an engaging and occasionally moving film starring Tom Tryon. The handsome, iron-jawed Tryon had previously played the sagebrush drifter Texas John Slaughter on a popular Disney television show. At the time Tryon was navigating the high chaparral on the small screen, he was concealing his real-life homosexuality from his employers, as homosexuality did not exist in the Old West and most assuredly not in the high, deeply Christian chaparral of the Lone Star State. Tryon, never a serious threat to Gielgud or Olivier, subsequently left the movie industry and became an extremely successful novelist, producing such varied late-Seventies fare as *The Other, Harvest Home, Fedora,* and *Lady.* His was quite the career. I never got around to reading any of his books, though I did see several of the films based on them. *The Other* was a hoot, I seem to recall, and *Fedora*, one of Billy Wilder's sign-off projects, was actually rather good. Tryon, a most un-usual man, died far too young.

I was proud of owning *The Cardinal*. Unlike many paperbacks of the era, which looked cheap, the paperback edition of Robinson's novel was shiny and elegant, with a Stendhalian black-and-white-and-red cover, altogether appropriate for the topic at hand. This was at the time when paperbacks were undergoing a trans-formation from disposable, off-the-rack detritus into what they remain today: inexpensive yet presentable objects suitable for any library. The book was published by Pocket Books. It cost seventy-five cents, more than twice the price of the Agatha Christie mysteries and the Alfred Hitchcock anthologies, which ran no more than thirty-five cents. I have checked the prices; my sister Ree still owns many of them.

The Cardinal was the first high-quality paperback I ever bought. I was really looking forward to reading it. But in the end, my plans were thwarted. I started it and tried getting into it, mostly at my father's behest, as in his youth he also had dreamed of taking the cloth, though his ambitions never spiraled as high as mine: No prelacy for him; he would have been more than happy to be a monk. The problem with *The Cardinal*, I soon realized, was that it was somewhat dense and took a while to get going. Much as I hate to admit it, it was a bit on the boring side. And to be perfectly honest, it was not entirely suitable reading material for a thirteen-year-old boy, as it contained a few racy passages where the hero, doubting his faith, briefly left the priesthood and hooked up with a perky Austrian *über*-floozy.

In the movie version of the book, which I saw later that summer, the *femme fatale* was played by Romy Schneider, a cunningly packaged vixen who also died young. At the time I was trying to read the book, my father was wearing out his 45 rpm recording of

"Stay with Me," the theme song from the movie, a powerful tune written by two songwriters who wrote no other powerful tunes I know of. It was belted out with uncharacteristic sincerity by Frank Sinatra, who often treated this kind of material in a breezy, almost contemptuous fashion. It was one of those songs that was not a hit in the wider world but was a legend inside our house. I loved that song and still do. It was a song about a man whose strength was buckling, who saw his world slipping away from him, and who hoped that his faith would abide. This was my hope at the time as well. But my faith did not abide.

I never finished reading *The Cardinal.* Our doltish, paranoid, antisocial mutt Frisky got hold of it one afternoon and gnawed it to pieces. My mother insisted that everything would be all right, that we could smooth out the pages with a steam iron, but I was having none of it. That stupid dog had gone and wrecked everything; wasn't the deliberate destruction of a book dealing with religious themes a perverse form of canine simony? I certainly thought so and hoped that God would make him burn in Hound Hell. I held on to the savagely mutilated paperback for years but never read it, in large part because by the following spring I had decided that I did not want to be a priest, so there was no possibility of ever becoming a cardinal. Doubling back to polish it off at that point would have been like reading *Mutiny on the Bounty* or *Two Years Before the Mast* after you had already decided to join the Air Force. The paperback hung around the house for years, a sad and vandalized reminder of dreams gone awry. Years after the fact, when Frisky wandered off one night and disappeared for the next three days, I refused to join the search party my father organized. He was no friend of the arts, that hapless cur, and as far as I was concerned, he could stay out there forever. Like the Nazis, he was a depraved sociopath, and like the Nazis, he had it in for books.

Another purchase from that same drugstore in that same general era was Joseph Heller's *Catch-22*. This was one of the most influential, widely discussed novels of my adolescence, a book that everyone read and everyone else talked about. I bought it, like many others, not so much because everyone was talking about it but because it had a striking steel-blue cover that was infinitely more eye-catching than anything I had seen up to that time. But *Catch-22* was another book I never got around to reading, again because of structural sabotage, though that wasn't the only obstacle. The big problem, at least at the outset, was that the book was too long and too long-winded. It had small, ugly type, a widespread problem in those days, though one that has since been corrected by publishing companies. And it was one of those books that got quoted so much in the years after it came out that it made you feel that you had already read it, that made you want to read something entirely different, like *Kid Colt and the Legend of the Lost Arroyo* or *Satan's Sorority* or even *Daniel Deronda*. One other high negative: The student activists in the college I later attended were always demanding that our teachers give *Hamlet* and *Absalom, Absalom!* the old heave-ho and assign *The Sirens of Titan* and *Catch-22* instead. A cultural reactionary from the word go, I had always treated the titans of the past with enormous reverence, so I thought these student activists were unlettered jackwagons. In the end, the whole Strawberry Statement *Kulturkampf* fiasco turned me against *Catch-22* for good.

Catch-22 was my first exposure to the concept of "this year's model," where everybody everywhere started reading the same book at exactly the same moment, even though a lot of them got only thirty pages into it before bailing out. It was one of those inescapable books that are universally revered until they get made into films. The films based on those books are always horrible and in some way tarnish their image. It seemed like the entire planet was talking about Dan Brown's *The Da Vinci Code* until Ron Howard's *Da Vinci Code* came out. Then the planet stopped talking about it. The same thing happened with *The Hours*, where Nicole Kidman sported that jarring prosthetic nose, and *The Shipping News*, where everyone was completely miscast, and Peter Jackson's cataleptic *The Lovely Bones*, fatally hamstrung by a shortage of Hobbits. There was also the curious case of *Atonement*, irreparably damaged by the disastrous decision to cast James McAvoy as the male lead, thereby prompting viewers on both sides of the Atlantic to side with the nasty little tyke whose lies destroy the protagonist's life.

It's not so much that the bad movies make the books seem less good; it's simply that the premiere of the bad movie signals that the high-water mark of the book's popularity has arrived, that its moment as a cultural colossus has now passed. By and large, a book will retain a certain grandeur and cachet so long as it has not been transmogrified into a bad film. After Hollywood gets its hands on it, the bad movie competes for attention with the good book. Until you see the movie *Catch-22*, you have an image of Yossarian in your head that is enticing, though vague. But once Yossarian becomes embodied in the person of the overbearing Alan Arkin, once the *Girl with a Pearl Earring* ceases to be a figure of mystery and romance and morphs into Scarlett Johansson, once the undernourished sparrow Penélope Cruz makes a complete hash of *Corelli's Mandolin*, the spell is broken forever. Only the greatest books can withstand the damage inflicted on their reputations by bad movies: *The Great Gatsby*, *Anna Karenina*, *Pride and Prejudice*. Hollywood has always been reasonably good at turning electrifying hooey like *Gone with the Wind* and *The Bridges of Madison County* into movies that are far superior to the novels that begat them. But it has trouble when it takes a run at *War and Peace*. Hollywood doesn't know what to do with serious fiction, so it does what it does best: It annihilates it.

Books designated as this year's model do have a certain value as props. One day, when I was carrying my *Catch-22* paperback around, trophy-like, hoping that some nubile teenaged girl would be smitten by my intellectual prowess, my friend Joe Alteari's sister, Joanne, asked if she could borrow the book. I said sure, be my guest, as I had never finished a book anywhere near as long as *Catch-22* and that situation was unlikely to change anytime soon. Joanne, I was sure, would make it straight through to the end. Joanne had a job at Sears Roebuck out on Route 1 and used to drive me to my summer job at the Naval Supply Depot, which sat directly behind that massive department store. I'd always liked her; she was a bit of a wiseacre. You never saw her without sunglasses. And she was a serious reader. A few weeks later, she returned the book, but it was now all dog-eared and matted. I was livid. Had she left it out in the rain or the snow or the sleet or what? She didn't understand what I was grumbling about; she said that paperbacks were always intended to be stuffed inside your back pocket or into your pocketbook; they were supposed to get jacked up. If you wanted a classy-looking book to add to your tragic little collection, you should go out and buy a hardback. She didn't seem to understand that the publication of *Catch-22* was a watershed moment in the history of the industry, as it marked the moment when paperbacks stopped being thought of as pre-fab refuse and started to be thought of as quality merchandise that could be displayed—proudly—in one's home. Actually, nobody realized that at the time, least of all me. Watershed moments only become apparent decades later. All I knew was that a classy paperback that had set me back six bits had callously been bent, folded, spindled, and mutilated and that I no longer had any desire to read it. So I never did. Years later I read *Something Happened* and *Good as Gold*, both of which I liked very much. But for some reason I never went back and read the book that made Joseph Heller famous. Whatever happened to that defiled, debased copy of *Catch-22*, I have no idea. But it was never replaced.

I have rarely been treated especially well in bookstores. I think this is because I do not look like a book lover. I look more like a cop. I certainly do not look like the kind of person who frequents serious cultural establishments. What it all comes down to is this: I do not look like I have ever read a book by Bill McKibben. Though it pains me to admit it, I look like somebody who can't make up his mind whether to buy the new Clive Cussler or the new W. E. B. Griffin. Bookstore personnel pick up on this. Spindly boys with thick Clark Kent glasses wearing ill-advised polo shirts and unpersuasive facial hair routinely come up to me and say, "Can I help you with anything?" as if I were a disoriented extraterrestrial or the last man to straggle home from Gettysburg.

Commercial bookstores are often staffed by transitory loners who are merely punching the clock, troubled youths and cast-off retirees who do not have all that much interest in books. Staff recommendations are pitifully generic—*Fight Club*, *Outliers*, *Infinite Jest*. It's like soliciting dessert tips from four-year-olds. Why doesn't the staff ever go out on a limb and select something by R. K. Narayan or Alan Sillitoe or Chrétien de Troyes? Oh, how many nights have I lain awake, gazing up at the stars, dreaming of the day I would stride into a bookstore and find a rack teeming with staff recommendations that might include such personal favorites as Octave Mirbeau's *The Garden of Torments*, Aidan Higgins's *Bornholm Night-Ferry*, Heinrich Böll's *Action Will Be Taken*? It would be even nicer if I walked into a Starbucks, a sort of para-quasi-bookstore, and stumbled upon a stack of books by Ward Just or Nathan Englander piled up to the ceiling. But I do not think this is going to happen.

Nor is it likely to happen in most independent bookstores. Independent bookstores, whatever their other virtues, are often staffed by condescending prigs who do not approve of people like me. The only writers they like are dead or exotic or Paul Auster. Independent bookstore employees have disproportionate respect for writers named Banana and Arno. If your name is Janos or Czeniew or Bjini, you're in like Flint. If your name is Joseph T. Klempner or O'Henry, you're not. People like this often like weird, obscure writers, but they never like the weird, obscure writers I like. Sometimes I think that I was born on the wrong planet, a planet where almost nobody reads and where the people who do read assume that I don't.

My unfortunate experiences in bookstores started a long time ago, when I was a student in Paris. Back then it was a rite of passage for aspiring young writers to visit Shakespeare and Company, the legendary bookstore on the bank of the Seine that is forever associated with Ernest Hemingway and James Joyce. In fact, the original bookstore—the one that got *Ulysses* published just in time for me to never finish reading it—closed its doors forever when the Nazis put in a surprise appearance in 1940; the bookstore I visited in the Seventies was a replacement in the fabled 5th Arrondissement named in honor of the original Shakespeare and Company. It was like the House of Burgesses down in Ye Olde Williamsburg: ersatz but iconic. The shop was filled with hirsute, emaciated, poorly dressed, poorly shod young men who were desperately trying to emulate the George Orwell of *Down and Out in Paris and London*. They looked famished, wan, and impoverished, some of them seemingly at death's door. You could never tell whether they'd gone to Phillips Exeter or Andover. The store was still being run by George Whitman, the successor to the mythical Sylvia Beach. I visited it twice, and both times I asked him what I thought was a reasonably serious question. Both times the grizzled bastard totally blew me off. He perhaps had me sized up as just another Papa Hemingway wannabe, just another F. Scott Fitzgerald *manqué*, just another would-be Henry Miller. But I did not want to be Ernest Hemingway, much less F. Scott Fitzgerald, much less Henry Miller, famously bald and ugly and mean. And I certainly had no desire to be Anaïs Nin. I wanted to be Nathanael West, the dyspeptic author of *The Day of the Locust* and *Miss Lonelyhearts*, who died in a car crash in El Centro, California, the day after Fitzgerald went to meet his maker. The date of West's death was December 22, 1940, the thirteen hundredth anniversary of the most recent burning of the Library of Alexandria. Obviously no one at Shakespeare and Company had any way of knowing of my arcane, improbable dreams. They treated me like scum anyway. So I stopped going there and bought all my books around the corner on the Boulevard Saint-Michel at a gigantic store called Gibert Jeune. It was a barn and nothing more, entirely without charm or mythology. It was actually a series of charm-free barns, each specializing in a different subject matter. But its books were cheap. I bought dozens of them there, all of which I still own: *Opéra* by Jean Cocteau, *Le diable au corps* by Raymond Radiguet, *La sorcière* by Jules Michelet, *Les caves du Vatican* by André Gide. And at least at Gibert Jeune, no one made a special point of being rude to me.

When I moved to New York, in 1976, everyone raved about the Strand, which had miles and miles of used books. In thirty-six years of living in or around Gotham, I have gone there only twice, because I never liked buying used books. People who have grown up poor don't like buying things secondhand, because they've already grown up wearing secondhand clothes and playing with secondhand toys. There isn't anything special about buying a used book; somebody else got that special rush first. I only buy secondhand books out of desperation, like the time I found myself stranded in downtown South Bend, Indiana, a hellhole if there ever was one, and saved the day when I unearthed a copy of Jean Anouilh's *Becket, ou l'honneur de Dieu* in a used bookstore. I think God Himself may have interceded here, compensating me for that long, hard year I spent in a seminary ten miles outside Scranton, Pennsylvania, which was also short on pizazz. But there is another dynamic at work here: Purchasing a secondhand book does absolutely nothing for a writer. Less than nothing. There is, it seems to me, a poverty of spirit about not wanting to purchase the shiny new book by Gabriel García Márquez. People should consider it an honor to pay full price for a book by Don DeLillo or Margaret Atwood. An honor.

My favorite bookstore in New York City was not any of the obvious ones, like the Gotham Book Mart or Rizzoli's or Scribner's or one of the dank crypto-commie bookstores in the East Village. It was the Commuter Book Centre, a dive that used to sit in the Lexington Avenue Passageway at Grand Central Terminal. It was literally a hole in the wall, roughly the size of your average bedroom. You had to climb up a couple of well-worn steps to get to it, and when you got inside, there wasn't a whole lot waiting for you. It was run by a big, relatively inanimate guy who sat at the cash register by the front door all day long and genuinely seemed to enjoy presiding over such a ragtag operation. He didn't say much, and you never saw him move. But whenever you bought a book, he looked it over carefully and then flashed you a knowing little wink that seemed to say: *Nice choice, bub. I can see I am in the presence of the literati.* The stock didn't turn over much; it looked like no fresh inventory had been added since Dickens put the finishing touches on *Little Dorrit.* All of the books were entombed in a thick patina of dust and grime. The store didn't have catchy window displays, and there were no author signings. It was not chic. It did not have that *je ne sais quoi* quality. Yet there was something so inspiring about this obstinately uninviting establishment that I could never resist visiting it. The store reminded me of my stogie-smoking, hard-drinking, guitar-strumming, saloon-singing Uncle Charlie: damned but saucy. I bought *Silas Marner* and *Ethan Frome* and *Lord Jim* and *The Idiot* there, among dozens of other titles, and I have never parted with them. All of these books told sad stories, as did *The Awakening* and *Billy Budd* and *The Castle.* I suspect that every single book in stock was heartbreaking, that the owner or manager or whoever was in charge deliberately refused to order any cheerful reading material like *Little Women* or *My Friend Flicka* because he feared that the store would lose its dyspeptic mojo. This was part of the store's allure. It was so forlorn and beaten down, with such a miasma of doom hovering about it, that it would have seemed inappropriate to buy something festive or upbeat like *A Connecticut Yankee in King Arthur's Court* there. It would be like asking for a fudge sundae halfway through Armageddon.

On New Year's Eve in 1991, without any warning, the bookstore shut its doors forever. It had lasted exactly thirty years, an eternity in New York. Apparently, the owner owed a ton of back rent and finally decided to call it a day. This was around the time the train station was getting primed for a face-lift, so the bookstore probably couldn't have lasted much longer anyway. I never found out what happened to the manager or owner or whoever it was who camped out by the front door every day. But I knew that an important part of my life was gone. It was the same way I felt when the Great Jones Diner just off Lafayette Street got shuttered or when the department store B. Altman's got taken over by scumbags from Toronto and imploded shortly thereafter. The bookstore was succeeded by a dandy little shop on the other side of the terminal called Posman Books. It is a much better bookstore than the one it replaced, with a far more engaging, personable staff, and I have purchased lots of reading material there. But I miss the Commuter Book Centre. It is broken-down and dirty and entirely without pretense. It was a dump for the ages.

I sometimes wonder whether all bookstore stories must end badly. Scribner's, an upscale operation on Fifth Avenue, closed its doors. So did the pip-squeak French bookstore that used to ply its trade in Rockefeller Center. Also down for the count went the Gotham Book Mart, a venerable institution in New York's Diamond District until the axe fell in 2007, after eighty-seven glorious years. For that matter, all those Borders stores I used to visit all across America are gone. There was also a first-rate bookstore in my wife's hometown in England. Every summer when we went over to visit her relatives I would stop by Alan Tucker's shop and come back lugging a dozen or more Penguin Classics: *Picture Palace* and *The Family Arsenal* by Paul Theroux, *The Suffrage of Elvira*, *The Mimic Men*, and *A House for Mr. Biswas* by V. S. Naipaul, *Hermit of Peking* by Hugh Trevor-Roper. A lot of these books had orange spines, and for some reason I thought they were beautiful. People said I was insane to buy books in England and then carry them all the way back to the United States, especially if they were orange. But people like that are peasants. Even if they are right about the insanity business. The way I looked at it, as soon as I owned the books, I was well on my way to reading them, even if it took me ten years to get around to it. These were days tinged with euphoria. When you are young, you think that if you read enough Penguin Classics, you can learn everything. You cannot. You will also forget much of what you have learned and never get to some of the books you always wanted to get to. And you will discover, as Samuel Johnson observed, that not all wisdom is to be found in books. But an awful lot of it is.

My daughter went to college with a boy whose Russian-Jewish parents left the Soviet Union in the late Brezhnev era and moved to the suburbs of Boston. When their suitcases were inspected at Logan Airport in Boston, the immigration officers were surprised to find that they were filled with books. "We took our books with us when we left Russia," Gregory's father once explained to me, "because in Russia books were like gold." This was the way I felt about those treasures I used to cart all the way back from the west of England to the east of the United States. The whole time I was in the air, I would keep pulling them out to inspect them, to caress them, rhapsodizing about how much pleasure they would give me when I got back home. Not one of those books disappointed me. I have never parted with a single one of them; they are all right there in my living room or office; I will be rereading them the day I die, and their physical presence will remind me of those days in Stroud when I was young and the world was new. This is another thing you cannot do with a Kindle.

I used to have spirited, engaging chats with the bookstore owner in Stroud, and looked forward to our annual visits. Conversely, I never patronized the W. H. Smith bookstore right around the corner, because it was venal and crass and sold candy and cigarettes and books by Jilly Cooper. A few years ago, I arrived in Stroud and found that the bookstore that sold the Penguin Classics had closed its doors. The W. H. Smith is still there. This is the way of the world.

My most memorable bookshop experience took place in Canada. Few people can make this claim. It was not even in a particularly fashionable part of Canada. My wife had an elderly aunt who lived in a small town in Ontario about a hundred miles east of Toronto. She may actually have been a cousin. She was one of only two people I have ever met who was entirely without malice. She never met a nutritionally suspect pastry she would not purchase or a bucket of Kentucky Fried Chicken she would not serve, sometimes to confused and chagrined guests. Aunt Adah was the closest thing to a grandparent that my children ever had, as my wife's parents died shortly before I met her, my father was an alcoholic with whom the children had little contact, and my mother was an emotionally distant manic-depressive who had only slightly less interest in her three grandchildren than in her own four children. She was Irish and then some.

Every couple of summers we would make the ten-hour trip from Tarrytown to Ontario to see Aunt Adah, widowed before my children were born, who lived alone in a cute little house on a bay that fed into Lake Ontario. We would not take the major routes to reach her but would meander northwest on local roads along the old Mohawk Trail, wending our way up from Albany until we reached Watertown, a once-flourishing but now barely extant city. A few miles north of Watertown lies Cape Vincent, a pokey fishing village where a ferry plies its way back and forth from Wolfe Island, halfway between the United States and Canada. We would clamber aboard the ferry, then drive the seven miles around Wolfe Island, and then take a second ferry to Kingston, a thriving city on the Canadian shore. The children loved the ferry rides. From there it was a two-hour drive down Highway 401 to Adah's house, where the twenty-piece bucket of Kentucky Fried Chicken would be waiting. Sometimes thirty-piece. The kids did not enjoy the drive on 401; it was unremittingly uninteresting. But they enjoyed the fried chicken.

At the time, our vacation destination boasted an active downtown, with a movie house, a public library, a jeweler's, an appliance store, several quaint restaurants, and a bookshop. These are now mostly gone, replaced by unsightly dollar stores. Dollar stores are like those tiny white stones one sees on unmarked Civil War graves: *Someone once lived here, but we do not know who, and we can no longer remember when.* While the town thrived, the bookstore thrived. In 1980, on my first visit, I struck up a conversation with the owner. He noticed that I was looking at books written by Canadian authors and made a few recommendations. Until then, I was only familiar with the work of Margaret Atwood, Mordecai Richler, and Brian Moore, though Moore is probably more Irish than Canadian. The owner recommended that I try *Bear* by Marian Engel and *This Side Jordan* by Margaret Laurence. I read them as soon as I got back to the States and loved them, though I was somewhat surprised that this straitlaced Canadian would recommend a book about a lonely female historian who treats herself to a short, ergonomically implausible love affair with a bear. The bear was a bit surprised, too. These two books will remain in my collection forever. The next time I passed through town, we had another confab or two about Canadian literature, and he said I should give Ethel Wilson's *The Equations of Love* and Alice Munro's *Friend of My Youth* a try. I did, and they were both outstanding. They, too, are permanent fixtures in my collection.

One summer, late in the 1980s, the man who owned the bookstore asked if I had ever read Morley Callaghan, who lived in Paris at the same time as Ernest Hemingway and F. Scott Fitzgerald and Gertrude Stein, and who had written a memoir called *That Summer in Paris*, which was basically *A Moveable Canadian Feast*. This book he actually gave me. For me, the Canadian Connection opened up a secret garden of delights, but it was also useful when I would find myself engrossed in conversations with English-speaking Canadians, people who would naturally assume that I knew nothing about Canadians except that they played ice hockey and drank Molson. They were particularly impressed—more like bewildered—that I had also read a number of French-Canadian authors, like Gabrielle Roy and Marie-Claire Blais. They certainly hadn't. English Canadians don't read that kind of stuff. It's not in them. Especially the men. Aside from my *tête-à-têtes* with that gregarious Ontario bookseller, I have never had a wide-ranging conversation about Canadian literature with anyone. Nor do I expect to.

My kids started to grow up, and for a few summers in a row we went over to France and England, so we did not get up to Canada. But the next time we visited Aunt Adah, I was overjoyed to see that the bookstore was still a going concern. I went in to see my old friend, eager to pick up where we had left off, but he did not seem to remember me. I visited several times that week, and we eventually swung back into the rhythm of things, and the day before I left for home, he gave me a copy of W. O. Mitchell's *Who Has Seen the Wind*. It was not a very good book, but on the inside flap are written the words "A gift of the shopkeeper." As with all my previous gifts, I will cherish it forever.

The next time we drove north, I returned to the bookstore I loved so much. But the conversation did not flow. I realized now that the shopkeeper had no idea who I was. He did not remember our conversations, and he did not remember the gifts he had given me. The store had fallen on hard times; books were going dirt-cheap, especially the black-bordered Penguin Classics. So I bought thirty-six of them. I bought *History of the Franks* and *The Confessions of Saint Augustine* and *Meditations* by Marcus Aurelius and *The Prince*. I bought *Burmese Days* and *Spanish Testament* and *The Road to Wigan Pier* and *Keep the Aspidistra Flying*. I bought *A Burnt-Out Case* and *The Ministry of Fear* and *Our Man in Havana* and *England Made Me*. I bought *The Rainbow* and *Women in Love* and *The Annals of Imperial Rome*. I bought Plato and Herodotus and Livy and Henry Fielding and Isaac Babel and Robert Graves and V. S. Pritchett. I also bought a copy of *The Iliad*, even though I already owned three copies. And, just for old time's sake, I bought one final book by a Canadian author: *The Whirlpool* by Jane Urquhart. These books line the shelves in my bedroom closet to this day. So may they always.

One day at age ninety-four, Aunt Adah died, and we stopped going to Canada. Her family felt that the time had come to put her in a nursing home, but she had other plans. The next time we visited, many years later, the town had become unrecognizably ugly, and the bookstore was on its last legs. Now it is gone. And, as was the case when the bookstore in Tarrytown closed its doors, the town was the worse for its passing.

Last spring I had a bookstore experience that more than made up for all the bad ones I had ever had. It happened in a most unusual way. I had just finished lunch with an Australian friend I have known since the day we met in Paris in 1972. I had run into his French girlfriend in a store around the corner from my boarding-house, and as soon as she realized that I was American, she told me that her boyfriend was not all that crazy about the French and would welcome a chance to converse in his own language. She invited me over for dinner that Thursday night. The three of us became fast friends; in fact, a few years later we all lived together for a month in a spooky, otherwise unoccupied high-rise in the southwest corner of France. The building housed German tourists in the summer; the rest of the year it housed no one. Living there was like being in a French horror film, perhaps *Le Shining*. Mick eventually went back to Australia to visit his ailing father, and a few years later he and Claudine broke up, and I did not see him for the next twenty-one years. But we stayed in touch, as I did with Claudine, now a longtime resident of Berlin. When I went out to visit Mick in Sydney with my family in 1997, it dawned on me that he was one of my closest friends, even though we had not seen each other since 1976. The time we spent in France together—drinking, watching midnight screenings of classic films at the Cinémathèque, drinking—had cemented our friendship for life. France is like that.

A few years ago, in his capacity as a flight attendant for Qantas, Mick began flying to New York every two weeks. Prior to that, there was no regular Sydney–Los Angeles–New York flight. We would now meet for dinner on Tuesday night, then reconvene for a Wednesday lunch, after which he would fly back to Los Angeles and then to Sydney. One afternoon after our usual sumptuous repast, I watched him disappear down the stairs at the 68th Street–Lexington Avenue subway station. It just so happened that there was a bookstore, Shakespeare & Co., directly across the street. At the time I was in the market for a novel by Ali Smith that a friend at *The Wall Street Journal* had recommended. Back in Paris, as previously indicated, Shakespeare and Company had never been especially cordial to me. In fact, they had been downright nasty. But that was long ago and in another country, so I figured I should let bygones be bygones. Anyway, I wasn't even sure that the two establishments were related, the Gotham bookstore choosing to distinguish itself by the use of an ampersand. I entered and asked the Irony Boy at the front desk if the store had a book by Ali Smith, called—now what was the name? Oh, yes: *There But for the Grace of God* . . . or something to that effect. Irony Boy said, "If we have it, you'll see it on the shelves." Now, why hadn't I thought of that? I did not see it on the shelves, at least not under the "s's" in the fiction section, so I returned to the front counter and, just for the sake of argument, asked if he would mind tearing himself away from whatever he was doing and look up the title on the computer. He did so with the worst will in the world, as if I were asking him to euthanize a particularly charismatic dachshund. He fumbled about for a bit, then hit pay dirt.

"The actual title is *There But for the* . . . ," he said.

"*There But for the Grace of God* is in the ballpark," I replied.

"It's a new book," he went on. "It's in the new-books section. That's why you didn't find it on the shelves."

That made sense. It really did. So we went off to find it. As luck would have it, it was stacked rather high on a shelf, out of his reach. He shuffled off to fetch a stepladder, but I said, "That won't be necessary." I reached up, without even needing to perch on my tippy-toes, and yanked the book right down off the shelf. That felt good. He could tell that I was going out of my way to be mean. But I couldn't help myself. He was an Irony Boy. And I'd waited thirty-nine long years to even the score with these snooty sons of bitches. Even if they weren't actually related to the snooty sons of bitches back in Paris. Now the moment of vindication had arrived. It was on. It was *so* on.

I paid for the book, and on my way out the door I spotted a title called *Paris Was Ours*. It was an anthology of stories by writers who had lived in Paris and included an essay in which I discussed my long-standing friendship with Mick. I walked out of the store and immediately collided with a man who was roughly my age, though better dressed, and slender. In my essay in *Paris Was Ours* I had talked about strolling into the Jardin du Luxembourg one evening in the late Nineties and bumping into an old friend from my student days that I had not seen in twenty-five years. In fact, I wrapped up the essay by describing that exchange, in which I asked him what he was doing in the gardens that day, and by extension, what he was doing in Paris, and he simply answered, "I could never get this place out of my head." He might have been talking about the Jardin du Luxembourg. But I think he was talking about Paris.

My friend's name was Jay Jolly. The man I collided with outside the premises of my old nemesis Shakespeare and Company—or a simulacrum thereof—that afternoon was Jay Jolly. Two weeks later Jay and Mick and I broke bread together for the first time since May 1973. We had a grand old time. It was as if no more than a day had passed since we had last seen one another, merrily knocking back drinks at the Alliance Française student cafe. This had all come about because I ventured inside a bookstore that was probably trying to pass itself off as the New York branch of a legendary Parisian bookstore that had always treated me like vermin, and spotted a book in which I mentioned both Mick and Jay, and all this happened just seconds after I had put Mick on the subway so that he could fly back to Australia, and just seconds before I crossed paths with Jay for the first time in more than a decade.

I don't think this kind of stuff happens with a Kindle.

CHAPTER FIVE

Prepare to Be Astonished

A while back, a friend whose unpredictable behavior I usually hold in high esteem handed me a book entitled *Father John: Navajo Healer*. By the looks of things, he expected me to read it, even though I am not really a Navajo healer autobiography kind of guy. Flummoxed but civil, I took the book home and positioned it on a shelf in a dark, virtually inaccessible corner of my office, right alongside all the other books that friends have forced upon me over the years.

This collection includes *Loose Balls: The Short, Wild Life of the American Basketball Association, The Frontier World of Doc Holliday*, and both *Steve Allen on the Bible, Religion, and Morality* and Allen's somewhat less Jesuitical *Hi-Ho, Steverino! My Adventures in the Wonderful Wacky World of Television*. If I live to be a thousand years old, I am not going to read any of these books. Especially the one about the American Basketball Association. I have not always been successful at conveying this fact to other people, but I am deadly serious about the way I parcel out my reading time. I may have time for this, but I do not have time for that. Several years ago, I calculated how many books I could read if I lived to my actuarially expected age. The answer was 2,138. In theory, those 2,138 books would include everything from *Tristram Shandy* to *Le Colonel Chabert*, with titles by authors as celebrated as Goethe and as obscure as Juan Filloy. In principle, there would be enough time to read 500 masterpieces, 500 minor classics, 500 overlooked works of pure genius, 500 oddities, and 168 examples of first-class trash. But by trash, I am referring to material that is so stupid it makes your heart start pounding and your teeth start chattering. Nowhere in this utopian future would there be time for *Hi-Ho, Steverino!* Unadulterated stupidity, in the hands of true professionals, can be exhilarating. Lameness is merely lame.

True, I used to be one of those people who could never start a book without finishing it, the compulsive type who could never introduce a volume to his library without making plans to eventually read it. Or to eventually peruse it. Familiarity with this character flaw may have encouraged others to use me as a cultural guinea pig, perversely burdening me with books like *Damien the Leper* (written by Mia Farrow's father) or *The Habit of Being: The Letters of Flannery O'Connor*, just to see if they were worth taking a stab at. (The second one was; the first one wasn't.) These forced reconnaissance missions came to an end the day an otherwise likable friend sent me *Accordion Man*, the self-published autobiography of Electro-Vox legend Dick Contino. Though I revere Mr. Contino for his unparalleled rendition of "Arrivederci, Roma," and his scintillating solo on "Lady of Spain," it disturbed me greatly that my friend would have mistaken my affection for Mr. Contino's music with an interest in his prose. Listening to his compact discs is fine: You can easily read *Death in Venice* or Pascal's *Pensées* while "Roll Out the Barrel" is rumbling along in the background. But if you spend too much time reading how Contino finally came to record "You'll Never Walk Alone," you will never get to Junichiro Tanizaki's *Some Prefer Nettles*. And *Some Prefer Nettles* is No. 1,759 on my list.

After I calculated how many books I could polish off between the present moment and my death, I became much more selective in my reading habits. With time's winged chariot now nipping at my heels, I knew that I needed to pick up the pace, making me less and less likely to read a book just for the sake of reading a book. Life, which in my youth I found unstintingly entertaining, now felt more and more like a Smith & Wesson cocked at my head, so if I had plans to read *The Decameron* and *Finnegans Wake* before I checked out for good, I would have to start being a bit more choosy. Logically, this meant that there were great books out there that I already knew I was never going to read. Some, like *Arrowsmith* and *Manhattan Transfer*, were books that I was actually looking forward to not reading. *The Last of the Mohicans*, too. Barring unforeseen circumstances, I have probably seen the last of Nathaniel Hawthorne, John Steinbeck, Upton Sinclair, Gertrude Stein, Richard Sheridan, Mikhail Sholokhov, George Sand, Plautus, Terence, Anatole France, François Mauriac, Laura Z. Hobson, and Henry Wadsworth Longfellow. If I live to be eighty, which I do not expect to do, I might set aside a year to read all the books I long ago decided that I would never read. But I suspect that reading Thomas Wolfe, Thomas Mann, and Thomas Hardy all in one year might kill me. It has surely killed others.

I believe that serious, or let us say *obsessive*, readers all have some sort of clock or meter running in our heads. We have a rough idea of how long we expect to live, and we have structured our reading habits accordingly. Once you reach the age of sixty, as I have, it is debatable whether there is still time left for Pliny the Elder, but there is certainly no time left for Pearl Buck. Any book you read from that time on could be your last. You wouldn't want it to be *The Good Earth*. It is said that a few hundred years ago, in the time of Thomas Jefferson, for example, it was possible for a person to read every book that had ever been printed. It is still possible to read every *great* book that has ever been printed; it would take about three years. Maybe four. Five, if you're a slow reader. But once you expand that universe to include the near-great, or the not-so-great, or so-so efforts by authors who had written other books that were great, the task becomes much more arduous. Something has to give. I love *Men Without Women* and *In Our Time*, but have no great desire to read *Across the River and into the Trees*. *David Copperfield*, *Hard Times*, and *Great Expectations* are among my favorites; *The Mystery of Edwin Drood* I am prepared to take a rain check on. *The Good Soldier* is a small miracle; I suspect that the lesser works of Ford Madox Ford are not. John Collier, James Hadley Chase, Sax Rohmer, Erle Stanley Gardner? Maybe next lifetime. There is, it must be emphasized, nothing wrong with any of these authors. But I no longer have time to read them.

Reading is intensely personal. This is why I do not like it when people try to force books into my hands. If I wanted to read Philip K. Dick, I would have probably gotten around to it by now. Ditto William Gibson and Ursula K. Le Guin. Book lovers are engaged in the ceaseless reconfiguration of a Platonic reading list that will occupy their free time for the next thirty-five years: First, I'll get to *War and Peace*, then *Ulysses*, then that juggernaut by Proust, and finally *Finnegans Wake*. But I'll never get to *Finnegans Wake* if I keep stopping to read books like *The Frontier World of Doc Holliday*. Even though it is quite an entertaining little affair.

I am certainly not suggesting that all gifted or lent books should be ridiculed, pulped, mothballed, or incinerated. My sisters have impeccable taste in crime fiction and know precisely which Ruth Rendell title to pass along next. But that's about it. Acquaintances and neighbors, I do not trust. Well-wishers I find even more suspect. Sadly, these people are often unaware of my feelings. In many instances, they try to pass along books as a probing technique to answer the question "Is he really one of us?" That is, you can't possibly care about the poor pre-Columbian denizens of this hemisphere unless you've read *1491* and its prequel, *1490*. Correct. And you're not really interested in the future of our imperiled republic unless you've read *The No Spin Zone*, *The No Spin Zone for Children*, *101 Things Stupid Liberals Hate About the No Spin Zone*, and *Anne Coulter on Spinoza*. Again, right on target.

Some people may wonder, Why don't you simply lie when people ask you about the books they've lent you? There are two problems with this sort of duplicity. One, lying is a mortal sin. Two, experienced off-fobbers of books will invariably subject their targets to the third degree: Were you surprised at Father Damien's blasé reaction when his fingers started to rot off? What did you think of that snappy little ermine number Parsifal was wearing when he finally wrapped his pudgy little fingers around the Holy Grail? Were you caught off guard by those weird recipes for *Sachertorte* in *The Tipping Point*? How did you react when you found out that Father John was a Mescalero and not a Navajo? After reading *The Frontier World of Doc Holliday*, do you have more or less respect for Ike Clanton as a money manager? Pity the callow lendee who falls for the trick question and is unmasked as a fraud.

Because I live in a small town where I cross paths with profligate book lenders all the time, I have lately taken to hiding in subterranean caverns, wearing clever disguises while concealed in tenebrous alcoves, and feigning rare tropical illnesses such as Sabu's Apnea to avoid being encumbered by any new reading material. Were I a younger man, I would be more than happy to take a peek at *Holy Faces, Secret Places: An Amazing Quest for the Face of*

Jesus, or Bob Weir's intimate history of The Grateful Dead. But time is running out, and if I don't get cracking soon, I'm never going to get to *Gunpowder and Firearms in the Mamluk Kingdom*, much less *The Golden Bough*.

Of course, the single greatest problem in accepting unsolicited books from friends is that it may encourage them to lend you others. Once you've told them how much you enjoyed *How the Irish Saved Civilization*, they'll be at your front doorstep with *How the Scots Invented the Modern World*, *The Gifts of the Jews*, *Indian Givers: How the Indians of the Americas Transformed the World*, and one day *How the Bulgarians Invented Hip-Hop*. If you tell them that you liked *Why Sinatra Matters* or *Why Orwell Matters*, you're giving them carte blanche to turn up with *Why Vic Damone Matters* or *Why G. K. Chesterton Still Rocks!* When I foolishly lied to a friend about how much I enjoyed Kinks lead singer Ray Davies's "unauthorized autobiography" *X-Ray*, she then upped the ante with a copy of Dave Davies's *Kink: An Autobiography: The Outrageous Story of My Wild Years as the Founder and Lead Guitarist of the Kinks*. Surely, *The Mick Avory Story: My Life as the Kinks' Original Drummer* and *Pete Quaife: Hey, What Am I, the Kinks' Bassist or a Potted Plant?* cannot be far behind.

This is why I finally had to tell yet another friend that I hated a mildly interesting police procedural he'd dropped off. The novel dealt with a fictitious organization called the Vermont Bureau of Investigation and was actually quite good. But when I found out that there were at least eleven other books in the series and realized that my friend might own all of them, I feared that I would never, ever get to Miguel de Unamuno's *The Tragic Sense of Life* at this rate. And at No. 2,127 on my list, Unamuno might only just get in under the wire anyway.

· · · · · ·

My reading habits, deranged or not, are colored by regional and class bias. I will not read books where the main character attended private school. *The Catcher in the Rye*, *A Separate Peace*, *A Good School*, and the Harry Potter books are all beyond the pale, as are *Goodbye, Mr. Chips* and *The History Boys*. I also will not read books by P. G. Wodehouse, a poncey aristocrat who played footsie with the Nazis during the fall of France. There are crimes that can be forgiven—arson, bestiality, cheating on one's income taxes—but this is not one of them. I do not enjoy books by authors who seem to assemble their novels brick by brick, like Thomas Mann and Sinclair Lewis, and I avoid at all costs books about melancholy WASPs, teens with social anxiety disorders, and immigrants who simply will not take no for an answer.

A couple of years ago, a friend gave me a copy of David Benioff's *City of Thieves*. The novel had come highly recommended to me, and as I had already seen Spike Lee's affecting film *25th Hour*, which is based on Benioff's first novel, I was really looking forward to reading the book. *City of Thieves*, set during the Nazi siege of Leningrad in 1941, deals with a Russian teenager who will be shot by Stalin's police unless he can get his hands on a dozen eggs that will be used to bake a wedding cake for a Russian colonel's daughter. Since cannibalism has already broken out in the city, eggs are clearly going to be hard to come by. So, as I opened to the first page, I was primed for a rip-roaring adventure.

But almost immediately, my elation faded. The narrator, the young boy's grandson, reveals on page two that after the war his grandfather came to America and became a "devout" New York Yankees fan. I found this revelation crushing. The idea that someone who had lived through the awe-inspiring siege of Leningrad would then voluntarily join the evil empire in the Bronx struck me as morally repellent. So I set the book aside and donated it to my library. Maybe some Yankees fan would enjoy it. I sure wouldn't.

I do not object to Yankees fans in principle, so long as they are homegrown, preferably natives of the Bronx or Yonkers. (Yankees fans born in Queens or Brooklyn, it goes without saying, are Iscariots.) But those of us who grew up in rabid, inbred sports towns like Philadelphia, Cleveland, Chicago, St. Louis, and Boston cannot stomach the kind of parvenu, out-of-town front-runner who becomes a "die-hard" Yankees fan without any moral, cultural, ethnic, genetic, or geographical connection with the team. Particularly repulsive are the ones in pink Yankees caps that you routinely run across in Tangier, Zagreb, Mombasa, the Hague.

In the case of *City of Thieves*, it struck me that a survivor of the heroic Siege of Leningrad—an underdog par excellence—would have a moral obligation to become a Dodgers fan and then perhaps later morph into a Mets fan after the Bums deserted Flatbush, because these teams are famously downscale and downtrodden and Democratic. The man's arrival in New York would roughly coincide with the opening scene of Don DeLillo's *Underworld*—a book I have read—which has the Dodgers facing off against the Giants at the Polo Grounds. Even though I grew up hating both these teams, neither of them is what you would call "evil." Nor are the Mets, who are merely annoying. But it is simply unconscionable that a survivor of the Nazis' Siege of Leningrad would later become a Yankees fan. Stalin would have been a Yankees fan. There's a guy who loved to gang up on the weak and defenseless. There's a front-runner if there ever was one.

My refusal to read books about the Yankees or their slimy fans also extends to books written by supporters of the team. Thus, when I learned that Salman Rushdie had taken a shine to the Yankees, it eliminated any chance that I would ever read *The Sa-*

tanic Verses, no matter how good it is. This vindictive attitude is rooted partly in principle and partly in pathology: I, like most Americans, resent the Yankees' success, wishing that my own cheapskate teams would also go out and purchase championships by the fistful. But I further reject the notion that Yankees fans experience the thrill of victory and the agony of defeat the way the rest of us do. They are fans who have not paid their dues. Yankees fans, not to put too fine a point on it, suck, and the rest of us do not. Rooting for the Yankees, as a friend of mine who roots for the Cubs says, is like rooting for the air. It's about as daring as rooting for a pack of ravenous pit bulls in a showdown with a blind, one-legged bunny rabbit.

My revulsion does not end with the Yankees. I also refuse to read books whose characters or authors have any affiliation whatsoever with the Dallas Cowboys, the Los Angeles Lakers, the Duke University men's basketball team, the University of Southern California football team, or Manchester United, the Yankees' vile, English, soccer-playing twin. All of these entities are irredeemably wicked. So implacable is my hatred of Man United—glamour boy David Beckham's old team—that when I met the gifted mystery writer Val McDermid at the Dublin Writers Festival a couple of years ago and found out that she was a Manchester United fan (even though, to the surprise of exactly no one, she is not from Manchester), I immediately unloaded all of my Val McDermid mysteries and started bad-mouthing her work to my friends. I'm dead serious about this stuff.

Happily, there are precious few novels that mention the Yankees, the Lakers, the Cowboys, or Manchester United. This is no accident. Editors have long understood that allowing an author to link his characters with a widely execrated franchise would turn off millions of potential readers, so they have gently urged these authors to excise such references, particularly if they occur early in the book, when the reader is still making up his mind whether it is worthwhile plowing ahead. Here are a few examples of passages that were wisely deleted from famous writers' manuscripts before they went to the printers:

> It was the best of times, it was the worst of times. Charles Darnay was rooting for the ripping side fielded by the Jacobins while Sydney Carton was all agog about those first-rate chaps from Manchester United . . .
>
> —Charles Dickens, *A Tale of Two Cities*

> For a long time I would go to bed early and conceal myself under the covers, munching stale *madeleines* my governess had secluded in her apron, all the while reading about the latest thrilling exploits of the Bronx Bombers . . .
>
> —Marcel Proust, *Swann's Way*

> He lay flat on the brown, pine-needled floor of the forest, and high overhead the wind blew in the tops of the trees, making it hard to pick up the radio broadcast of the Michigan-USC game.
>
> —Ernest Hemingway, *For Whom the Bell Tolls*

> There was no possibility of taking a walk that day. So Rochester suggested that we all take in the Spurs–Man United Cup Final.
>
> —Charlotte Brontë, *Jane Eyre*

> Maman died today. Or yesterday, maybe. I don't know. I got a telegram from the home: "Mother deceased. Funeral tomorrow. Lakers tickets still available."
>
> —Albert Camus, *The Stranger*

In my younger and more vulnerable years my father gave me some advice that I've been turning over in my mind ever since. "Whenever you feel like criticizing any one," he told me, "just remember that all the people in this world haven't had the advantages that you've had. Like Gehrig batting cleanup."

—F. Scott Fitzgerald, *The Great Gatsby*

You can see what I mean about this thing.

One day a few years back, I stumbled upon a remarkable book called *The Talisman of Troy*. Penned by Valerio Massimo Manfredi, the book chronicled the adventures of Diomedes, a second-tier character in *The Iliad*, after the fall of Troy. Bristling with prose like "Anchialus shuddered: in that boy was the awesome power of the son of Peleus, but not a crumb of his father's piety, nor his hospitable manners," *Talisman of Troy* advanced the theory that Helen of Troy had not really been abducted by Paris, son of Priam, but had deliberately gone to Asia Minor in order to get her hands on a sacred totem—the talisman of Troy—that would enable women to rule the world. The book was thus one of life's unalloyed pleasures: an uncompromisingly stupid novel in a world filled with stupid novels that do make compromises. And, by virtue of its faux-Hellenophilic inanity and all-purpose Delphic hootiness, it was a powerful weapon in the hands of those of us who work night and day to resist the tyranny of the good.

Most of us are familiar with people who make a fetish out of quality: They only read good books, they only see good movies, they only listen to good music, they only discuss politics with other Democrats, and they're not shy about letting you know it. They think this makes them smarter and better than everybody else, but it doesn't; it makes them mean and overly judgmental and miserly with their time, as if taking off fifteen minutes to page through *The Da Vinci Code* is a crime so horrific, an offense in such flagrant violation of the trans-celestial laws of intellectual resource management, that they will be cast out into the darkness by the Keepers of the *New York Review of Books* Meta-fictional Flame. In their view, any time spent reading a bad book can never be recovered, but far worse is that this misappropriation of precious minutes and even seconds also constitutes a crime against humanity. People like this also act as if the rest of humanity is monitoring their time sheet.

Those of us who occasionally delve into extraordinarily bad books like *The Talisman of Troy* recognize that such prissy attitudes are neurotic and self-defeating. Bad, bad, bad, bad, bad books are an essential part of life, as entertaining and indispensable as extremely bad clothing (retro polyester shirts, two-sizes-too-small hockey jerseys on fatsoes), unbelievably bad music (*John Tesh at Red Rocks*, Phil Collins anywhere), incredibly bad trends (metrosexuality, deliberately not using toilet paper for a year), and stupefyingly bad politicians (take your pick). I started reading extremely bad books as a boy when my beloved but slightly unhinged Uncle Jerry lent me the classic Reds-under-the-beds screed *None Dare Call It Treason*, and I have been reading them ever since.

Indeed, one of the reasons I became a book reviewer was that it gave me the opportunity to read a steady stream of hopelessly moronic books and get paid for it. One of my first assignments was to review Wess Roberts's jubilantly idiotic *Leadership Secrets of Attila the Hun*, which contained the line "Our songs, dances, games, jests and celebrations must always remain steadfast as propitious opportunity to renew our allegiance and identity as Huns."

I can well remember my breathless reaction when I was handed this assignment by my editor: "Let me get this straight: I'm going to get to read sentences like 'Being a leader of the Huns is often a lonely job,' and you're going to pay me for it?" For, to be perfectly honest, *Leadership Secrets of Attila the Hun* was so bad I would have read it for free.

But people who only read good books cannot understand such a mentality.

"Why would you read *Star: A Novel* by Pamela Anderson when you could read *The Savage Detectives* by Roberto Bolaño?" they ask. The answer is: "I would *not* rather read *Star: A Novel* by Pamela Anderson than *The Savage Detectives*. But I would rather read *Star: A Novel* by Pamela Anderson than one more novel about an enigmatic woman in a famous painting or one more book where the main character suffers from Asperger's syndrome or Tourette's and gets on everybody's nerves for 350 pages. Anyway, I already read *The Savage Detectives*, and I need a night off."

I do not read bad books frequently, and now that I am in the autumn of my life, I tend to limit my down-market diversions to extravagantly bad books that I have taken great pains to pick out myself. But I will never completely stop reading bad books, just as I will never completely stop ordering the disgusting curly fries at Arby's. Shockingly bad books have an important place in our lives, because they keep our brains active. Good books don't make you think, because the author has already done all the thinking for you, but a terrible book can really give your brain a workout, because you spend so much time wondering what incredibly dumb thing the author will say next. One caveat: As with bad movies, a book that is merely bad, but not exquisitely bad, is a waste of time, while a genuinely terrible book is a sheer delight. It is the difference between movies starring Stallone and movies starring Van Damme. This is what made the late, great Mickey Spillane so memorable: He never tried to be a poor man's Raymond Chandler; his work was unadulterated swill. I feel the same way about the *Loins of Telemachus* and *Cuirass of the Myrmidons* books: It is the fact that they are so clunky and dumb that makes them so much fun. The more unreadable, the merrier.

Let me stress that in making my pitch for impossibly bad books, I am not being camp. "Camp" is an intellectually duplicitous posture derived from the idea that something indisputably bad can be transmuted into something good by virtue of the reader's knowing, "ironic" perspective on its breathtaking atrociousness. That is not what I am talking about here. At no point do I ever lose sight of the fact that bad books are truly bad. But it is their very badness that reminds us of the good books of which they are pallid copies; they are like the mud that reminds us of the absent splendors of the sun. *The Bridges of Madison County* is a corn shucker's *Madame Bovary*, *The Talisman of Troy* is *The Odyssey* without Odysseus, Newt Gingrich's *1945*, where the Nazis have won the war in Europe, is a Bizarro World version of Philip Roth's *The Plot Against America*. Sometimes you feel like a nut; sometimes you don't.

Woefully bad books fall into three broad categories: the stupid, the mega-stupid, and the ones written by O. J. Simpson. Each has its own inimitable charms. Stupid books range from anything with the word "rapture" in the title to investment guides linking the yield curve with the teachings of Nostradamus. Mega-stupid books try to explain how to hold better meetings or motivate slackers by imitating the cruel but well-organized Shaka Zulu. And then there are cultural oddities like O. J. Simpson's obscene *I Want to Tell You: My Response to Your Letters, Your Messages, Your Questions*. In it, the then-imprisoned Simpson said of his wife, who perished under mysterious circumstances that still leave the experts stumped: "Like every person, Nicole had her faults. She blamed other people for her problems when she was unhappy. But the way she treated our kids when they were born, that made up for all the rest of it." No sirree, no aficionado of insanely bad books will want to be without a copy of this humdinger.

I am certainly not suggesting that all bad books are as boundlessly entertaining as these monstrosities. Despite being one of the worst books ever written, *Atlas Shrugged* is no fun at all, and the uninterrupted stream of inert balderdash that flows from Jimmy Carter's pen provides even fewer laughs than his presidency did. This is because famous people tend to write bad books in a predictable, tastefully dreary style, or to have run-of-the-mill bad books written for them by routinely crummy ghostwriters, whereas rank amateurs and ding-dongs pull out all the stops and go for the gold, venturing into forbidden territory where rank professionals would fear to tread. Jimmy Carter couldn't write a book as bad as O. J. Simpson if he tried.

One of the main reasons those of us who love bad books go out of our way to make our sentiments known is that it is a way of resisting the hegemony of good taste. If slaves to quality had their way, there would be no thrillers by Marilyn Quayle (*Embrace the Serpent*), no children's books by Madonna (*Lotsa de Casha*), no autobiographies by Geraldo Rivera (*Exposing Myself*). If goodness fetishists were in control of the publishing industry, nothing more hair-raising than Darryl Hannah's autobiography would ever make it into print. That's right, no books by Shaq, no memoirs by Susan Boyle or David Lee Roth or Rue McClanahan, no collections of racist ruminations by Dinesh D'Souza. Sound like a world you'd want to live in?

Garrison Keillor once wrote: "A good newspaper is never quite good enough but a lousy newspaper is a joy forever." The same goes for bad books. Some people would identify a passion for bad books as a guilty pleasure, but I think of it as a pleasure I do not feel the least bit guilty about, even though I probably should. Bad movies, bad hairdos, bad relationships, and bad Supreme Court rulings merely make me chuckle. Bad books make me laugh. And if they ever stop writing books with lines like "Being a leader of the Huns is often a lonely job," I don't think I want to be here anymore.

I used to wonder why it took me so long to get around to reading certain books in my personal library. Why was I rereading and then re-rereading *Portnoy's Complaint* and *The Great American Novel* and *Death Comes for the Archbishop* and *The Go-Between* and even *Flashman* when I still hadn't gotten around to reading Nabokov's *Bend Sinister* and Ernest Renan's *The Life of Jesus?* Then one day I hit upon the answer when I took a copy of *The Adventures of Huckleberry Finn* on a trip to Los Angeles. I had not read Mark Twain's *chef d'oeuvre* since my teens but had fond memories of that most unlikely of high school experiences—reading an assigned work I did not loathe. Now, decades later, I had every confidence that this experience would be repeated.

It was not. This, however, was not Twain's fault; I simply could never get physically comfortable with the book. The problem was the packaging. My copy, which was lying around the senior citizen center that my wife runs out of the goodness of her, though certainly not my, heart, was a traditional Bantam Classic, but the cover was a photo from the 1993 Walt Disney film version of the novel. It was typically nauseating Disney iconography, depicting a promiscuously cute little Huck, played by a very young Elijah Wood, and a surprisingly dapper Jim (Courtney Vance) sashaying through the woods into a gorgeous sunset. Tucked inside were photos of Huck sucking on a corncob pipe, dickering with the duke and the dauphin, posing as an English valet. Every time I picked up the book, my eyes were lured back to those fulsome photos of Sugarplum Huck. I do not know what Huck looked like as Twain imagined him, any more than I know how F. Scott Fitzgerald pictured Jay Gatsby. But Gatsby cannot look like Robert Redford, and the most memorable character in American fiction cannot look like the very young, very cuddly Elijah Wood. Cannot, cannot, cannot.

I ditched the Bantam edition of *Huck* and, when I returned home, fished out a second copy I owned. But the experience was exactly the same. The cover of the Signet Classic was a drawing of a ruddy-cheeked scamp, buckteeth prominent, clutching an apple, sporting a perky little tam cocked at a saucy Depression era angle. Here Huck bore an alarming similarity to Jerry Mathers of *Leave It to Beaver*. Revolting. So once again my efforts to polish off this peerless classic were stymied. I could never get more than a few pages into the book before the illustration on the cover made me sick.

All this prompted me to think more closely about magnificent books I had resisted reading over the years. The first to come to mind was Arthur Miller's *Death of a Salesman*. When I was in high school, the assigned version of Miller's seminal play had a grim, depressing green-and-brown cover depicting a stubby, doomed man with his back to the viewer, clutching a case filled with merchandise for which no buyer could possibly be found. I was living in a sub-par neighborhood at the time, and my dad was out of work, so it never seemed like that play was going to be as uplifting as *The Black Arrow*. So I never read it. A few years ago, when the New York Public Library mounted an exhibition of famous book covers—*The Catcher in the Rye*, *Catch-22*, *Soul on Ice*—I avoided the building until the show closed.

Spurred on by this recollection, I recently conducted an inventory of my collection to see how many unread books had unsightly, off-putting covers. The results knocked me for a loop. In one bookcase sat rows and rows of beautiful Penguin Classics. Beneath them sat my favorite novels, all of which had very nice packaging, ranging from the catchy (Haruki Murakami's *Norwegian Wood*) to the elegant (Andrea Barrett's *Ship Fever*) to the ominous (Robert Olmstead's *Coal Black Horse*). And beneath them were a few dozen gorgeous art books.

But in the next room, in the cabinet where I keep my unread books, I was stunned to realize how many of these neglected works were eyesores. Some were bland or ugly because they dated from earlier eras, when little effort went into packaging, or because they came from England. Particularly ghastly was the 1951 hardcover edition of Edward Bellamy's *Looking Backward*, a putrid aquamarine collection of Patrick White stories called *The Cockatoos*, and an uninspiring-looking collection entitled *The Portable Dorothy Parker*, adorned with a photo that made Parker look like the least amusing woman who ever lived, with the possible exception of my intransigently dour Aunt Norah.

What shocked me most was that some of the least appetizing covers were relatively new. Louise Erdrich's *Love Medicine*, issued in paperback in 1985, was chartreuse, orange, and baby blue, a lethal combination even Milton Avery would have shied away from. My Reagan-era edition of Grace Paley's *Enormous Changes at the Last Minute* suggested an out-of-date employee handbook: *A Handy Guide to Your Feminist 401-K!* The decrepit Vintage edition of Gertrude Stein's *Three Lives* that I own looked worse than she did.

It all added up. Until now, I'd thought that I had set these books aside for so many years because they were too daunting or, in the case of Thomas Mann, too dull. Now I realized that this was not the explanation for the long delays. What these books had in common was that they were ugly. Really, really ugly. The 1987 hardback edition of Georges Perec's *Life: A User's Manual* is a drab rip-off of a Balthus street scene. The 1991 hardback edition of Thomas C. Reeves's *A Question of Character: A Life of John F. Kennedy* looks like some flunky in the design department pasted clip art onto the cover just seconds before the galleys were being shipped to the printer. A 1997 edition of *The Bad Seed* comes adorned with a photograph of a creepy doll that bears an odd resemblance to a girl I sat next to in fifth grade.

Gradually, I realized that the books I had put off reading for so long were united not by being too demanding or too turgid but by the fact that their covers literally screamed: "Pulp me! Pulp me!" I'd owned Jorge Luis Borges's *A Personal Anthology* for thirty-five years but had never opened it, because the cover looked like somebody had smeared Gulden's mustard all over it. Unsightly covers may also be the reason I'd never taken a crack at *Celtic Fairy Tales*, *A History of the Global Stock Market from Ancient Rome to Silicon Valley*, or the classic Kingsley Amis romp *Girl, 20*. Graphic vileness was also the common denominator linking *Stock Market Logic*, *Three Plays by Sean O'Casey*, *Can You Drill a Hole Through Your Head and Survive?*, *History of the Conquest of Peru*, *The Crying of Lot 49*, *L'Assommoir*, and even *The Satanic Verses*. Though in that case the author's passion for the New York Yankees was also a major contributing factor. The double-whammy effect, as it were.

I was overjoyed to make this discovery. For years I thought I'd put off reading *The Gulag Archipelago* because of concerns that it might depress me. Wrong. Now I realized why I had never gotten very far into Willa Cather's *The Troll Garden*. At long last it became clear why I had so long resisted taking *Climate: The Key to Understanding Business Cycles* or *A History of Taxation and Expenditure in the Western World* or *The Story of Stupidity: A History of Western Idiocy from the Days of Greece to the Moment You Saw This Book* out for a test drive. It wasn't the subject matter that had deterred me, lo, these many years. It was the packaging.

Elated that I had solved this mystery, I raced out and bought a copy of *Huckleberry Finn* with a passable cover. I loved it! Then I did the same with *Nicholas Nickleby*. Fantastic! I then moved on to *Dr. Faustus*, a book I had tried to plow through a half-dozen times. No problem! That only left one more magic mountain to climb. I raced off to the library, checked out a copy of *Death of a Salesman* that came with perfectly inoffensive packaging, and retreated to my bed for a nice, long read.

I hated every word of it.

So much for that theory.

For most of my life I trusted the frothy kudos that appeared on the backs of books and would consult them before deciding whether or not to read the book in my hand. If Barry Hannah, a writer I admired, said that James Crumley, a writer I did not know, "works with fever on the brow," I'd go out and see if this was true. It was. If Michael Ondaatje said that Alistair MacLeod was Canada's best-kept secret, I would buy one of his books to see if this was in fact the case. It was. It was comments by noteworthy, reliable, honest writers that led me to W. G. Sebald, Anne Michaels, James Salter, Primo Levi, Dara Horn, Hjalmar Söderberg, and Jean-Patrick Manchette.

When I was in my mid-thirties, an enthusiastic comment by

John Updike introduced me to William Trevor. Prior to reading Updike's praise, I had never even heard of Trevor. I took his comments so seriously that I read all of Trevor's books over the next eighteen months. He immediately became one of my favorite writers. Interestingly enough, I had always admired Updike as a critic, particularly as an art critic, but had never warmed to him as a writer. Too much Keystone State angst. Trevor, I think, is a better writer than Updike. Updike may have known this; he praised Trevor to the skies anyway. I never encountered another writer whose judgment I trusted as much. Ethics-wise, most writers could give the Whore of Babylon a run for her money.

I also liked Updike the man. I once met him in the green room of a television show, and we chatted for half an hour. We mostly talked about art. His segment had been delayed so that a cabal of political hacks could gasbag with choreographed anguish about a colleague's death. The dead man later had a street named after him in Washington, D.C. Updike, now deceased, did not. But the novelist, unlike the stone-dead bureaucrat, will be remembered. Updike, I recall clearly, was anything but full of himself. He was, I think, the only famous person I have ever met who did not seem like a velociraptor. He was certainly the only writer.

A few times over the years, I have discovered writers because of an enthusiastic appraisal of their work in a newspaper or magazine. One day I read a review declaring that Penelope Fitzgerald was the greatest living English-speaking writer. To be fair, the competition was not especially stiff—basically, just William Trevor. This was the first I'd ever heard of Penelope Fitzgerald, and by the time I got my hands on *The Bookshop*, she was dead. She had not begun writing fiction until she was sixty years old, a great misfortune for all of us. I read *The Bookshop* first and liked it so much that I immediately moved on to *Offshore* and *The Golden*

Child and my favorite, *Human Voices*, and within a year I had read eight of her nine novels.

I have saved her ninth novel, *Innocence*—a book I have yet to lay eyes on—for a later date. The others I have now gone through at least twice. Obviously, if I wanted to complete the set, I could go online and order the book. How plebeian. To order the book online, to procure it by overnight shipment, would wreck everything. It would strip my life of all the magical, unscientific qualities I most value. It would remove it from the realm of serendipity, the only place I have ever felt truly comfortable. If I went out of my way to acquire *Innocence*, rather than waiting to stumble upon it or have someone break down and buy me a copy just to get me to shut up about it after so many years, it would cast everything I hold dear into doubt. Thereafter, the world would be structured and sensible and unbearable. One day, when I least expect it, I will duck out of the rain into a bookstore in Harrisburg or Laguna Beach or Walla Walla and happen upon *Innocence*. It will be one of the great events in my life. It will confirm my belief that the book has been waiting for me all these years, biding its time, keeping a low profile, confident that I would one day wander in and snap it up. The pilgrimage is everything. The destination means nothing.

Until that moment, I will have to make do with my emergency reserves. Prior to trying her hand at fiction, Fitzgerald wrote three well-received biographies. One was about the Pre-Raphaelite painter Edward Burne-Jones. I own it. I despise the Pre-Raphaelites, with all those marinated Ophelias and frizzy-haired waifs; where did these jokers get off criticizing Raphael? Andrew Lloyd Webber collects Burne-Jones, and it's not hard to see why. But I will eventually read the book anyway, because Fitzgerald has given me so much pleasure over the years. Perhaps she will change my mind about the Pre-Raphaelites. I doubt it. She will certainly not change my mind about Andrew Lloyd Webber.

Being handed a map leading to buried treasure like Penelope Fitzgerald is an increasingly rare experience today. Critics are mostly servile muttonheads, lacking the nerve to call out famous authors for their daft plots and slovenly prose. Academics fear that an untoward word will hurt them somewhere down the line when their own daft, slovenly books come up for review. Blurbs in particular can no longer be trusted. Usually they are written by liars and sycophants to advance the careers of bozos and sluts. In many cases authors will call in favors from friends who praise books they know to be dismally inadequate. This is volitionally cruel, because writers know that other writers hate writing blurbs. They hate it when their editors ask for them, and they hate it when agents ask for them, and they really hate it when their friends ask for them. Being asked to write a blurb for a friend is like being asked to give a friend's gross, dysfunctional kid a summer job. *I may like you; that doesn't mean I have to like your swinish progeny.* The reason writers hate writing blurbs for friends is because, no matter what they say, their friends will be upset that they did not shower them with even more immoderate praise. And in any case, envious trolls who will never be in a position to roll logs in a generally whorish manner will accuse them of being log-rolling whores. Conversely, writers hate writing blurbs for strangers, because it forces them to read books they do not want to read, at a point when time itself is running out on them. All blurbs should be written before the age of fifty; after that, one should never read a book one does not want to read, unless there is money in it.

Purists can decode blurbs to see the procrustean contortions a writer had to put himself through in order to be able to praise a friend without actually praising his book. "No one sets up a scene better than . . ." is how Trevor once described a book of short stories by a writer I like too much to criticize here. This may or may not be true. Whatever the case, the stories themselves were dull and undistinguished. Trevor, to his credit, never said that the book was any good. He merely said that the author was good at setting up scenes. He didn't say that he was good at finishing them. The ability to praise a colleague without actually recommending his work is sometimes referred to in the trade as Pirandello's Last Finesse. Colleagues will gaze at such ingeniously obtuse wordplay and marvel.

"This dude hasn't lost anything on his fastball," they will say. "He can still bring the ambiguous thunder."

Quotations clipped from book reviews that do not identify the author are worthless. *The San Francisco Chronicle* did not say that a newly published novel evoked both Lao-Tzu and Groucho Marx. Some writer said it. The Cleveland *Plain Dealer* did not find a book miraculously prescient. Some journalist did. *El Correo, Westdeutsche Allgemeine Zeitung, El Mundo, Blekinge Läns Tidning, Berner Zeitung,* and, of course, *Leben und Glauben* are not in a position to pass judgment on anything. They are amorphous. If a quote doesn't have a name attached to it, it doesn't mean anything. It's of no use to anyone if some unidentified churl at *El Globe & Mail de Santiago* rakes Isabel Allende's latest novel over the coals. For all we know, the person writing the review could be Augusto Pinochet's spiteful, out-of-wedlock grandson, Paco.

Once upon a time, book reviewers used a panoply of adjectives to describe books. All that changed on February 11, 1997, when a top-secret directive from the National Academy of the Arts was issued to American book reviewers stipulating that they must use the word "astonishing" at some point in their review or they would not get paid. "Astonishing" is a much better word than "luminous" or "incandescent," because it is gender-neutral, whereas "luminous" and "incandescent" and even "wise" are code for "Only divorced middle-aged women with cats who listen to *Fresh Air* every afternoon will enjoy this book." The problem with incandescent or luminous books is that they veer toward the provincial and the abstruse, focusing with alarming frequency on bees, Provence, or Vermeer. I prefer books that go off like a Roman candle. When I buy a book, I don't want to come away illuminated. I want to get blown right out of the water by the author's jaw-dropping pyrotechnics. I want to come away astonished.

Several years back, literally overwhelmed by the flood of material unleashed each year by the publishing industry, I decided to establish a screening program whereby I would only read books that at least one reviewer had described as "astonishing." Thus, I was overjoyed by the great news that Alice McDermott's new novel, *After This*, was absolutely astonishing, because while I'd heard terrific things about her previous books, I could never recall anyone using that specific term to describe them. As a result, I'd never tried any. Having recently picked up Alice Munro's *The View from Castle Rock*, which the *Seattle Times* described as "astonishing," and Nobel laureate J. M. Coetzee's *Slow Man*, deemed "an intense, astonishing work of art" by no less an arbiter of taste than *O, The Oprah Magazine*, I was rounding out the year with a troika of masterpieces that promised to be nothing short of astonishing.

And the hits kept coming. Typical was the treatment accorded Orhan Pamuk, winner of the 2006 Nobel Prize for literature, whose novel *The New Life* was described by *The Times Literary Supplement* as "an astonishing achievement." This happened at roughly the same time that Ayelet Waldman came out with *Love and Other Impossible Pursuits*, which, while not astonishing in and of itself, did include a character that reviewer Andrew Sean

Greer described as "astonishing." Almost simultaneously, Abigail Thomas published *A Three Dog Life*, singled out by *Entertainment Weekly* as "astonishing," an "extraordinary" love story—"Grade: A." Personally, I find the Grade A business a smidgen redundant; if a book is astonishing, you're obviously not going to give it a B.

Some people may protest that it is ridiculous to make book-buying or book-reading decisions purely on the basis of a single adjective. Perhaps. But let me stress that while I only cozy up to books that have been designated "astonishing," I do not read every single "astonishing" book. For example, I shied away from M. T. Anderson's *The Astonishing Life of Octavian Nothing, Traitor to the Nation*, even though it won a National Book Award for young people's literature. Just because the author himself used the term "astonishing" to describe his subject doesn't automatically make the book astonishing; it could be merely stellar, sensational, a real page-turner, or absolutely, positively unputdownable. For somewhat different reasons, I avoided "an astonishing thriller" I read about in an ad in *The New Yorker*, because this assessment came from one Linda Grana of the Lafayette Bookstore in Lafayette, California. Linda Grana may be a critic of the first water, on the same level as Samuel Johnson and Scott Peck and Oprah, but if the word "astonishing" does not appear as part of a review by a designated cognoscente in a mainstream publication, I do not buy the putatively astonishing product. I can't be buying books just because somebody in a bookstore somewhere said they were astonishing. I'd go broke.

Are there ever times when I worry that my obsession with the word "astonishing" prevents me from reading a great book? Sure. But the truth is, if nobody describes a book as astonishing, it probably isn't astonishing, and if it isn't astonishing, who needs it? When Marilynne Robinson's long-awaited *Gilead* finally appeared a few years ago, it was variously described as "poignant," "absorbing," "lyrical," "meditative," and "perfect." It was also called "magnificent," "a literary miracle," "Grade A," and, yes, "incandescent." But nowhere did I see anyone refer to it as "astonishing." I've already explained how I feel about incandescent books; if I had a nickel for every incandescent novel I've ever read, I could retire tomorrow. But I don't, so I can't, and I sure as hell am not going to keep falling back into the same old habits. First book that doesn't leave me astonished, *your* mistake; second book that doesn't leave me astonished, *my* mistake.

I do not mind when blurbs or pull-quotes are misleading. I do mind when they are absurd. In recent times, I have discovered that the snippets of praise that adorn books have taken on a preposterously hyperbolic tone. The *fawnatisti* now routinely resort to untenable, indefensible, and sometimes ludicrous analogies that do a disservice to both the author and the reader. I have lost track of the number of times I have seen contemporary writers described as "a latter-day Chekhov." Perhaps the *blurberistas* have simply reached the conclusion that everyone in this society is a dope and no one is keeping score. But some of us are keeping tabs on things. We owe it to ourselves, we owe it to other readers, and we owe it to Chekhov.

Last year I read a book of short stories called *There Are Jews in My House*. It was the work of a young Russian writer who emigrated to New York in 1994. What initially attracted me to the collection was the incredibly enthusiastic comments that appeared on the dust jacket. "Lara Vapnyar is Jane Austen with a Russian soul" is how resident *New Yorker* sage Louis Menand put it. Chimed in André Aciman, author of *Out of Egypt: A Memoir*: "One is tempted to name Anton Chekhov, or Nina Berberova, or Katherine Mansfield, but the book that springs to mind is *Dubliners*."

Wait a minute: Whose mind does that temptation spring to? Not mine. And are we talking about *Dubliners*, as in James Joyce's *Dubliners*, the greatest collection of stories ever written? Or are we talking about Fast Eddie McGettigan's *Dubliners*? Because if we are talking about James Joyce's *Dubliners*, my reaction would be: *Whoa, Nelly*. Consider the material. The title story in *There Are Jews in My House* deals with a Russian gentile who briefly offers a hiding place to a Jewish friend during the Nazi occupation of Russia, even though she secretly resents her friend's happier marriage, curvier figure, and more outgoing personality and isn't all that broken up when her friend finally shoves off. Another centers on a prudish young math teacher who is given the mortifying assignment of teaching a sex education class for young girls. A third features a little boy in Brooklyn who suspects that his grandfather might be having it off with an old flame from back in the land of the sultry Babushka. They are all good stories, nicely written, all touching in some way, all just this side of sentimental but never mawkish. But none of them in any way brings to mind the caustic, unsentimental, highly stylized, and somewhat over-the-top work of Jane Austen, and none of them even vaguely suggests the work of James Joyce. Particularly nonevocative of Jane Austen are the sentences from Vapnyar's story "A Question for Vera": "Vova Libman didn't care if he was a boy or a girl; he cried all the time. He cried, and when he calmed down, he picked his nose and ate his boogers."

I don't know how much of *Emma* and *Persuasion* and *Sense and Sensibility* Louis Menand has read, but let me tell you this: There are no boogers in the work of Jane Austen. Not a one. How on earth could critics manage to jump from Lara Vapnyar to Jane Austen without so much as a pause for Eudora Welty or Katherine Anne Porter? How did they get from *There Are Jews in My House* to

Dubliners without making a pit stop for Lorrie Moore's *Birds of America* or *The Ballad of the Sad Café and Other Stories* by Carson McCullers? This criticism is no reflection on the talented Lara Vapnyar. It is, rather, a reflection on a passel of critics and *blurbmeisters* that have simply lost their minds.

However nice and generous it may be to compare young writers who are just getting out of the starting gate to the undisputed titans of Western literature, it isn't really fair to the writers themselves, and it isn't really helpful to anyone else. Rookie first basemen who break in with the Yankees do not automatically get compared to Lou Gehrig. First-term presidents are not immediately likened to Honest Abe. Twenty-something painters are never spoken of in the same breath as Velázquez. Scientists who have just earned their Ph.D.'s are not discussed in the same terms as Albert Einstein. In most fields of human endeavor, you have to get a few points on the scoreboard before anyone starts talking about you as if you were the second coming of Alexander the Great or Leonardo da Vinci or Werner Heisenberg or Pelé or even Cher. Comparing freshly published authors who are still wet behind the ears to James Joyce and Jane Austen and Anton Chekhov isn't just unfair to the dead; it's unfair to the living. No one can measure up to that kind of homage. Not even Jonathan Franzen.

This brings us to the least-discussed subject in the world of *belles lettres*: book reviews that any author worth his salt knows are unjustifiably enthusiastic. Writers frequently complain that a critic who reviewed their book is vicious, crass, and ignorant. But that is only when they are talking about me. In my own experience as a reader who pays heed to reviews, I take an entirely different tack. To me, book reviewers in general are just too darned nice. And I know whereof I speak. A few years ago Bruce McCall wrote a flattering notice about my book *My Goodness: A Cynic's Short-Lived*

Search for Sainthood. I was gratified by the praise, particularly coming from someone I admired and envied. But toward the end of the review, McCall said something that caught me totally by surprise. "Somewhere," he wrote, "Mencken is beaming."

No, he wasn't. H. L. Mencken, a self-absorbed curmudgeon and all-purpose snob, wouldn't have thought much of my piddling efforts. He looked down his nose at everybody, especially those not to the manor born. And he hated the Irish. So in generously asserting that Mencken was beaming at my efforts, McCall could not have been more wrong. H. L. Mencken, now or then, dead or alive, couldn't have cared less what some pathetic third-generation Mick like me wrote. He wouldn't beam at my writing if his life depended on it. He was from Baltimore, where they keep the beaming at other people's work to an absolute minimum.

Anyway, the book wasn't all that good.

This is not the sort of thing you will hear from most writers. Authors like to bellyache. Authors are always complaining that critics missed the whole point of *Few Mourn the Cameriere*, or took the quote about the merry leper ballerinas out of context, or over-looked the allusions to John Millington Synge and Hildegard von Bingen, or didn't mention that the author once jilted the critic after he kept begging her to go out on a double date dressed as one of the Boleyn sisters but maybe with an eye patch. Authors are always complaining that reviewers maliciously cited the least in-candescent, least Pushkinian passages in the book; or have a grudge against them because of something that happened the night the Khmer Rouge or Joy Division broke up; or said mean things only because the author went to Georgetown while the re-viewer had to settle for Villanova.

What makes all this grumbling so unseemly is that the vast majority of book reviews are favorable, even though the vast majority of books deserve no praise whatsoever. Authors know that even if one reviewer hates a book, the next ten will roll over like compliant pooches and insist that it's the most thought-provoking novel since *The Idiot*. Reviewers tend to err on the side of caution, fearing reprisals down the road. Also, because they generally receive but a pittance for their efforts, they view these assignments as a chore, serving up reviews that read like term papers or lightly reworded press releases, churned out by auxiliary sales reps masquerading as critics. This is particularly true in the mystery genre, where the last negative review was written in 1943.

There is nothing wrong with a needlessly effusive notice, nor any reason to suspect that the reviewer is being excessively servile because he seeks the author's hand in marriage or expects similar treatment when his own book, *Would That the Khedive Had Not Overslept*, comes out in paperback. This does not alter the fact that such reviews are unfair to the reader, who may be hornswoggled into thinking that Raymond Chandler really *would* crack a smile and tip his hat at the author, or that the fledgling novelist *has* gone toe-to-toe with Joseph Conrad and given the ornery old cuss a proper thrashing. Books are described as being "compulsively readable" when they are merely "okay," "jaw-droppingly good" when they are actually "not bad," "impossible to put down" when they are really "no worse than the last three." Authors are described as an alchemical synthesis of Madame de Staël, Alcuin of York, and Arthur Conan Doyle, or are said to write like Charlotte Brontë on acid or to have out-Dostoyevskyed Dostoyevsky and horsewhipped Heine, when they are in fact more of a cross between Candace Bushnell and Ngaio Marsh, or write like Nora Roberts on Robitussin-DM, or have narrowly out-Scottolined Lisa Scottoline and were lucky to play Anita Shreve to a draw.

The same authors who mope and whine about a negative comment here and there are only too glad to accept praise that is not warranted, accolades they do not deserve. But how often does an author ever come out and admit that the praise showered on his book was excessive, ill-considered, unseemly, or flat-out wrong? That's the sort of thing that takes real moral fiber, real integrity, real guts. You know, like admitting that H. L. Mencken wouldn't have been caught dead beaming at your book.

The worst thing about premature semi-hysterical adulation is that it places an enormous burden on the author to live up to expectations he himself did not create. The Angolan-born novelist José Eduardo Agualusa (*Creole, The Book of Chameleons*) has been extolled thusly: "Cross J. M. Coetzee with Gabriel García Márquez and you've got José Eduardo Agualusa, Portugal's next candidate for the Nobel Prize." To which I say: Cross "Let's not go overboard here" with "Hold on a cotton-pickin' second" and you've got "Yeah, maybe when pigs sprout wings."

Just as authors dread being labeled "a poor man's Francine du Plessix Grey" or "Moloch's errand boy," many authors live in fear of praise that is discomfitingly intimate or jarringly visceral. I for one would never want my work referred to as "a big dish of Beluga caviar, sailing in on a sparkling bed of rice, with a mother-of-pearl spoon," as Alice Munro's *Runaway* once was. I just wouldn't. Personally, I do not feel that it is acceptable to describe someone's writing as a big dish of beluga caviar sailing in on a sparkling bed of rice, even if it is. There's a sinister chumminess to this kind of writing, suggesting that the reviewer may actually be daydreaming about the author in graphic cetacean terms. If I were Alice Munro, I'd add a couple of locks to the door. Dead bolts, in fact.

If you can't trust the reviewers anymore, whom *can* you turn to? Well, one superb innovation of recent times is the readers' review section on Amazon.com. Here jes' plain folks get to voice their opinions, acting as selfless, intrepid cultural watchdogs seeking to shield their fellow book lovers from duds. Certain individuals have built quite a reputation for themselves online, their trenchant, witty *aperçus* vying with the phoned-in ruminations of the snooty, burned-out hacks who masquerade as professionals at our top magazines and papers.

Of course, some reviewers can get a bit coarse and personal in the rough-and-tumble world of Internet facials, sending stunned top-flight authors home to lick their information highway wounds. But for the most part these gifted amateurs inject a much-needed breath of fresh air into the reviewing process. Most appealing is their absolute fearlessness when it comes to trashing high-profile authors whom mainstream reviewers would hesitate to mix it up with. Beholden to no man, cloaked in righteous anonymity, these reviewers do not hesitate to take even the brightest stars—Joyce Carol Oates, Elizabeth Barrett Browning, Maeve Binchy—to the woodshed. This is what makes citizen reviewers such a welcome addition to the body politic: Their courageous sniping from behind the bushes, emulating Ethan Allen and the Swamp Fox back in 1776, reaffirms that democracy functions best when you fire your musket and then run away.

It's always fun to go back in time and speculate on what might have happened had Jack the Ripper or the Venerable Bede been on Facebook, or had Pharaoh's army been kitted out with state-of-the-art amphibious equipment. This is why I cannot help wondering what a typical Amazon.com review might have looked like had the Internet existed centuries ago:

King Lear: Average reader rating: ★★. The author tells us: "As flies to wanton boys are we to the gods; they kill us for their sport." Oh, right, like I didn't know that? Like I didn't know that to be or not to be is the question? Like I didn't know that the fault lies not in us but in the stars? Tell me something I don't know, Mr. Bard of Whatever.

Oedipus Rex: Average reader rating: ★★★★. Sophocles is a satisfying author who writes in clear, snappy prose. Youngsters in particular could learn a lot by imitating Mr. Rex, until he goes a bit off the rails toward the end. Nothing earth-shattering here, but zippy stuff. Have to admit I'm still puzzled by the icky subplot involving Mr. Rex's mother.

The 120 Days of Sodom: Average reader rating: ★★★★★. So I like totally preordered this book based on the title, which just happens to be the same as my maiden name—Marquis de. Yeah, a sketchy reason to buy a book, but I was pumped. But when it got here, I didn't understand it at all. It just didn't go anywhere. It just kept repeating itself. I went through it a few times more, searching for some deeper, awesome meaning, but just ended up totally bummed. Actually, some parts of it were kind of gross.

The Aeneid: Average reader rating: ★★. Whine, whine, whine! Okay, so your hometown burned to the ground and your family got wiped out, but do you have to keep bellyaching about it? Where's that gonna get you, Mr. Grumpy-Biscuits? Basically, Virgil is a poor man's Tacitus. He goes on and on about Priam and Dido and Zeus, when all the reader wants is to get to the good part when the Trojans start teeing off on the Vestal Virgins. And talk about a rip-off: He doesn't even include the story about the one-eyed giant who can turn pigs into Greeks.

On the Revolutions of the Celestial Spheres: Average reader rating: ★★★½. Those who have read my countless reviews elsewhere know that I am a mathematician, astronomer, polyglot, and philosopher in my own right and therefore uniquely qualified to discuss everything from Zeno's Paradoxes to the Gordian knot. Mostly, I think my fellow polymath Copernicus has done a pretty solid job here. The thing most laymen don't realize—unlike mathematicians/philosophers/astronomers/polymaths like me (as those familiar with my numerous other reviews can tell you)—is that people like Copernicus are really good with numbers. Just as I am. Really, really good. (Me, that is.) Readers seeking more of my unique insights can reach me at Igor@mymommysbasement.com.

Deuteronomy: Average reader rating: ★★★. I don't get it. I've read most of the books in this series, and they totally kick butt, but this one leaves me scratching my head. Is there a story here? Am I missing something? Why so much talk about clean and unclean beasts? The author really got on a roll with *Genesis* and *Exodus,* and I was on the edge of my seat when I read *Numbers.* But this one runs out of gas early. Now I'm glad I skipped *Leviticus!*

And finally:

Mein Kampf: Average reader rating: ★. Lively writing, but just too, too depressing. Why does he keep using big words that normal people can't understand, like *Lebensraum* and *Oberkommandant* and *Wienerschnitzel*? Hey! I own a thesaurus, too! And what's up with the Jewish thing?

In the end, I would still like to believe that the praise printed on the covers of books is not without value. At least some of it. If we are going to be disappointed, it is nice to know that we did not plunge into the tiger pit of our own free will, but were tricked into taking that blind leap and that's why we wound up impaled on those razor-sharp spikes. Dipped in curare. And python venom. And dung. If I have to waste a few days reading a book that I'm going to end up hating, I'd prefer to do it because of somebody else's recommendation. I don't want this thing to be accidental. And I don't want to take all the heat myself.

Sometimes our experiences stun us. Two years ago I read an amazing novella called *Beauty Salon* about a gay, cross-dressing Mexico City hairdresser who turns his business establishment into an AIDS hospice. I only picked *Beauty Salon* off the shelf because of a quote on the back cover written by Francisco Goldman, saying that Mario Bellatín's books seemed like "gifts from the future." I found this description disarmingly beautiful. It sounded like Goldman really meant this. He had crafted a gorgeous turn of phrase and given it away to another writer. This was breathtakingly generous.

Since Goldman had been so right about Bellatín, I decided to go ahead and read Goldman's novel *The Ordinary Seaman*. It was about a group of luckless Central American rejects who find themselves marooned on a rat-infested ship all the way down on the Brooklyn docks. The ship will never see the high seas again, as it is nothing more than a prop in an insurance scam. The novel was based on a true story and was incredibly sad. It was a remarkable book. So then I decided to read a novel by an author—not a critic—whose considered praise—no phone-in jobs, please—accompanied the paperback version of *The Ordinary Seaman*, just to see how far I could go with this thing before I finally ran into a book I did not like. It never happened. The trail from Goldman led me to Oscar Hijuelos and later to Selden Rodman and Seán

Virgo, and then on and on to a half-dozen other authors, and each time the aleatory daisy chain introduced me to yet another wonderful book.

The blurb trail ultimately led to a fantastic little novel called *The House of Paper* by the Uruguayan novelist Carlos María Domínguez. *The House of Paper* is a literary mystery in which a man comes upon a Joseph Conrad novel mailed to a recently deceased friend and travels all the way to Argentina to find out why it was sent to her. His quest leads him to a bibliophile so obsessed with his collection that he one day decides to hire workmen to build him a house on the oceanfront that will consist entirely of his books. But then a woman with whom he had a one-night stand in Mexico City at a literary conference many years in the past writes and asks for a particular book. The man cannot find it. He is beside himself. He tears the house apart, literally destroying it in the process, and when he finally locates the requested title, he ships it off to London. Alas, the woman who asked for it—the woman he spent that memorable night with in Mexico City fifteen years earlier—has just been run over by a car while daydreaming about Emily Dickinson.

I can readily imagine myself as one of the characters in this novel. That would be so much preferable to the life I am living now. I would love to build a house using books instead of bricks. I would love to be run over by a car while daydreaming about Emily Dickinson. Or maybe not "run over" so much as "plowed into" or perhaps even "ever so lightly grazed." Either way, this sort of dramatic sign-off beats lung cancer any day of the week. I love reading books that I stumble upon in this way. It turns life itself into a jigsaw puzzle.

I found *The House of Paper* so mesmerizing that I did not need to follow the critical trail any further. I had made my point. Maybe someday I would come back and repeat the experiment. But not now. What I feared, perhaps, was that this was already turning into another one of my obsessions, that I would spend so much time following one highly recommended book to the next that I would never finish the dozens of other books I am currently working my way through, never finish off the Modern Library list of the 100 Greatest English-Language Novels of the Twentieth Century, never finish *Ulysses*, never find out how *The History of the Decline and Fall of the Roman Empire* turns out, and never reach the final page of *Middlemarch*.

I already had enough obsessions.

CHAPTER SIX

The Stockholm Syndrome

I sometimes try to think of specific instances where a book has made a huge difference in my life. I am not talking about the disastrous role a book like *A Separate Peace* or *The Catcher in the Rye* can play in turning one of your best friends into a suicidal ninny, or the way discovering a copy of *The Female Eunuch* on a girlfriend's nightstand can bring a torrid, acrobatic romance to a screeching halt. No, I am talking about books that affected me so powerfully at the time I read them that they literally changed my life.

Frankly, I can't think of all that many. Yes, you can definitely get pointers from books like *The Iliad*, in particular the horrific scene where Achilles mutilates Hector's corpse and Homer admonishes similarly inclined human-rights violators across the ages: *When you get to the end zone, act like you've been there before.* And you can learn all sorts of things from *A Journal of the Plague Year* and *A Briefing for a Descent into Hell* and even *The 120 Days of Sodom* that will stand you in good stead later in life. At the very least, the cumulative effect of reading an enormous number of great books will rescue you from the blithe savagery that is the default mode for so many of your compatriots. But if I had to pick out a specific book and say that it was responsible for this or that development in my life, I'd be hard-pressed to come up with a title. I liked *Robinson Crusoe* and *Persuasion* and even *Moonraker* at the time I read them, and they definitely made me feel more sophisticated and worldly. But I can't say that any of them changed my life. Perhaps my life would have been completely different if I'd read *Middlemarch* at an early age.

The closest I can come to a candidate here is Henry de Montherlant's *La reine morte*. Montherlant is a slightly-less-than-immortal French writer who is basically unknown in the United States. Born on April 20, 1895, and breathing his last on September 21, 1972, Montherlant was an extremely dour novelist and playwright whose most famous works are the plays *La reine morte* and *Port-Royal*, though he also wrote several very fine, if dour, novels, including *Les jeunes filles*, *Les célibataires*, and *Le Chaos et la Nuit*. I read *La reine morte* while studying French in college, and to this day I am not sure why. I do remember that I used to love riding home from college on the J bus on Friday afternoon, congratulating myself on being the only passenger who was reading Jean Giraudoux and André Malraux and Henry de Montherlant, either in the original French or in translation. It was the thrill of the newly converted, the thrill of reading something esoteric in a foreign language, the thrill of being admitted to the ranks of the cognoscenti. It was the thrill of the sophomore. The J bus continues to ply its way across Philadelphia to this day, and I am sure that if I boarded it this afternoon, the vehicle would continue to be Montherlant-free. Philadelphia is just not an Henry de Montherlant kind of town.

Intimate familiarity with the work of Henry de Montherlant is an achievement, to be sure, but it is not the sort of thing one undertakes in the expectation that it will reap huge benefits down the line. In the normal course of events, my late-adolescence dalliance with Montherlant would have remained interred in a cultural sepulcher amidst fleeting associations with the *oeuvres* of Paul Morand, Henri Troyat, Elsa Triolet, and Patrick Modiano, gifted French writers who, like Montherlant, are not household names in the United States. Yes, I might have pulled these kinds of names out of my hat at some point later in life, perhaps to fashion a witty quip—"I take my text today from the immortal Hervé Bazin . . ." "As Roger Peyrefitte so aptly put it in one of his trademark *aperçus* . . ."—but these writers would have played no further role in my existence.

Henry de Montherlant was the exception. It just so happened that he died shortly after I arrived in Paris in 1972. Going blind, he shot himself, but he also swallowed a mouthful of cyanide, just to be on the safe side. His adult life was ending just as mine was beginning. At the time I was staying in a charming boardinghouse run by a gaunt, humorless widow I will identify only as Madame C. It had once been a private home nestled inside a private courtyard, and was located on a quiet, nondescript side street one block south of the Boulevard Montparnasse. At some point the residence had been converted into a boardinghouse that was now filled with effervescent French-Canadian nurses who were doing internships at the nearby Children's Hospital. The nurses were all about five to ten years older than me. They took a shine to me; they liked to have me tag along and serve as their personal security detail when they visited the seedier parts of Paris at night; they adopted me as their mascot. Just before they flew home, they would leave me their unused Métro tickets. No woman has ever done me a greater service.

One Friday evening I came in to discover Madame C sitting in the living room, gravely sipping her *tisane* and gazing at the television, where a hifalutin program honoring the dead Montherlant was being aired. This was on prime-time TV, a slot occupied back in the States by *The Brady Bunch* and *Baretta*. I poked my head in, and in my halting, very bad French—which has never actually gotten all that much better—asked if I could take a peek, too, volunteering the information that I had read Montherlant's work in college. Specifically, *La reine morte*.

You could have knocked the poor woman over with a feather.

Madame C was not a nice person. She was terse and sullen, with a harsh voice, a severe hairstyle, an imperious carriage, and a vicious little dog named Monsieur Digue. She was the first termagant of my acquaintance. She looked like one of those commerce-minded French people who may have been sorry to see the Germans go in the summer of '44; the Nazis, unlike the *putes* and *salauds* from Picardy, always paid on time. People in the boardinghouse feared her; she was constantly scolding the nurses about keeping late hours or leaving the lights on in the subterranean kitchen or making too much noise as their high heels clickety-clacked up the stairs late at night. She was like their mothers, or their aunts; she had arrogated to herself the right of *in loco parentis*. If things did not improve, it always seemed, grounding was an option.

For whatever reason, Madame C was always nice to me. Not bubbling over with warmth and motherly affection, no, but not explicitly horrible, the way she was with the visitors from Spain and Venezuela, whom she despised, or with the French-Canadian nurses, whom she seemed to view as apprentice sluts, with their afterthought miniskirts and excruciating rustic accents. She really didn't care for the smart-aleck cop from Yugoslavia. Yet, inexplicably, she didn't seem to mind me. She gave me a great deal on the room overlooking her garden, which is where I stayed the first month I was in Paris. It was the nicest place I had ever lived in my life. Then, after a disastrous trip to antiseptic Grenoble, where I considered enrolling at the local university, I beat a hasty retreat to the City of Light and specifically to her *pension*. By no means displeased to see me back on the Rue Mayet, she let me move into a teensy-weensy room with no view of the garden or anything else for a paltry twelve francs ($2.40) a day. I stayed there for the next eight months, in a state of seraphic, low-budget bliss. The room was a glorified alcove and gave out onto an airshaft and reeked of powerful, sometimes sickening, cooking odors billowing up from the basement kitchen, but I was living no more than thirty yards from the legendary Boulevard Montparnasse and right around the corner from the Duroc Métro, and the building was filled with convivial French-Canadian nurses whose families were always sending them fragrant DuMaurier cigarettes, which they were only too happy to share with a fellow native of the New World. So Madame C's *pension* was A-OK with me.

As is only to be expected, I was a great carouser in those days, forever staggering in drunk at three o'clock in the morning from mysterious nightclubs I could never find again after I had sobered up. I sometimes had trouble getting my key into the lock; and I made a lot of noise dragging myself up the stairs; and I would listen to tempestuous music by Slade and T-Rex at all hours of the day and night; and I occasionally brought girls I had scraped off the sidewalk back to my lair of iniquity, which was strictly prohibited; and sometimes I didn't even bother to bring girls back, because I was already sleeping with one of the Canadian nurses, which was even more strictly prohibited; and to top things off, I was American and therefore a barbarian. But through all of this, Madame C chose to look the other way when I contravened one of her house rules. I was coarse and insensitive and immature and generic, but it didn't seem to bother her. True, she did march upstairs and rap on my door one night and demand an explanation for the series of shrill sounds the Catholic, crypto-fascist bachelor down the hall kept complaining about, and she must have known from the way I blocked the door that I had a penniless Spanish girl who needed a place to sleep for the night scrunched up against the wall, though she may not have known that the girl was Spanish, much less penniless, but she let that go, too. Anyone else she would have turfed out into the street, *bonita muchacha* in twain. But in my case, she didn't.

In the end, I think it was because of Henry de Montherlant.

It was one thing for a French person to have read Montherlant. But for an American to have read his work, and a young American at that, and to have known the exact date of his birth, and then to have patiently and respectfully sat in the living room for a few minutes watching his colleagues give him a big send-off, and to seemingly mourn his passing, was inconceivable. You can easily game the French; just slip in a few nice comments about Coco Chanel and Pepin the Short every so often and you're home free. That memorable night back in September, I had paid homage to Henry de Montherlant, and by extension to France itself. I had not read Montherlant back in college calculating years in advance the advantages that might accrue to me because of this sortie into the French literary wilderness, but it worked out in the end. Again and again, through one domestic crisis after another, it was Henry de Montherlant who saved my bacon.

That said, I never enjoyed Montherlant's work. Too dour. Maybe the people on the J bus back in Philadelphia were on to something.

I developed a series of fixed routines the year I lived in France. They mostly involved writers. I would fork over a buck and a half and sit way up in the cheap seats at the Comédie-Française three times a week, hoping that Molière's sense of humor would rub off on me. The walls of the theater were lined with busts of the immortal French playwrights—Corneille, Racine, Hugo, Musset, and a few less recognizable dramatists whose fame has not carried very far beyond the shores of France. The building was saturated, perhaps infested, with history, some of it pulmonary. Molière started coughing up blood during a performance of *Le malade imaginaire* at the Comédie-Française on February 17, 1673, and died later that evening. Being on the outs with the Catholic Church—*Tartuffe*, his savage attack on the French clergy, really got up their noses—he was buried under cover of darkness at Père Lachaise, the final resting place of Beaumarchais, La Fontaine, and Apollinaire, not to mention Oscar Wilde and Jim Morrison. It was quite a town.

You couldn't get away from famous writers in Paris. Everywhere you went, you saw evidence that they'd been there. Victor Hugo's house in the Place des Vosges reminded you. The church across the street from the Panthéon where Racine was buried reminded you. The Hôtel de l'Avenir, where Oscar Wilde died, reminded you. The plaques on the sides of buildings, memorializing Paul Eluard and André Breton and George Sand reminded you. The French idolized writers the way Americans idolized switch-hitters who could occasionally drill the ball into the gap. Everywhere you turned, there were streets named after writers. Everywhere you turned, there were bookstores, carrying all the masterpieces by Flaubert and Montaigne and Rabelais, and they stayed open late. French bookstores didn't look all that different from jewelry stores; they enticed and beguiled and astounded you. Paris, it soon became apparent, was a city built for writers. Famous writers wrote their famous books in Paris. Famous writers got buried under cover of darkness in Paris. Famous writers be-

came famous in Paris. We had nothing like this back in Philadelphia. For that matter, we had nothing like this back in America.

Throughout my time in Paris, I adhered to a number of snappy
little rituals involving famous writers. Everyone did; everyone
had the same rituals. If a friend was visiting from the States, you
took him to the Café de Flore, the old stomping grounds of the
major postwar French intellectuals, or to Les Deux Magots,
where Camus helped Sartre and Simone de Beauvoir invent exis-
tentialism one unseasonably mild evening in February 1946. Or
you might drag them up to the Boulevard Montparnasse and have
a kir at La Rotonde or La Coupole or Le Dôme, forever linked in
lore and legend with Hem and F. Scott and Zelda and all the other
starters on the Lost Generation's first team. These places were
horrifyingly expensive. If things went well, your friend picked up
the check. If not, since you were living on twenty-three francs a
day and twelve of them were earmarked for your rent, you did not
eat for the rest of the day. You were in effect reenacting scenes
from *A Moveable Feast* and *Quiet Days in Clichy* and, if things took
a really bad turn, *Les Misérables*. It was exhilarating. The writers
and intellectuals were long gone from these places—the cafés
were teeming with tourists and phonies and prep school hand
jobs and people like you—but it didn't matter. You visited these
places as a way of honoring the great writers of the past. You
weren't showing off; you were paying homage. You were even using the infuriating second-person voice because that was the way
Hemingway wrote. Eventually you would get over it. Visiting
those cafés was like visiting the Colosseum of Rome. It didn't
matter that the gladiators were no longer there. The gladiators
had been there once. They had never been to Philadelphia.

Shortly after I arrived in Paris, I started visiting famous writers' graves. In the Cimetière Montmartre you could pay your re-

spects to Stendhal and Zola, though Zola's remains were later moved to the Panthéon. In Père Lachaise, the marquee names included the aforementioned Molière, Wilde, Beaumarchais, Apollinaire, and Morrison, but also Gertrude Stein. And Edith Piaf. And Isadora Duncan. And Jean-Baptiste Camille Corot. And Honoré Daumier. And Jules Michelet. And not just Héloïse but Abélard, too. The Cimetière du Montparnasse, the most centrally located yet peaceful of the cemeteries, was home to everyone from Guy de Maupassant to Baudelaire (and later to Sartre and de Beauvoir and Samuel Beckett and his wife, Suzanne, not to mention Brancusi and Tristan Tzara and Maréchal Pétain's long-suffering wife, Annie). I had read all of Maupassant's stories in college and loved them, but Baudelaire's tomb was much more impressive. It sat all by itself off in a corner of the cemetery, with a solemn rendering of the poet's body carved in stone. Above it was poised a sinister gargoyle who seemed to be lost in thought, as if he were trying to remember something that was right on the tip of his tongue, perhaps *le mot juste*. I would visit the gravesite about once a week; it seemed like the sort of thing an aspiring young writer should do. There was nothing about Baudelaire's style that would ever be of any use to me; I have never been terribly interested in poetry, and Baudelaire's work is dreamy and cryptic and drug-addled and hard to read in the original. Also, he wore silly clothes. But Baudelaire had a great reputation and great style, and he invented expressions like "the wind of the wing of imbecility," so I thoroughly enjoyed those visits to his grave. He also had that wonderful name: Baudelaire is a thousand times more evocative than Bergson or Baudrillard. And it certainly has more of a ring to it than Beattie. I never went to Paris on any of my thirty subsequent trips without visiting the tomb of Baudelaire, and I suppose I never will. Subconsciously, I suspect, it was all a way of reminding myself how far I had come from that down-market housing project in Philadelphia, and from the City of Brotherly Love in general. In Quaker City housing projects, when I was growing up, nobody cared about Charles Baudelaire, much less his *Flowers of Evil*. They felt the same way about Baudelaire that they felt about Jean Giraudoux and Henry de Montherlant. French guys. Off with their heads.

One day, after I had been in Paris for about six months, I decided that I needed a change of scenery. Paris is gray and mournful in February, and my French-Canadian girlfriend had just gone back to Montreal to get on with her life and I knew that I would never see her again, so a grand gesture seemed in order. I decided that I would hitchhike to eastern France and visit Arthur Rimbaud's hometown of Lunéville. Lunéville was not my ultimate or even my primary destination; I planned to visit a friend, all the way over near the German border, whom I knew from back in college. He was a French major and simply adored the French language, with a particular soft spot for *le futur antérieur*, and in fact he had been intoxicated by the very idea of France since childhood. He'd stopped by my boardinghouse on the way to Strasbourg a few months earlier and later sent me a postcard inviting me out for a spin around Alsace-Lorraine. Or maybe just Alsace. So I was off.

The trip was one I would never forget. It was drizzling the morning I set out, not a great day for hitchhiking, but a few minutes after I started waving my sign on the side of the road at the Porte de Vincennes, a fortyish man in a shiny new blue Ford sedan pulled up. It may have been a Ford Torino; it was certainly bigger and flashier than the bland, box-like French cars on the road. The man was wearing a pink jumpsuit and a coonskin cap, like a Eurotrash Davy Crockett unexpectedly resurrected from a fey French frontier underworld. He was also wearing dark sunglasses, even though it was overcast that day and the sun never once put in an appearance. I could not see his eyes, but I could see the coonskin cap and the jumpsuit. I got into the car anyway. I was twenty-two, not all that well-versed in the ways of the world, a *tabula rasa*.

The car, I immediately noticed, smelled like it had just rolled right off the assembly line; it had only a couple hundred kilometers on the odometer. The man, whose name I did not catch, spoke French with a pronounced German accent and had the radio tuned to a station that specialized in curiosities like Horst Jankowski's inexplicable 1965 hit, "A Walk in the Black Forest." The jaunty *Deutsche*-hayseed music did not fit with the man's look. He was, he explained, delivering the car to a friend in eastern France, somewhere in the Strasbourg region. He did not say why. He did not explain the jumpsuit or the coonskin cap, much less the shades. He drove really fast. It was incredibly misty that day, and much of the time we found ourselves on a serpentine two-lane ribbon of highway where you couldn't see more than fifty yards in front of you, but all day long he kept flooring it so he could overtake slow-moving vehicles. It was as if he had a train to catch and kept forgetting that he had a car. Several times we narrowly avoided being wiped out by oncoming tractor-trailers. Luckily, the car accelerated quickly and handled well, and he was an excellent driver, so we escaped intact.

I have no idea what we talked about that day, but he did buy me a tasty lunch in a well-appointed *auberge* on the outskirts of Châlons-sur-Marne, where Attila the Hun was defeated by an unlikely alliance of Romans and Visigoths in A.D. 451. It didn't look as if much had happened around there since. It was the first time I had ever eaten rabbit. At some point I told my benefactor and erstwhile chauffeur that I was interested in visiting Lunéville because it was the town where Arthur Rimbaud had grown up. He asked who Arthur Rimbaud was, and I said, "The French Jim Morrison," and then he asked who Jim Morrison was, and I must have said something like "the American Johnny Hallyday," and we let it go. He dropped me off in busy downtown Lunéville around four in the afternoon, said goodbye, and was on his way. I never forgot him, though I never caught his name or nationality and for the life of me cannot recall whether we conversed in French or English. I do recall the outfit, as only stood to reason. I had a couple of stiff ones, then reported to the local tourism office and discovered that Rimbaud was not born in Lunéville but in Charleville, about fifty miles to the north. Maybe more. So this leg of the junket had been a complete waste of time.

Confirming in advance pertinent details about places I soon intended to visit would never be my strong suit in life. Many years later, I would drive all the way across America, eating exclusively at Hooters restaurants, and make a special detour hundreds of miles out of my way to Dodge City just so I could call my son and say, "I'm going to go visit the O.K. Corral, but then I've got to get out of Dodge." Alas, while a rootin', tootin' statue of a pistol-packin' Wyatt Earp could be found smack-dab in the center of Dodge City, as could the vaunted Boot Hill, the O.K. Corral was located hundreds of miles to the southwest, in Tombstone, Arizona. You would have thought I would have learned to check things in advance from my earlier experience in Lunéville, but I did not.

I don't remember how I got from Lunéville to Strasbourg, but when I turned up early that evening, my friend was nowhere to be found. The concierge said that he had packed up a month or so earlier and returned to the States and was not coming back. I later found out that as soon as Mike arrived in Strasbourg, he made the alarming discovery that he hated the French. So he went home to South Jersey to sell real estate, and I never saw him again. I would now have to spend the night in some crummy student hostel. I took in the sights of Strasbourg, a doleful little town, for a few hours the next day, then headed back to Paris. The entire adventure had been a bust.

Still, I think that Rimbaud would have been impressed by the epic futility of my pilgrimage. Prodigiously gifted, one of the most influential poets of all time, but a class-A screwup, Rimbaud would have gotten a kick out of my account of the mysterious driver, the flirtation with automotive tragedy, the pinkness of the jumpsuit, the coonskinnedness of the cap. After all, Rimbaud had once been shot in a Brussels hotel by his lover Paul Verlaine, had ended up abandoning poetry and running guns in Africa, and had passed away at age thirty-seven when a pain in his knee that was originally diagnosed as severe arthritis turned out to be cancer. So it wasn't like he was clicking on all cylinders, either. I could have been killed that day, but it would have been worth it to know that I breathed my last in an eight-car collision while on my way to visit what I erroneously believed to be Arthur Rimbaud's hometown in eastern France. Had I been on the way to Joyce Kilmer's hometown in New Jersey and gotten flattened by a tractor-trailer, I think I would have been livid, albeit dead. But had I been on the road to Joyce Kilmer's hometown, New Brunswick, which would have involved hitching up the Jersey Turnpike, I doubt very much that I would have accepted a ride from a man in a pink jumpsuit, a coonskin cap, and opaque shades. I think I probably would have packed it in and taken the bus.

Since that afternoon in 1973, I have never made it to Charleville.

. . . . . .

I am not and have never been a fetishist about writers. With the obvious exception of Baudelaire. And Rimbaud. And Hugo. And Molière. And Beckett. And one or two others. Generally, I try not to go overboard. For example, I have no desire to spend a week in the very room in Oxford where Lewis Carroll wrote *Alice's Adventures in Wonderland*, as my daughter's fourth-grade schoolteacher did one summer. I do not like hot weather or people who wear plaid shorts, so even though I admire Ernest Hemingway, I have no intention of visiting his house in the Keys, much less the saloons he frequented in Havana. I would never set off on one of those sugarplum literary excursions around England, where participants get to visit Jane Austen's tomb and Anne Hathaway's cottage and the pub where A. S. Byatt's cribbage league dukes it out every Thursday night. I would be even less interested in loping through Germany with a bunch of hard-core *Wanderjahr* aficionados, where the big payoff might be a chance to have a few jolts in Young Werther's favorite *Brauhaus* and find out what he was so sorrowful about. And if such a thing exists in Rumania— say, a lycanthropic literary ramble through the Carpathians—it is unnecessary to send me the brochure. I feel the same way about anything involving the haunts, furniture, appliances, writing implements, or meerschaum pipes of C. S. Lewis. If it's got anything to do with the author of *The Screwtape Letters*, count me out.

I have, it is true, visited the Paris subways in memory of Jean Valjean and Inspector Javert. They were disappointingly sanitary. And I have attended several concerts at the Paris Opéra, where Gaston Leroux's *Phantom of the Opera* is set. Also, I once took a train to Le Havre, where Sartre wrote *Nausea*, but I went there to rendezvous with my future wife, not to confirm whether Le Havre was the kind of city that would induce nausea. It was. I have also visited Honoré de Balzac's house in Paris—I have in fact done so several times—but it is not because I am obsessed with Balzac. I simply like the house. It is beautiful yet austere, with a spare, lovely garden out back. It sits on a quiet street in the fashionable 16th Arrondissement, no more than a fifteen-minute walk from the Arc de Triomphe and the Eiffel Tower. The house, now a museum, has two separate entrances. Balzac, who made enormous amounts of money but spent even more, was always in trouble with his creditors, so whenever he heard them pounding on the front door, he would scurry out the back. Once, when two grizzled Franco-repo-men intercepted him at the rear entrance, he denied being Honoré de Balzac, insisting that he was only the gardener. A very fat, very well-dressed gardener. The repo men must have been quite a pair.

There are some writers whose work you can connect with their surroundings—Georges Simenon, William Faulkner, A. E. Housman, Jean Giono, Allen Ginsberg, and of course Henry Miller, Ernest Hemingway, and F. Scott Fitzgerald—but Balzac is not one of them. Balzac's house is tasteful and petite and charming and refined, adjectives that could never be used to describe Balzac himself. Balzac was a fat slob who gorged himself on oysters and snails and profiteroles and whatever else happened to turn up on the lazy Susan at dinnertime, and never exercised and kept himself awake all night by drinking vats of coffee and didn't take care of himself. Consequently, he didn't last long. Balzac put his body through so much abuse that when he died, his organs resembled those of an eighty-year-old man. In fact, he was only fifty-one.

The thing you learn from visiting Balzac's house is that the genius of the author cannot necessarily be adduced from the physical surroundings in which he supposedly did his work. What you adduce from visiting a famous writer's house is a great deal of information about curators and interior designers and docents. Balzac's house is an altogether relaxing and tasteful environment. But Balzac himself was neither relaxed nor tasteful. There are very nice caricatures and paintings on the walls, and beautiful carpets, and that lovely garden out back, and the house is undeniably filled with Olde World Charm. But none of it has anything to do with Balzac.

This is just as true of the houses or apartments or neighborhoods associated with Victor Hugo and Charles Dickens and Samuel Johnson and Samuel Beckett and my personal favorite, Chatterton. You can visit their homes and prowl around their bedrooms and inspect their pens or typewriters or ink pads or thesauruses or arsenic vials, but it will not lead you to a richer understanding of their work. Nor is the spirit of the work always reflected in the neighborhood it was written in. When writers are writing, they are not really in Paris or London; they're inside their own heads. The bourgeois *arrondissement* in Paris where Beckett lived would not be the most obvious place to write *Waiting for Godot*; the grubby, proletarian neighborhoods on the northern edge of the city would have been more like it. There is nothing about the Place des Vosges that would make you think Victor Hugo had written *The Hunchback of Notre Dame* there. He had to write *The Hunchback of Notre Dame* somewhere. It might as well be the Place des Vosges.

In the many years that have passed since my Parisian adventures, I have continued to visit writers' homes in France and England but not so much in the United States. This may be because England and France are economy-sized countries and most of the great writers—like Dickens and Jonson and Tennyson and Hugo and Zola and Baudelaire and Colette and Voltaire and Sartre and

Apollinaire and Morrison—are buried in or around London and Paris, whereas you have to drive all over the place if you want to see the final resting places of Sherwood Anderson and Zora Neale Hurston. As for Edna Ferber, just forget it; she was cremated and no one knows where the ashes wound up. I have, over the years, managed to slip in visits to Edgar Allan Poe's room at the University of Virginia, and the Edgar Allan Poe Museum a few blocks away, and the Edgar Allan Poe Museum in Baltimore, Maryland, and Edgar Allan Poe's cottage in Philadelphia, and Edgar Allan Poe's cottage in the Bronx, though I have never actually made it all the way up to that library in Buffalo that used to display Edgar Allan Poe's watch until it got purloined on June 7, 1906. I have made these trips not so much because I am a passionate Edgar Allan Poe fan as because Poe, like Victor Hugo and Christopher Columbus and Stonewall Jackson, seems to have been buried in about seventy-five different places. So if you happen to find yourself in Steubenville, Ohio, or El Paso, Texas, with nothing to do one afternoon, there's a good chance that you'll find an Edgar Allan Poe Museum somewhere in the greater metropolitan area where you can while away a few hours. For a writer who didn't produce all that much and who died young and destitute and drunk, Poe certainly has an awful lot of museums attached to his name. Maybe if he'd been able to buckle down and stay in one place, he would have been more productive. Probably not the Bronx.

Poe was one of those writers who exerted a decisive influence on me as a kid, because after I read "The Premature Burial" at age twelve, I begged my three sisters to jam hat pins into my corpse before the morticians sealed up the coffin just to make sure I was really gone. I was also aware at a fairly early age that with "The Murders in the Rue Morgue" Poe had invented the detective novel, though this in itself is a mixed blessing, as detective novels, with few exceptions, are piffle, and even the exceptions only just barely qualify as literature. Poe's work qualified. And he did have that mystique. He was a huge influence on Baudelaire and the Symbolists, and like Baudelaire, he had a very catchy name. He was one of those Americans, like Frank Zappa and Jim Jarmusch and John Fante, whom the French overvalue, placing them on a gilt pedestal in a personally handcrafted pantheon of the Parallel United States of America dominated by Screamin' Jay Hawkins and Richard Brautigan and Lawrence Ferlinghetti and Chester Himes, a pantheon that does not include Ronald Reagan and the Daughters of the American Revolution and Faith Hill and NASCAR. It is an invented—nay, concocted—America that works for the French but does not work for anybody else, because it is out of scale and false and ridiculous. The French have taken a slice and elevated it to the majesty of a loaf. The French are like that.

My first job in journalism was editing a broadsheet, direct-mail magazine called *Uncle Sam*. It was a magazine that celebrated America but did so on the cheap. To put out the magazine every month, we had to rely on dirt-cheap visuals, like blurry photos of Crazy Horse Mountain or the graffiti that vandals had spray-painted all over the boulders on Mount Saint Helens. We obtained these pictures by cajoling accommodating park rangers and underappreciated housewives into going out and snapping them for us, gratis. One day in the spring of 1982 I read about a "ghost" that made a habit of visiting Poe's grave at the Poe Museum in Crabcake Corners every year since 1949, always leaving behind three roses and a half-drunk bottle of brandy as a birthday gift. It sounded like an inside joke of some sort. I called up the museum's curator, Jeff Jerome, and asked if he would stake out the gravesite for me. He did, and when no one had showed up by 11:15, he took a quick break to grab something to eat. When he got back, the mysterious stranger had come and gone, leaving behind his usual tribute. A few days later, I received a photo of Jerome, looking a bit the worse for wear, standing next to Poe's tombstone, clutching the bottle of brandy. I still have that picture. It is *prima facie* evidence of the first truth I ever learned about my chosen line of work: that when the chips are down and a journalist finds himself backed into a corner, Mr. John Q. Public will always come to his rescue.

Jerome, who tried but never succeeded in intercepting the visitor in the many years that followed, was skeptical of the notion that only one person, or only one visitor from beyond the grave, was involved here. "People actually think this person comes and drinks a toast over Poe's grave," he told me at the time. "But I know there has to be more than one person involved, because if I put away a half-bottle of brandy, I wouldn't make it outside the cemetery gates."

In 1998 the visitor stopped coming. It is now believed that he is dead, if human, or has resumed his otherworldly slumber, if spectral. No one can say for sure. This is one of those cases where it is preferable not to know the truth, nor to see it treated in some sardonic fashion on YouTube. We do not know why Ingram Frizer killed Christopher Marlowe in a victualing house in 1593, nor do we need to. We do not even know what a victualing house is. We do not know why Jane Austen never got around to writing her book *The Magnificent Adventures and Intriguing Romances of the House of Saxe Coburg*. We do not know what John Stuart Mill's daffy maid was thinking of when she used the only copy of Thomas Carlyle's history of the French Revolution as kindling for a fire. Nor do we know why Carlyle hadn't taken better care of the manuscript or inquired of Mill in advance whether his household staff included any first-rate numskulls. We do not even know if

William Shakespeare's plays were written by William Shakespeare himself or by some first-rate chap who went to Eton and Cambridge, the way first-rate chaps who went to Eton and Cambridge would like us to believe things happened. We do not need to know everything; it takes all the joy out of life. Personally, I prefer to believe that it was the ghost of Edgar Allan Poe himself who kept stopping by that Crabcake Corners cemetery every winter for all those years, and that for some reason he finally decided that the joke had worn thin. Poe was always hard to get a read on.

There are a couple other writers whose homes I have visited: Emily Dickinson's house in Amherst, Massachusetts; Washington Irving's Sunnyside, right down the road from my home in Tarrytown, New York. Neither of them made much of an impression on me. They don't feel like places where writers lived and worked. They feel like mausoleums. Washington Irving is a particularly sore point with me, mainly because of the continuing regional fallout from the publication of *The Legend of Sleepy Hollow*. Irving, we are told, was the first American writer who was taken seriously in Europe, but he was quickly surpassed by more exciting writers like James Fenimore Cooper and by more gifted writers like Nathaniel Hawthorne and Herman Melville. I once read that on his deathbed, Franz Schubert implored his brother to run out and fetch him one last James Fenimore Cooper novel before checkout time; on the subject of Washington Irving's work, he was notably silent. People who live in Sleepy Hollow, New York, the town that adjoins Tarrytown, are misinformed about Irving's stature; they think he is on a par with Homer. They are altogether delusional.

For 122 years Sleepy Hollow was known as North Tarrytown, a mostly working-class community that was home to a sprawling General Motors plant. But in 1996, a *junta* of parvenu Yuppies seized control of the tonier districts of the village—Philipse Manor and Sleepy Hollow Manor. Shortly thereafter a plebiscite was held, asking residents if they would like to rename their village Sleepy Hollow. The old people wouldn't, and the young people would. There were more young people, including hundreds of carpetbaggers who'd slithered up from Gotham, and so the name North Tarrytown passed into history. People who grew up in North Tarrytown were livid. It was not so much that they objected to the new name's Satanic prissiness; it was because they felt disenfranchised. Subsequently, when old people would die, their families would insist that the obituary identify their birthplace as North Tarrytown, not Sleepy Hollow. Sleepy Hollow is a good name for a book or a legend or an orthopedic rehab center or even a high school, but it is a bad name for a town. Even more laughable was the name a slow-witted developer gave to a beleaguered condo unit he planted along the river: Ichabod's Landing. By the looks of it, the developer was unaware that Ichabod Crane was a dork who came to a bad end at the hands of the Headless Horseman. Christening an American condo complex Ichabod's Landing is like naming a European development Polonius Close or Sancho Panza Vistas or Uriah Heep Manor. No matter. The scheming Yuppies and their odious hench-developer friends perhaps thought that the moniker Sleepy Hollow would make prospective home buyers overlook the fact that the student body at Sleepy Hollow High School was more than 50 percent minority and that the principal thoroughfare in the village was lined with thriving Ecuadorean, Peruvian, Chilean, and Mexican bodegas.

No way, José.

Tarrytown itself has a sliver of connection with literary fame: Mark Twain bought a mansion called Hillcrest high atop the village and lived there for two years, or for part of two years, or maybe he only slept there that one night, depending on which fragment of local apocrypha you choose to believe. In any case, he quickly unloaded the joint following a dustup with local tax assessors. It is now a restaurant. I admired Twain from the time I was a boy, because, just as Frank Sinatra was the only singer my parents liked whom I didn't hate, *Huckleberry Finn* was the first book a teacher assigned me that was actually fun to read. One day when I was in my forties, a friend and I drove to Hartford, Connecticut, to visit Twain's house. My friend was a native of Hartford, and she was eager to show off the crown jewels of the Yankee State. That didn't take long. Harriet Beecher Stowe's house was right next door to Twain's house, but we never got to it, as the Twain visit wore us out. Hartford was also home to the great poet Wallace Stevens, who, when asked by a literary magazine for a biographical profile, replied: "I am a lawyer and live in Hartford. But such facts are neither gay nor instructive." His wife, Elsie Viola Kachel, would later stagger the schedule of her evening constitutionals so she did not have to spend any more time than necessary with her husband. But before things went sour, she had been the most beautiful girl in Reading, Pennsylvania, and served as the model of the goddess Liberty for the now-extinct Mercury dime. This is, to my knowledge, the only instance in which anyone even tenuously connected with a living American poet was immortalized on a piece of American currency. In France this kind of stuff happens all the time.

Mark Twain's house was dark and depressing. It had a lot of nice woodwork and more fireplaces than you could shake a stick at, but it was still dark and depressing. Once you entered the building, the staff locked you in, forcing you to take the official guided tour with a docent. Luckily, the docent was not dressed in a white suit and a panama hat with a stogie protruding from beneath a heavily mustached upper lip. That would not have looked at all good on her. Nor was she one of those insufferable Mark Twain impersonators who sputter things like "The reports of my death have been greatly exaggerated" all afternoon. A few years later I would attend a dinner in Hartford where a conscienceless Twain impersonator would mercilessly torment the defenseless guests the entire night. A friend who had accompanied me to the event, a very fine writer in his own right, at one point inquired whether the man had other literary impersonations in his repertoire, if he could perhaps switch to Henry David Thoreau or Clifford Odets or even Milan Kundera to give the rest of us a breather. When he said that he could not, Doug and I hatched a plot to jump him in the parking lot right after dinner and slit his throat. No charges, we were sure, would ever be brought against us; the police would deem it a victimless crime. But our nerve failed us, and Hartford has had to live with the consequences ever since.

Though no distaff Samuel Taylor Clemens impersonator she, and thankfully not clad in ponderous Gilded Age period costume, the docent that day was an intense, middle-aged woman who was a bit slow on the draw. She seemed more interested in the house than in Mark Twain. I began to suspect during the course of our visit that she may not have been entirely clear who Mark Twain was. She seemed to think that he was some irascible old coot most famous for giving Alexander Graham Bell the bum's rush when he turned up, hat in hand, seeking seed capital for some ditzy invention. An old coot whose principal claim to fame was that he had left behind an amazing house. The house was less amazing than depressing. As we wended our way through it she would quiz us on the myriad treasures we had seen in previous rooms. She may have been keeping score. How many windows have we seen? How many desks? How much inlaid marble? When we got to the top floor, which housed Twain's billiard room, she stared directly at me and said: "How many fireplaces have we now seen?"

"Two hundred and forty-seven," I replied.

She shook her head.

"Wrong," she said. The correct answer, I seem to recall, was seven. Her tone was one of mild disappointment and resignation rather than pique. She did not think I was being snarky or mean by suggesting that the house contained 247 fireplaces. She merely thought I was misinformed.

I will never forget the time we spent in the nursery shared by Twain's two youngest daughters. An older daughter, his beloved Susy, had succumbed to spinal meningitis at age twenty-four while he was away in Europe, though, after seeing the way her father had decorated the place, I was kind of surprised she'd lasted that long. After her death, Twain could no longer live in that house. He almost certainly never returned to the upstairs bedrooms, and it wasn't hard to see why. The walls of the nursery were covered with faded, macabre wallpaper, depicting scenes from a famous nursery rhyme. After running through her well-rehearsed spiel, the docent turned to us and said, "Surely you all remember the famous 'Mister Froggy Went a'Courtin'?"

No, in fact, not all of us did.

She took this as a cue to transfix us with her stare, slip into full-tilt pedagogic mode, and then, in a reedy soprano, begin singing:

Now, Mister Froggy went a'courtin, uh-huh.
Mister Froggy, went a'courtin, uh-huh.
Now, Mister Froggy . . .

And so on and so forth until the little ditty had reached its conclusion. I gazed into her eyes, and just slightly to the left in each retina I could see the gates of Hell. They were ajar. Actually, it looked like they were now swinging wide open. That woman scared the bejesus out of me and everybody else in that room, and after that I never went on a guided tour of a writer's house again.

There was, however, one other occasion when merely being in a writer's house scared me out of my wits. That's when I was invited to give a talk at James Thurber's house in Columbus, Ohio. In fact, I was asked months in advance whether I would like to spend the night at the celebrated humorist's home. I said yes, that sounded like loads of fun, but it most certainly was not. I did not know at the time that Thurber's house was a Victorian building in a neighborhood that was completely deserted at night. All of the adjacent buildings, I would soon learn, emptied out at sundown. I also did not know that gale-force winds were expected to rip through town that evening. My presentation at Thurber's house went well enough, as did my talk at a local arts center. But after my talk, while I was signing books, two young men came up and wished me a happy birthday. I asked how they knew it was my birthday, and they said that they knew all kinds of things. What's more, they had a birthday present for me, a wafer-thin object bundled up in convenience store wrapping paper. Although they had thoroughly enjoyed my book *Red Lobster, White Trash, and the Blue Lagoon*, in which I spent a year exploring the lower depths of American pop culture trying to find something worse than *Cats*, they felt that I had been needlessly mean to their favorite rock band, Rush. So they hoped I would give Rush a second chance. I said I would think about it, though I could barely remember who Rush was.

Shortly thereafter I was deposited back at Thurber's house in the middle of a monsoon. My hosts departed, and I was alone.

Now the house went to work scaring the hell out of me. It would have scared the hell out of Nosferatu. I kept hearing lightly padding footsteps upstairs, which I took to be ghosts or poltergeists. Possibly a wraith or two. Definitely a few zombies. It was impossible to sleep, so I started working on the computer. Foolishly I engaged in a bit of research about the house and found out that it was built on the site of an insane asylum that had burned to the ground in 1868, with seven inmates perishing in the fire, and that a man may have blown his brains out in the upstairs bathroom shortly after the present structure was erected around the turn of the century. Thurber himself, who left Columbus on the dead run in his twenties and didn't seem in much of a hurry to come back, had even written a ghost story about the house. The storm railed against the house all night, and the winds howled, and I kept waiting for paranormal entities to crawl out of the basement and drag me straight to Hell or, failing that, Cincinnati. I finally got to sleep about four o'clock in the morning and almost missed my eight o'clock flight to Washington, D.C. While rummaging through my overnight bag on the plane, I found the gift the two young men had given me. I undid the wrapping paper to find that they had burned me a copy of Rush's greatest hits, accompanying the compact disc with the lyrics to such perennial favorites as "Tom Sawyer" and "Working Man." For the first time in my life, I literally felt my heart stop. I had suffered through a night of abject terror in James Thurber's chilling ancestral abode, but had I opened that package during the dark night of the soul while I was still trapped in that sinister building, I think the sheer horror would have been more than my poor heart could have borne. Spending a night in a haunted house is one thing, but spending a night in a haunted house in a deserted neighborhood in the middle of a raging storm, knowing that two Rush fans are out there somewhere—fans who know that you're spending the night alone in a haunted house in the middle of a raging storm in a deserted neighborhood where no one can hear you scream—is too terrifying to contemplate.

One memorable excursion involving writers required a summer jaunt to Pennsylvania. It was a state I had long ago fled but had never stopped loving, like a fondly remembered first wife who would have made a perfect lifelong companion if she'd only had a bit more money. Moolah was a relevant factor here, for in recent summers many cash-strapped Americans had been opting for a "staycation": a slimmed-down getaway where folks stick close to home. A staycation might take you to Cooperstown or Manassas or to a town associated with luckless witches. But it would not take you to Machu Picchu or Pompeii.

Typically, staycations combined edification with retail: You visited a battlefield or a museum and then hit the amusement park and the outlet stores. All this sounded too prosaic for me. Instead I designed myself a "Keystone State literary staycation." My destinations were Reading, where John Updike's *Rabbit, Run* takes place; Pottsville, where the prolific John O'Hara set fifty of his *New Yorker* stories and several of his novels, though always identifying his hometown as Gibbsville; and Scranton, where Jason Miller, who won the Pulitzer Prize for theater in 1973 for *That Championship Season*, grew up. All were within two hours' drive of my New York home. The idea was to combine local color and cuisine with culture while holding down the expenses by staying at the Ramada Inn. Throughout the trip I planned to reread the works that had made these men famous. Personally, I thought it sounded like great fun. But in the end, I had to do the trip on my own, because I couldn't get my wife or even one of my kids to accompany me. Staycation, be damned. They'd rather just stay.

Scranton was my first stop. Motoring into town, I came face-to-face with the deserted junior high school where a pivotal scene from the film version of *That Championship Season* occurs. Then I headed downtown to Nay Aug Park—designed by Frederick Law Olmsted, of Central Park and Plains of Abraham fame—where the opening scene of the film was shot. After that I spent an hour driving around the grungy streets of North Scranton, where much of the action is set. It was all very illuminating, but as I drifted from one place to the next, a number of unsettling thoughts gripped me. One, *That Championship Season* is a downbeat play, in which four high school basketball stars are united with their coach twenty-five years after they won the state title and the results are not pretty. Life has not worked out for these guys—one is an inept politician, one is an alcoholic, one is sleeping with his best friend's wife, the coach himself is a racist scumbag—and in a way the play eerily presages the author's own career: a stunning debut, an inability to repeat the success of *That Championship Season*, an acting career that began with the classic horror film *The Exorcist* and ended with the unimaginably hokey *Rudy*, and finally a return to Scranton, where Miller died, broken by alcohol, at age sixty-two.

All these thoughts were with me as I drove around Scranton. The cultural element in my staycation was working out nicely, but emotionally this was turning into a bit of a downer. I rectified this by paying a visit to Steamtown, the superb downtown train museum, where I took a ride on a vintage diesel train. For just three bucks. Three bucks! After that I waltzed across to the Trolley Museum, whose crown jewels include a Philadelphia Transit Commission streetcar I probably rode on as a child. Maybe the 47.

Or the 6. Gosh, another dirt-cheap delight! I finished up that day with a jim-dandy meal in the Caffe Classico, followed by a drink in the Radisson Lackawanna, the spiffy hotel that had recently risen from the ashes of the derelict train station in the film version of *That Championship Season*. By the end of the day, I'd completely forgotten how much the play and the circumstances of its author's premature demise depressed me.

The next morning, after a diversionary expedition up Route 6, a local road that ultimately leads to the vastly underrated Grand Canyon of Pennsylvania, I hooked southeast to Pottsville. In the early part of the twentieth century, Pottsville had two claims to fame. One, the famous novelist John O'Hara had grown up there. Two, the Pottsville Maroons had been the 1925 champions of the fledgling National Football League, until they got stripped of the title on a cheesy technicality by more powerful, less honorable owners. That was about it for the Maroons. Banners honoring the otherwise forgotten hometown heroes could be seen everywhere. Judging from my brief visit to the town, the Maroons were still a whole lot more popular than the novelist.

"He was a spoiled brat," said Dr. Peter Yasenchak, executive director of the Historical Society of Schuylkill County, an institution whose halfhearted tribute to the novelist consisted of a book-case containing perhaps ten of his books, none signed by the author. O'Hara, who didn't have much nice to say about the town where he was born, left early and didn't come back. I had just driven all the way up Mahantongo Street, the street that appears as Lantenengo Street again and again in O'Hara's stories, and been impressed by the many fine houses that lined it. There was actually a plaque outside the building where the author was born. But there was no Bard of Avon ambience in this humble burgh. After all, Pottsville had been a big numbers-and-prostitution center in the prewar era, when coal was king, and almost by default O'Hara's fiction focused on gangsters, barflies, bookies, murderers, floozies, two-timers, louses, dipsomaniacal doctors, craven adulterers, and all-purpose creeps. No American writer ever introduced fewer likable characters than O'Hara. None, by my last count. This may have been because O'Hara went to Rutgers. The author, whose father's early death crushed his son's dreams of attending Yale, was a bitter, bitter man. The pain did not mellow with age.

"Nobody really knew him," said Yasenchak. "He stayed up there on Mahantongo Street and never came down into town before sundown. And he was only interested in writing about who was playing footsie with whom at the country club. He was kind of a strange cat."

Dismayed by this lingering antipathy toward Pottsville's most famous author, I retreated to the local diner for a psychologically defibrillating chocolate milkshake. The Garfield Diner contained all sorts of Garfield the Cat memorabilia—plaques, signs, clocks, stuffed animals—but it was not in fact named after Garfield, also kind of a strange cat. It was named after the martyred president, James Garfield. It was a swell place, the kind of cheery eatery that you never encounter in O'Hara's morbid, oppressive fiction. If Julian English, the doomed protagonist of *Appointment in Samarra*, had only had the good sense to drop by the Garfield Diner and treat himself to a bacon double-cheeseburger with fries on the side and then wash it all down with a chocolate milkshake, he might have reconsidered his decision to asphyxiate himself in his car. That's how yummy that milkshake was.

Reading was the last stop on my itinerary. In the interests of historical accuracy I visited Shillington first, because that was where Updike was born and spent part of his youth, but Shillington was a bland, run-of-the-mill suburb. Reading may have been a city whose best days were behind it—and whose best days may not have been all that great—but cities, even hard-pressed ones, are inherently more interesting than suburbs. Reading's one top-shelf tourist attraction is the colorful pagoda that sits, in anomalous splendor, atop the mountain poised at the edge of the city. In *Rabbit, Run*, Updike renamed Reading Brewer and ditched the pagoda in favor of a fancy mountaintop hotel, but nobody was fooled. The mountain peak appears again and again in the novel. It symbolizes a pinnacle Rabbit cannot attain, as well as a shadow he cannot escape. I think.

Reading's city fathers made a really smart decision when they green-lighted that pagoda in 1908. The day I visited, tourists from Singapore and Japan and points west were getting their pictures taken in front of it. Their unabashed joy helped lift my mood after all the drinking and failure and marital infidelity in Updike's novel, not to mention the scene where Rabbit's soused wife accidentally drowns her newborn baby. Thank God somebody in Reading wasn't moping the day away.

There is one other thing worth seeing in that part of the Keystone State. While I was visiting the University of Scranton, the library's circulation clerk, Kathleen Rinaggio, told me that she had appeared as an extra in the 1982 film version of *That Championship Season*. "They were all so nice—Robert Mitchum, Martin Sheen—and my daughter played the whole five days with Paul Sorvino's son," she recalled. Rinaggio then directed me to the Piazza dell'Arte, which sits right next to the Lackawanna County courthouse. The square contains tributes to assorted famous Scrantonian writers and artists—Jean Kerr, W. S. Merwin—but it is the bust of Jason Miller that dominates the plaza. Beneath it are written the words "I could not be prouder of my roots. . . . In coming home, I have discovered who you are. . . . You are my people." Inspecting the reverse side, I noticed the name of the sculptor. Paul Sorvino.

This unexpected little moment was the high point of my staycation. The city of Scranton, ridiculed without mercy in *The Office*, had erected a charming, vest-pocket plaza in honor of a native son who had paid tribute to it on stage and screen and refused to cave in when Hollywood leaned on him to set the story elsewhere. In other parts of the square stood standard-issue statues of Christopher Columbus and Tadeusz Kosciuszko and Philip Sheridan. They were all terrific fellows, but none of them hailed from Scranton. Anyone can put up a statue to a general or a patriot or an explorer. Putting up a statue to a writer shows more imagination and class. It's the sort of thing they do in France.

There are places on the face of the earth that we have no great desire to visit, but when we do visit them we come away the better for the experience. This is what happened to me when I went to Stockholm. I trekked to the frozen north to do a radio program about cities that had been immortalized by crime writers. In this case it was Stieg Larsson. I was one of the early proponents of Scandinavian *noir* in my social circle, raving about Mankell and Håkan Nesser and Kjell Eriksson and Åke Edwardson and Karin Fossum—the lone Norwegian in the bunch—long before anyone else I knew was aware of their existence. I was also the first person I knew to bang the drum for the outstanding Icelandic writer Arnaldur Indriðason. My friends soon tired of this schtick. One of the finest living mystery writers lives in Reykjavik? Knock it off.

I stumbled upon the Nordic Gumshoe Genre in the mid-Nineties, while dawdling in a Philadelphia bookstore. Informing one of the clerks that I was tired of mysteries set on Mulholland

Drive or down in Little Italy or in the dainty English countryside, where unspeakable depravity lurked behind every primrose bush, I asked if she could recommend something a bit more exotic.

"Try *The Dogs of Riga*," she said.

I did. Though *The Dogs of Riga* sounded like a thriller by Martin Cruz Smith, it was actually a mystery by the Swedish novelist Henning Mankell. And a first-class mystery it was, the latest in a series featuring the clinically depressed police detective Kurt Wallander. Wallander is a divorced middle-aged man whose daughter is a mess, who has a tense relationship with his elderly father, and who is not in great health. He is a diligent, plodding copper who usually needs a lucky break to crack the case. Based on this description, it was hard to see how Mankell's books would stand out in any way from the herd.

But Mankell—who is also the director of the Teatro Avenida in Mozambique—proved to be a gifted writer who uses the humdrum mystery format to address the disintegration of Swedish society, the horrors of old age, the very meaning of being a policeman. In this he resembles, without equaling, the formidable Franco-Belgian novelist Georges Simenon, whose Inspector Maigret series stands second only to Arthur Conan Doyle's Sherlock Holmes series in the mystery canon. I was so taken by *The Dogs of Riga* that I went out and bought eight other Mankell books and within a few months had polished off his entire subarctic *oeuvre*. After that, I moved on to his formidable antecedents Maj Sjöwall and Per Wahlöö, whose 1968 novel, *The Laughing Policeman*, was made into a listless movie starring Walter Matthau a few years later. Over the next few years, I began gobbling up Mankell's numerous protégés and/or imitators: Mari Jungstedt, Jens Lapidus, Camilla Läckberg. I even started giving Swedish murder mysteries to fellow mystery lovers as Christmas presents. They got a much warmer reception than *The Man Without Qualities*. Everyone found the grim atmosphere beguiling. Everyone liked the way the story was sometimes viewed from the perspective of the murderer. Scandinavian mysteries, they quickly learned, possessed a seductive charm all their own. Part of their appeal was their reverse exoticism: the unrelenting bleakness, the zero tolerance for chuckles, and the ferocity of the crimes—the Swedes really go in big for decapitations, scalpings, disembowelments, tattooed torsos floating to the surface of foreboding lakes. All this makes the books much darker and spookier than those glib *mafiosi* capers set in Bologna and Bensonhurst. And the Swedes do not write conventional whodunits; they are obsessed with understanding why people become axe murderers in the first place. Mostly, it's because of something that happened to them as children growing up on the mean streets of, well, Stockholm.

The anomic prose, the general avoidance of generic gangland motifs, and the absence of the wisecracking that characterizes so much contemporary American crime fiction were also a welcome change. Wallander did not wear flashy clothes, and he did not have a dazzling record collection that included rare bootlegs by Hüsker Dü and Kraftwerk, and he did not have any cool friends, and he was not a master chef or an expert on truffles or a closet oenophile. He was an old-fashioned cop trying to figure out why scalped, disemboweled, tattooed corpses kept turning up all over town. This was true of Mankell's peers and protégés as well. None of their characters were even marginally cool. They were all deadbeats.

From the moment I discovered Mankell, I constantly told friends that they were missing out on something big if they continued to overlook the Scandinavian Whodunit Boom. They sneered at me. They continued to dismiss the genre until *The Girl with the Dragon Tattoo* rolled off the presses. Then they couldn't get enough of it. Now everyone was jumping on the Viking bandwagon. A few years later, I went back to that Philadelphia bookstore to thank the helpful employee for introducing me to Mankell, and she said that she had no idea what I was talking about. As noted in an earlier chapter, my experiences in bookstores have often been less than ideal.

I rattled on so much and for so long about the subject that the BBC finally broke down and let me do a program about it. The premise was to determine the extent to which a crime novel or series of crime novels evoked the city in which they were set. I was planning to do a whole series of these things, but the BBC must have figured out that it was all a scam to visit fabulous places like Rio de Janeiro and Tokyo, so they only ponied up for two programs. The first was the nation's capital, where I spoke with a retired FBI agent nicknamed Dr. Death, the single most fascinating person I have ever interviewed. I also had a spirited conversation with mystery writer George Pelecanos in his Silver Spring, Maryland, home, the author taking pains to remind me that, while there could be no denying that his dark, violent novels captured the essence of his hometown, Washington, D.C., he still really liked the city.

Stockholm was a different story. Sometimes described as the Venice of the North, Stockholm is not a particularly rough town. Despite all the violence in the books that are set there, Stockholm doesn't have the grit of Marseille or Glasgow or the East End of London, where the Krays once ruled the roost, and it isn't scary in the way that East New York and East Los Angeles and East St. Louis and West Philadelphia are. To the naked eye, it has all the grit and menace of Santa Fe. I suspect that this may be true of Sweden in general. It is just not a scary place.

By the time I turned up in Stockholm, *The Girl with the Dragon Tattoo* frenzy was in overdrive; the national art museum actually had the office belonging to the main character in Larsson's books on display, the way previous curators might have honored characters dreamed up by Strindberg or Bergman. *The Girl with the Dragon Tattoo* trilogy had already sold twenty-seven million copies, three books for every citizen of Sweden. People were going to night school to learn how to write Scandinavian crime fiction, with amazing success. Things were getting out of hand.

Unless you are a complete idiot, genre fiction will eventually tire you out. You will eventually grow tired of vampires, werewolves, sorcerers, demons. You may even grow tired of succubi. You will definitely get your fill of Klingons, dark ops, warlocks, the Dark Knight, the Knights Templar, knights in general. Something like that now happened to me with crime fiction set in exotic climes. Their basic selling point was their colorful settings, not their prose or plotlines; few writers from Italy, Holland, Brazil, or anywhere else could match Harlan Coben and Michael Connelly and Dennis Lehane for ingenuity, pacing, and thrills, or Elmore Leonard for dialogue, or Ross Macdonald for atmosphere, or James Ellroy and Raymond Chandler for ingenuity, pacing, thrills, atmosphere, plotlines, dialogue, and style. Americans like Poe and Dashiell Hammett had invented the genre, and to this day only a handful of foreigners could even hope to compete in that league.

When push came to shove, there was nothing special about Alicia Giménez-Bartlett's police procedurals set in Barcelona or Patricia Hall's Yorkshire mysteries, which could have taken place anywhere. Cara Black's French thrillers were neither particularly gripping nor particularly evocative of Paris, and she wasn't much of a writer. Alexander McCall Smith's good-natured Ladies' Detective Agency series were not especially tantalizing; it was only their offbeat Botswana setting that set them apart. More and more, the exotic thriller was starting to seem like a con job, a ploy to make a humdrum tale seem more compelling, when in fact the only thing it had going for it was that it was set in some oddball place. Oslo. Transylvania. Or Laos, home to the gripping Dr. Siri series. Yes, *that* Laos.

The truth is, I myself had oversold the Nordic mystery genre. For years I'd been telling people that they were missing out on something really good if they didn't take a crack at Scandinavian mystery writers. But they weren't missing out on something *great*. *The Girl with the Dragon Tattoo* is badly written and is for all intents and purposes voyeuristic porn. The nonsense about Lisbeth Salander as a feminist role model is twaddle; she's a sociopath with piercings. Stieg Larsson's books had come along in the right place at the right time, when the zeitgeist was ready for them, but Stieg Larsson as a writer wasn't in a class with Mankell. And in any case I was tired of them all. I was fast approaching my sixtieth birthday and getting too old for this kind of stuff. For most of my life I had enjoyed high-class mysteries—P. D. James, Ian Rankin, Ruth Rendell—but only as a breather. I never honestly believed that crime fiction transcended the genre; it might be beach reading of a very high order, but it was beach reading all the same. I now realized that I'd had it up to here with bumbling middle-aged coppers and dysfunctional hackers and Swedish serial killers. Now that I was working my way back from the end of my life and counting the days, I didn't have time to waste on Scandinavian *noir*. Every minute I spent reading about Lisbeth Salander's tattoos was time I could have spent reading about Queequeg's tattoos.

This was a classic case of disappointment when you discover something absolutely wonderful, and then everybody else gets into the act, and then the person or thing you enjoy becomes more popular than it has a right to be, and then things get completely out of scale, and then you get sick of the whole thing. Still, I did have one unforgettable experience in Sweden. That was the afternoon I went to interview a police officer who handled questions from the media. Thoughtfully, he had arranged for two female police officers to join us. We had a nice long talk about crime and crime fiction, and then he produced a chocolate cake purchased in honor of my visit. I did a double-take, assuring him that nothing like this would ever happen back in New York, much less Los Angeles. As we were finishing up our conversation, the two officers offered to take me for a spin around downtown Stockholm. We climbed into their squad car and spent about forty-five minutes looking for hardened criminals. We drove hither. We drove yon. But we met with no success, for nary a hard case was to be found anywhere. I felt a bit sorry for them, because they knew that I was on the prowl for baby killers and neo-Nazis and fiends who specialized in decapitating choirboys while they were still singing, but we couldn't even find a goddamn pickpocket. Eventually they got a call about a brouhaha in a Burger King and they were on their way. And I was on mine. Based on my experiences, I think that Americans reading Stieg Larsson and Henning Mankell and Åke Edwardson and all the rest are going to be terribly disappointed if they go to Stockholm seeking murder, mutilation, and mayhem. For best results, stick to Washington, D.C.

Some time back, on a pleasure trip to Paris, I paid my usual visit to Baudelaire's grave. I was standing there, gazing at the tomb I knew so well, when a man approached me from behind.

"It's not his tomb, you realize," he said. He was about thirty-five, good-looking, obviously French. "This is only his cenotaph.

His body is buried in the family tomb on the other side of the cemetery."

I thanked him, making the usual small talk about great, dead French poets. He then offered to show me the Baudelaire family tomb. I said that would be a real treat, not entirely sure why. I wondered if Baudelaire's cenotaph was some kind of French trysting place, or if I was being lured into a crafty mortuarial ambush and would soon be relieved of my wallet. It was reassuring that the man seemed to be a bona fide sepulcher buff, and the cemetery was reasonably well traveled, so I gamely tagged along. We arrived at the Baudelaire family tomb, gave it the once-over, chatted some more.

Abruptly, we were joined by a woman well into her sixties who seemed to be conducting some routine mausoleum maintenance. She, too, was impressed that I knew who Baudelaire was. She asked whether I'd like to see where Maréchal Pétain's wife was buried. Annie, you mean? Annie Pétain? I sure would! Who wouldn't? Along the way, we paused for a moment by the graves of Constantin Brancusi and Jean-Paul Sartre and Simone de Beauvoir and Guy de Maupassant. My companions were impressed that I not only knew who they were but had read their work. Well, not Brancusi.

The French, alas, can only resist condescension for so long. As our little procession wended its way through the cemetery, the two of them began to grill me about dead French luminaries I had never heard of. Was it possible that Delphine Seyrig, a radiant movie star of the Nouvelle Vague era, was unknown in America? Tsk, tsk. Had I never heard of the trenchant social critic Roland Topor? *Mon Dieu.* Could things have reached such a dire impasse that an ostensibly cosmopolitan American such as I was unfamiliar with the work of Yves Mourousi, whom I took to be the French

Wolf Blitzer? In other words, by the time our little tour was over, I had been ground right into the dirt, casually dismissed as a Francophile *manqué*, a mere dilettante, just another hapless, would-be *idiot savant*. Once again, I'd succumbed to the classic Gallic rope-a-dope tactic, sticking my head out just far enough to get it lopped off.

But then the woman pointed at the final resting place of Gisèle Freund, a photographer who once took a famous head shot of—you guessed it—my old bosom buddy and personal savior, Henry de Montherlant. The photograph, which I had seen in several exhibits, made Montherlant look absolutely horrible. Dour to the last, the crotchety old son of a gun had asked her to shoot him that way.

"Boy, oh boy, did that guy ever know how to put pen to paper!" I exclaimed. "Let me tell you, September 21, 1972, was one of the most heartbreaking days in my life. After I read *La reine morte* in college, I was sold on that guy for good. And here I've got to be completely honest with you: I never really recovered from Henry de Montherlant's passing. Of course, I guess a lot of people feel that way."

You could have knocked them over with a feather.

CHAPTER SEVEN

Other Voices, Other Rooms

A reading life, a friend once told me, is an adventure without maps where you meet unexpected soulmates along the way. Those soulmates may include your children. When your children are born, it is by no means inevitable that they will share your tastes or values, any more than that they will share the proceeds of your will. Neither of my children seems smitten by jazz. My son has to date shown no great interest in the visual arts. But both my children have been fanatical readers since childhood. As they have grown up this has enabled us to trade anecdotes back and forth about common experiences. One is our seemingly congenital dread of the high school syllabus.

The gnashing of teeth never stopped when my fifteen-year-old son brought home *A Tale of Two Cities* as his summer reading assignment. According to him, the forced march through Dickens blighted June, devastated July, and obliterated August. "It was the best of times; it was the worst of times" is what he wrote in his report that summer. "Sorry, Chuck, it's either one or the other. Make up your mind." Thus, at back-to-school night in September, when his teacher told the assembled parents that our gifted, enthusiastic children—every last one of them a joy to work with!—loved Dickens, I knew that she was lying. I didn't know how other students felt about it, but my kid hated *A Tale of Two Cities*.

For decades well-meaning pedagogues have been sabotaging summer vacations by forcing high school kids to read novels like *Lord of the Flies, Brave New World, The Red Badge of Courage*, and *The Grapes of Wrath*. These books may be the cornerstones of our civilization, but they're certainly no fun. One reason the average American reads no more than four books a year may be the emotional trauma suffered while trying to hack his way through *Wuthering Heights* at age fourteen. I myself have never recovered from reading *The Return of the Native*, not only because Thomas Hardy's bleak vision and stifling prose made me feel bleak and stifled but because it was my first exposure to the extravagant cruelty of which teachers were capable. If my teachers had had an ounce of human decency, they might have assigned us *Macbeth* or *Rob Roy* or Caesar's *Gallic Wars* back in high school, knowing that the good-natured carnage would have at least held the boys' interest for a while. Or they could have chosen *The Stranger*, which had the mitigating charm of being depressing and hard to decipher and would thus keep the kids who were obviously going to Antioch and Oberlin happy. But by insisting that we write a full report on an uncompromisingly depressing nineteenth-century novel by a writer who never allowed a single ray of sunshine to brighten his work, the powers-that-be at Cardinal Dougherty High School were literally taunting the student body.

"Don't mess with us, for there is no torment too excruciating for us to contemplate," they seemed to be saying. "If you even once complain about how boring and irrelevant *The Return of the Native* is, next summer we'll make you read *Tess of the d'Urbervilles*. Just try us, punks."

Forty-five years after being pistol-whipped into submission by Thomas Hardy, I am amazed that the infamous summer reading list continues to exist. In a society that has dispensed with every other laudable cultural more—kids didn't used to come to school dressed like they worked the night shift for Murder, Inc.—it bewilders me that students still allow adults to fish-gut their summer vacations by forcing them to feast on the trivial glibness of *The Catcher in the Rye* or mind-numbing kitsch like *The Alchemist*. I am not saying it is necessarily a bad thing that schools require students to read books during the summer: Culture, like vitamins, works best when imposed rather than selected. I am simply recording my amazement that in an age when urban high schools use weapon detectors to check for pocket-sized Uzis, educators still try to get kids to read *The Scarlet Letter*.

And yet, the system seems to work. A while back, I conducted an informal survey among high school students I know, asking them to evaluate the books they had read over the past few summers. My polling sample was admittedly skewed, as I refused to speak to self-congratulatory illiterates or girls coiffed like Lisbeth Salander. Nevertheless, the results stunned me. Even though today's pandering, smorgasbord-style reading lists regularly include works by such non-Nobelists as Dean Koontz, along with pitchers of slop like *Shakespeare Bats Cleanup* and *The Earth, My Butt, and Other Big Round Things*, the kids I talked to had mostly spent the past few summers reading books that could reasonably be described as "good." Though they were not always bubbling with enthusiasm for these books, they generally used no term more euphemistically abusive than "interesting" to describe *Beowulf*. Though no one mentioned *The Return of the Native*, still on many reading lists, one college-bound senior did tell me that she actually enjoyed *Middlemarch*, even though it took all summer to wade through it.

"What I didn't enjoy was writing all the chapter summaries to prove that I'd read it," she says. "*Middlemarch* has eighty-six chapters."

I know. You don't need to tell me.

Other students were less enthusiastic but still reported enjoying the assigned books, if only because they got to read them in peace without having to examine them in the autopsy style that is the hallmark of the high school literature class. Of course, there was always the possibility that the kids were lying, merely telling an adult what he wanted to hear out of fear that any untoward comments would be reported to the authorities. But even if this was true, I ended up feeling a grudging admiration for what English teachers were trying to achieve. The theory seemed to be that smart kids would eventually outgrow featherweight homilies like *To Kill a Mockingbird* and move on to something slightly more culturally authentic, like James Baldwin or Richard Wright or Toni Morrison or Ishmael Reed, whereas if you could get less gifted kids to read anything at all, you were way ahead of the game. In this sense, fleeting favorites like *The Curious Incident of the Dog in the Night-Time* and Harper Lee's inspiring but historically suspect novel about Just the Nicest White Man Ever serve as a vital bridge between books that amuse and books that astound. Until I was sixteen I thought Agatha Christie was the greatest writer who ever lived. Then I found out that she wasn't. When I was in high school, I thought that *God Bless You, Mr. Rosewater* couldn't be topped. Oh, yes, it could. Nobody gets to Balzac and Proust without first going through Camus; nobody gets to *Moby-Dick* without first making the acquaintance of *The Old Man and the Sea.*

My sole remaining beef about summer reading lists was their cavalier juxtaposition of the titans and the knuckleheads, as if David Copperfield and David Baldacci were in the same weight class. It's possible that minor books can lure readers to major ones, functioning as a cultural Venus flytrap, but crummy books only lead to more crummy books. There is a direct line from *Slaughterhouse-Five* to *War and Peace*, from *The Red Pony* to *The Red and the Black*. *Sister Carrie* might pave the way for *Anna Karenina*, but *Carrie* would only pave the way for *Cujo*.

Even my son, who ended up studying classics in college, seemed to realize that summer reading was, on balance, a valuable experience.

"I hated *A Tale of Two Cities* until I got to the end," he told me a few years later. "I wasn't interested in the characters, and I didn't believe the history. But then when I got to Sydney Carton up there on the scaffold, I thought, *Wow, what a great ending.* I really liked it the second time I read it."

"You reread *A Tale of Two Cities?*" I exclaimed in disbelief. "After all that moaning and groaning about how much you hated it?"

"Yes," he replied. "It wasn't as good as *Great Expectations*, but those last twenty-five pages were amazing."

This admission impelled me to reevaluate everything I'd ever believed about summer reading. For more than four decades I'd been cursing the day my high school English teacher was born, convinced that the time I'd spent on *The Return of the Native* had robbed me of all hope of human happiness. But if my son's experience held true, perhaps it was simply a case of my being too young to appreciate Hardy's genius. Determined to clear up this matter, I picked up a copy of Hardy's rustic masterpiece and gave the Bard of Dorset a second chance. I got as far as page six, where my eyes alighted upon this sentence:

To recline on a stump of thorn in the central valley of Egdon, between afternoon and night, as now, where the eye could reach nothing of the world outside the summits and shoulders of heathland which filled the whole circumference of its glance, and to know that everything around and underneath had been from prehistoric times as unaltered as the stars overhead, gave ballast to the mind adrift on change, and harassed by the irrepressible New.

That's when I took it back to the library. Thomas Hardy had wrecked my youth; there was no way he was wrecking my golden years, too.

A person's relationship with books does not remain static throughout his life. As young people mature, they may outgrow authors they loved in their youth. But jilting one's first loves is an action that must be handled with delicacy, respect, and affection. You cannot toss Hans Christian Andersen or the Brothers Grimm onto the junk heap just because you've discovered Lewis Carroll. It's not fair.

Sometimes even the most loyal reader may feel a need to part company with a writer he once admired greatly. It is almost as if one is picking a fight, looking for an excuse to bid an old lover goodbye. This has happened to me with Henry Miller, John Cheever, and, more recently, Henning Mankell, whose last few books have been phone-in jobs. I was halfway through Ian McEwan's *Saturday* when I suddenly realized that every single character in the book revolted me. So did every character in his previous novels, *Amsterdam* and *Atonement*. I trial-ballooned this opinion and found that many of my friends felt the same way. The consensus was that McEwan was one of those writers who had steadily become less and less interesting as he became more and more famous. For some reason, this reminded me of Hemingway's line in *A Moveable Feast*: "He ends up rich himself, having moved one dollar's width to the right with every dollar that he made." Take that, F. Scott. Nothing McEwan had written in the past twenty years was on a par with *Black Dogs* or *The Child in Time* or *The Comfort of Strangers*. It didn't help that McEwan had taken on airs. It didn't help that he was starting to confuse himself with Flaubert.

I had not expected this reaction from my friends. I had not always been terribly interested in other people's opinions about books, but perhaps in the twilight years of my life I was prepared to widen my reading circle beyond its long-standing membership of one. It pleased me to know that so many of my friends had gotten off the train at the same station as me, that my dislikes were also their dislikes. I began quizzing them about this subject, though in truth it was more like grilling them. I sent seventy-five friends a detailed questionnaire regarding their reading habits, dreams, dislikes, passions. Were there books they could never get out of their heads? Did their taste in books affect their relationships with other people? I also warned them about the consequences of not responding: e-mails, phone calls, merciless satire. And then I sent them nagging e-mails and made follow-up phone calls to clear up specific issues. Their ages mostly ranged from forty to sixty-five, though there were also a few of my children's friends for whose opinions, inexplicably, I had developed a modicum of respect. I wanted the survey to be as scientific as possible, even though it obviously wasn't, because it only included people who have the same obsessive relationship with books that I do and studiously ignored the masses.

To some, my queries must have seemed like drudgery, homework that interfered with their reading. Usually they would start off with a curt, perfunctory "yes" or "no" to questions like "Are there books you feel that you need to read before you die?" without even bothering to supply the titles, which was the whole point of the exercise. Or, if they did, they mentioned something by Halldór Laxness or Elisabeth Kübler-Ross, which led me to believe that they were not entering into the spirit of things. But sooner or later, as they worked their way through the questions, something clicked. Sooner or later, one of the questions would pique their interest and they would jump all over it, raving about *Lolita* or *Pale Fire* or *Bend Sinister*, as if they had been employed by the marketing arm of Nabokov, Inc.

Typical was the response to the question "Did you ever stay home from work to read a book?" Yes, admitted quite a few, and "I wish I'd done it more often," said others. Four people in publishing said that they had deliberately chosen a profession that would allow them to stay home reading and pretend that it was work. I knew what they meant; I once skipped work for an entire week so that I could lie on the sofa and read ten Ruth Rendell novels, and then I tucked into three others she had written under the name Barbara Vine. The work I was doing at the time sickened me; I dreaded going into the office. And I am self-employed.

"One time, I was so engrossed in *Rosemary's Baby* that I let my husband go to a Christmas party alone," recalled a journalist friend.

Added an Englishman who had recently made a film about ethically suspect pet detectives: "When working at Princess Plastics in Yeovil on the night shift, I used to interfere with the programming of the metal press in order to read."

"I can't remember staying home from work, but I once ducked out of a funeral to finish a book," said a woman I have known for forty years without once suspecting that her most prized possession is the Golden Books edition of *Little Red Riding Hood* that her grandmother used to read to her until "her tongue got tired."

"Why did you skip the funeral?" I asked.

"They were burying my aunt, and I never liked her," she replied.

"Any particular reason?"

"She was always making snippy comments about me."

"Do you remember the book you read that day?"

That one seemed to stump her.

"Nineteenth century. Scott, maybe Hardy. Could have been Trollope."

"How old were you at the time?"

"Forty-two."

Friends constantly singled out writers they had outgrown or discarded. The same names came up again and again: Kurt Vonnegut, J. D. Salinger, Anaïs Nin, Jack Kerouac, Hermann Hesse, Henry Miller, and on two occasions, Mary Renault. That one caught me by surprise. Less surprising was when nobody reported outgrowing Shakespeare. My brother-in-law, a painter to whom I have sent eighty-seven books that I no longer wanted over the years, said that he loved *Catch-22* but hated everything else by Joseph Heller. Others mentioned special cases like Albert Payson Terhune and e.e. cummings, where something objectionable in the author's background later came to the surface, forcing readers to reappraise their relationship with the author. "After John Dos Passos and Erskine Caldwell started calling for the bombing of North Vietnam, I stopped reading them," said a French friend who is a painter and museum curator but who also publishes exquisite books about the history of the rhubarb and the leek at his own expense. A French intellectual *par excellence*, he added, "When you meet a fan of Richard Brautigan, it's almost as if we were speaking of a common relative."

At least half my friends owned a copy of every book they loved, and most of them still owned the physical copies of the books they worshipped as children.

"I own all my favorite books, and when I see secondhand copies in bookshops, I buy them and force them on friends," said a radio producer who grew up in the north of England.

"I collect volumes of *Cyrano de Bergerac*," said a literary agent who talked me into becoming a freelance writer and thereby changed my life. She was a waitress at the time. Or perhaps she worked in customer service. "I love that book so much that anytime I see it, I buy it."

"Any book that's a favorite, I own," said a magazine editor from London. "Although an exception: I don't have *A Confederacy of Dunces* anymore, because the copy I owned and read several times went missing from work and I haven't wanted to replace it with a copy which has less personal history."

"I still have all the books I grew up with," my son said, "but since I'm only twenty-five, it's too early to say which books shaped my life."

Were there books that people felt they had to read before they died? Oh, yes. Over and over, friends singled out *Remembrance of Things Past*, *Ulysses*, *Finnegans Wake*, *The Magic Mountain*, *War and Peace*, *The Brothers Karamazov*, *Tristram Shandy*, *Buddenbrooks*, *The History of the Decline and Fall of the Roman Empire*, Boswell's *Life of Johnson*, *The Rise and Fall of the Third Reich*, and *Middlemarch* as peaks they must one day scale, though they doubted that they would ever do so. A couple also mentioned Halldór Laxness, but again, I didn't take it personally. More than a handful listed the Bible as a dimly envisioned, long-term project, including a gifted author of bisexual erotic fiction who used to write melancholy country-and-western songs. The lead guitarist from my high school rock band, now a psychologist, said that he enjoyed the Old Testament but found the New Testament "stupid." His opinion must be taken with a grain of salt, however, as his last name is Goldberg. And he likes science fiction, so where he gets off calling *The Word of God, Version 2.0* "stupid" is beyond me.

Friends also listed daunting titles of more recent provenance, like *Gravity's Rainbow* and *The Savage Detectives* and *The Wind-Up Bird Chronicle* as looming fortresses that might ultimately prove impregnable. These were mountains that they badly wished to climb, but in order to do so, they were going to need Sherpas. Lots and lots of Sherpas. Most people said there were somewhere between one and five books they felt they had to read before breathing their last, though one listed thirteen individual titles, including *Pnin, Eminent Victorians*, and *The Moonstone*, plus a number of unspecified works by Vita Sackville-West, and such general categories as "all of Proust," "all of Gertrude Stein," "more Balzac," "more Tolstoy," and "more Dostoyevsky," rounding things out with "the complete works of Vivekananda." She is from Baltimore and dances to the beat of her own drummer.

Only three people had no desert island reading list. Two said they simply didn't care if they never got to Joyce and Proust, and the third, a young man who had just returned from a year's service as a Marine Corps intelligence officer in Afghanistan, remarked, "I'll be depressed enough about dying."

Another question in my survey asked: "How many people's opinions on books do you value?"

"Two, and one's dead," said the woman who stayed home from her aunt's funeral reading Sir Walter Scott. Or Thomas Hardy. Or Anthony Trollope. Others said: None. None. A few. None. Not many. None, and definitely not yours, not after you went on that Icelandic kick. Mostly they relied on book reviews or friends' tips when choosing a book, though one friend, a librarian, said that he insisted upon "a chorus of recommendations." "A chorus?" I asked.

"Yes, a chorus," he replied. "You know, as in 'listening to the tribal drums'?"

Okay. Sure.

An artist friend said that she would only buy a book if it had a beautiful cover. That left out the Bible. The artist paints beautiful pictures. I own six of them. In fact, she paints beautiful pictures of books that have beautiful covers. *The Princess Casamassima*, for one. All this is very postmodern.

A friend who works in educational publishing said that he never discussed books with strangers, because he found the subject "intrusive." Several said that they would launch preemptive strikes against people they had just met whose company they enjoyed but whose reading tastes they had reason to fear. They headed them off at the pass by announcing early in the relationship that they didn't read much and never accepted reading suggestions from anyone, because if they discovered that their friends considered *Lord of the Rings* or *Harry Potter* serious literature, they would find it difficult to remain friendly.

"I had to give up a friend because she insisted that I read Lee Child," said a magazine editor of my acquaintance. "And I am careful never to ask about *Eat, Pray, Love*, as I would like to retain some women friends."

"I wouldn't have any friends if I let them know what I think of their taste in books," said a retired language teacher. "Not any."

"I've never ended a friendship over a book recommendation," said a reformed publicist whose father's illness compelled her to spend several years in a section of northern Florida that was fiercely anti-intellectual, even by the standards of the Citrus State. While there, she joined five book clubs and lived to regret all of them. "I must say that whenever a woman started raving about *The Bridges of Madison County*," she recalled, "I could literally see her IQ dropping before my very eyes."

"I had a friend, now a former friend, who recommended some of the best books ever," said one of the few people I know whose tastes parallel mine. "Our friendship probably went on a lot longer than it should have just because I wanted regular access to her book recommendations. I wonder what she's reading now. Maybe it's time for détente."

In discussing books that could suffocate a burgeoning friendship right there in the nursery, the name Ayn Rand came up constantly. I even warned one of my daughter's otherwise sensible, intelligent, and even likable friends, who had infelicitously identified *The Fountainhead* as her favorite book, to purge this from her Facebook profile immediately. Otherwise, thirty years down the road, when she was being considered for the position as the first distaff chairman of the Federal Reserve, that information could come back to haunt her. The same went for *Atlas Shrugged*.

Only two people in the survey acknowledged writing in their books.

"You're not supposed to write in books," snapped a friend who has the copy of *The Silent Spring* that she read at age sixteen. "Books are sacred." But a man who once wrote speeches for George Herbert Bush—it didn't work—disagreed.

"I write in books indiscriminately," he reported. "So did John Adams. Have you seen his marginalia in his copy of Washington's Farewell Address? Hilariously mean."

My sister Eileen also writes in books. She works in the healthcare field, which I do not. But perhaps it is in our genes.

"If the editing is bad, I correct the mistake," she told me. "If there is a serious mistake, such as a direct contradiction of something that was said earlier, I underline it and write rude remarks. I do not take notes. I simply say the line or lines over and over again in my head when something strikes me as particularly well written."

Books seemed as real to people as anything else in life: food, career, relationships, modern dance. "If I were blind, I don't think I could live anymore," said a young book editor whose parents designed a quota system when she was a little girl, stipulating that if she sat at the table and spoke to adults for a fixed amount of time, they would let her go off and read. "My great-grandmother went blind in her early eighties and spent the next fifteen years without being able to read. She would always say, don't get old, don't lose your eyesight, nothing is more boring than knowing that you'll never be able to read a book again." Others said they would feel similarly bereft if they suddenly found themselves eyeless in Gaza.

"Reading reminds me what it is to be human," said a physicist friend.

"Reading means I can lead quadruple lives any old time I open a book," said a children's book writer. "I've learned as much about people, culture, science, history, politics, other lands—criminy, other universes—from books as from actual lived life. To paraphrase Emily Dickinson, there is no aircraft carrier like a book."

"Reading gives me hope," said a fellow journalist.

"Reading means that tomorrow may not be as bleak as today," said my daughter.

"What does reading mean to you?" I asked a friend who once produced a film about the Afghan version of *American Idol*.

"Being a human being," he replied.

The centrality of books to our existence cuts both ways, though. There are two books, or at least two passages in books, that I wish I had never read. The first is the rat scene toward the end of *1984*; everybody mentions that, including a close friend, a Vietnam vet, whose G.I. buddy woke up one morning to find a rat sitting on his face. My friend also had a rat living in his desk over there in Southeast Asia that he eventually had to beat to death with a hammer. The second passage that sticks out for me is an extraneous sequence in Haruki Murakami's *Sputnik Sweetheart*, where he discusses the death by impalement of the Greek freedom fighter Athanasios Diakos in 1821. Just for good measure, the Turks also roasted him on an open fire. It took him three days to die. Not all of this was in Murakami's book, but I looked it up on Wikipedia and now, for some reason, I have never been able to stop thinking about it. Perhaps if it had only taken him two days to die, I could. Amazingly, the flaying scene that occurs in the same author's *The Wind-Up Bird Chronicle* did not upset me in the least.

Others shared unnerving reading experiences. One woman said that six decades later she is still haunted by the woodcut drawings of hanging victims, their feet dangling in the air, that she happened upon in a copy of "The Ballad of Reading Gaol" when she was just seven years old. She was also fleetingly traumatized by a book about a woman who had an affair with a lizard.

"Is there a passage from a book that is a recurring nightmare to you?" I asked my correspondents.

"Yes, and for this reason I hate Jerzy Kosinski," said my sister Eileen.

"The description of domestic life in Willa Cather's 'Paul's Case,' which reminded me of my childhood, and not in a happy way," said an editor friend.

"Almost certainly something from the MCDP-1, the Marine Corps Doctrinal Publication *Warfighting*," said the young Afghan Theater war vet.

"The accident scene in *The World According to Garp*," said a woman who refuses to read books that are sad. Presumably, she did not finish that one. Then, from straight out of left field, came this remark from a man in the medical billing industry, who gave my son his first job: "I keep going back to that line from *Gatsby*, 'So we beat on, boats against the current, borne back ceaselessly into the past.' For some reason, I can't get it out of my head."

A subject cited by more than one person was marital discord stemming from divergent reading habits or incompatible tastes.

"My husband always hated it when he would come home and find me reading," said an environmentalist friend and teacher, who described herself as "a book widow," though in fact it was more the case that her book-loathing husband was a book widower. "He thought that I should live life instead of reading about others. He thought that I should devote more attention to him, that the book I was reading was actually competing with him. I should have divorced him sooner."

Volunteered another: "As soon as I saw my future husband reading *A Separate Peace* back in college, I should have known not to marry him."

"I would never end a friendship because of a book recommendation," said a retired New York City schoolteacher. "But my first husband did like *The Fountainhead*. Hmmm . . ."

Generally speaking, my friends' tastes did not overlap with those of their spouses or partners, and even when they did, there was sometimes an odd twist.

"Listening to my wife's thoughts on books is one of the joys of our thirty-plus years of being together," said a friend whose job in the educational field requires knowing everything there is to know about everything. "This was not the case with my starter wife in our four years of mutually induced misery."

"I met my husband in Shakespeare class, so that was an auspicious start," said the woman who was once locked inside Mark Twain's house with me. "We had shared authors we loved: Mark Twain, Oscar Wilde, Samuel Beckett, James Joyce, John Cheever, Graham Greene. I grew to love them more because he loved them. However, I worship the female greats: Willa Cather, George Eliot, Edith Wharton, Alice Munro. My husband has zero interest in women authors. Alas, the recommendations go in only one direction, from him to me."

Still, that was something.

"Do I value my husband's taste in books?" asked a friend who works in publishing. Her tone was one of incredulity. "You've met my husband."

A slightly different dynamic is at work in my house. I *do* value my wife's taste in books, but I choose not to mimic it. My wife and I, complete opposites in temperament, have very different tastes in books. This makes for a useful division of labor. She reads Anthony Trollope so that I do not have to, in the same way that she carries out staggering amounts of *pro bono* work in the community so that I do not have to do any. English by birth and disposition, she occasionally reads books about the Raj, some of which I have given her, none of which I will ever read myself. She reads books about intrepid if deranged explorers and incurable diseases and the plight of harried London midwives and the formative years in the life of Samuel Beckett before the gloom settled in for good, and is the only person I have ever met who has read not one but two William Gaddis novels. Sometimes she talks with me about these reading experiences, once again sparing me the ordeal of having to read the books themselves. In this sense she serves the same function as the seasoned, dependable book reviewer, telling the reader just enough about *The Recognitions* or

Carpenter's Gothic or *The Barchester Chronicles* or *2666* to make him sit up and pay attention but not enough to make him want to go out and buy them. Or read them.

My wife, who has the remarkable ability to read in bed with her head propped up on a pillow—an almost Tantric skill that I have never mastered—never recommends books to me, as she cannot figure out what I will like. She also does not care. For many years she would give me a book about Winston Churchill as an emergency Christmas present—*The Churchill Nobody Knows, with the Possible Exception of Yours Truly—Old Squiffy*; *Churchill Takes One for the Team*; *Winnie Saves the Day!*—until one year she found herself backed into a corner with no more Churchilliana left in stock at the local Barnes & Noble, save for *The Collected Speeches of Winston Churchill*. Which she then gave me. I like Winston Churchill the man, and I like books both by and about Winston Churchill—I have read *A History of the English-Speaking Peoples* twice—but too much of a good thing can be a bad thing, and that last Churchill volume was a bit on the dry side. The following year, I asked my children to serve as intermediaries and tell her to stop buying me books about Winston Churchill and instead give the money to some worthy cause: the Red Cross, the Children's Aid Society, Médecins Sans Livres de Churchill. After that she stopped giving me Christmas presents, period.

On rare occasions, my wife will read a book that I recommend to her, but she rarely finds the experience pleasurable. I was sure she would be bowled over by the elfin charm of Penelope Fitzgerald's *The Golden Child*, but she was not at all amused, finding the whole thing "a bit too precious, a bit too British." She was also disappointed by a Salman Rushdie novel I gave her, and was equally blasé about V. S. Naipaul. She did enjoy a short biography of Cary Grant that I passed along, and an oral history of the Beatles. We have been married for thirty-five years, and in that time she has read no more than seven books I have championed, which works out to one every five years. Yet she seems to like the books I buy her. This may be because I take great pains to buy presents for people that they will actually enjoy, meaning that I almost never buy presents that I would enjoy. Every year, when her birthday comes around, I try to find an Anthony Trollope novel she has not read or, failing that, a lesser-known work by Henry James. My wife is the most intransigently optimistic person I have ever met, yet before switching off the bedroom light every night she likes to read Henry James for forty-five minutes or so. It is all quite beyond me.

My son and I have the same taste in movies—films where things get blown up—but we do not have identical tastes in books. We both like books about Alexander the Great and Mark Antony and George Armstrong Custer, but we disagree on science fiction. My son adores books about outer space and parallel universes and events that transpired long, long ago in a galaxy far, far away. My failure to nip this passion in the bud is perhaps my only failing as a father. For years he has been trying to get me to read Frank Herbert, always falling back on the tried-and-true bromide "You can't criticize something if you haven't read it." To which I reply: "That's like saying that you can't make fun of Burning Man because you've never been there. You can imagine how much you'll hate it. You can extrapolate from the known facts." My son, to my horror, owns two copies of *Dune*. But he also owns two copies of *The Iliad*. In baseball, a .500 batting average will get you into Cooperstown.

"You want to leave your children well fixed at the end of your life?" says my friend who skipped her aunt's funeral. "Leave them with books."

My daughter, a neuroscientist, knows exactly what I like to read. She regularly gives me books about science and art and history. The science books are accessible items, geared toward the layman. She almost never gives me a novel. She plays it close to the vest. In return, I give her books like *A Death in the Family* and *The Periodic Table* and *Peter Pan*, books she often reads the same day she receives them. As with my wife, I give her superb, highly readable items that I am probably not going to get to myself. But it's nice that somebody in my family has. My daughter recently confessed to me that when she was around eleven or twelve, she used to duck under the covers at night and devour books about Jack the Ripper and Vlad the Impaler. I had no idea. Perhaps the student newspaper she put together, entitled *The Daily Bloodsucker*, adorned with the blaring headline "The Man with the Wooden Stakes" that has hung directly above my desk for the past sixteen years should have been a tip-off. Perhaps this is why she became a neuroscientist: to more closely examine the part of the brain that makes otherwise normal twelve-year-old girls want to read about Eastern European mass murderers.

My daughter, whose tastes are admittedly eclectic, hates libraries.

"They are everything bad about cemeteries without any of the redeeming qualities," she says. "When I read a book, it is an investment, not a loan. If you don't want to own books, it means you are an asshole."

She also does not understand the group-hug imperative where a friend gives you a book that he or she really, really loves and really, really hopes that you will love it, too. As if it were a litmus test. As if it were a matter of life and death.

"I buy books one at a time, because I want to read them right away," she says. "I want the right book at the right time. I do not want to stockpile them. I do not want to hoard them. I do not want people to give them to me. Each reading experience is personal. You have this moment now. It can only exist in the present. So it's stupid to think that you can re-create it for someone else."

When I asked my daughter if reading was escapism, she answered: "No, reading is the opposite of escapism. It is introversion so extreme that you come out the other side of yourself." When I asked for the list of books she was never going to finish, she rattled off *Moby-Dick*, *Tess of the D'Urbervilles*, *Ulysses*, *Finnegans Wake*, *The Brothers Karamazov*, and *Crime and Punishment*, which she has tried to read no fewer than six times. Four of those titles are on my list of books that I no longer believe I will finish. So, let's recapitulate: She despises people who borrow rather than buy books, doesn't like being lent books by other people, is probably not ever getting around to *Finnegans Wake* or *Ulysses* or *Tess*, and has a kid brother who owns two copies of *The Iliad*. I am starting to believe that a person's taste in books may be hereditary.

Of my sixty-five close friends, only two are not avid readers. One, a college basketball star who later led the European League in scoring, insists that the last book he read was *Bury My Heart at Wounded Knee*. I cannot tell whether he never came across another book that proved equally appealing or if he hated the book so much that he simply nixed the reading habit for good. But I understand one thing: Athletes are all tuckered out at the end of the day, so the last thing they want to do before bedtime is to snuggle up with Henry James. Also, athletes do not need to escape to a more exciting world; they have already lived in one. A second friend, whom I have known since I was thirteen, would not read a book if you paid him. I did offer to pay him, and he still wouldn't read a book. Despite these unbridgeable gaps in our reading habits, I like these two much more than I do some people I know who read Jonathan Franzen and Jonathan Safran Foer and Jonathan Lethem and assorted writers named Colm. Books do not make the man, though they certainly help. That said, as a maniacal reader, I am curious to know what it is like to never read books. I asked the two if was possible for a person who didn't like reading to pick up a book and enjoy the experience. The answer was no. I then asked if reading was torture for them. The answer was yes. As one explained it: "Reading good books is like eating rich food. If you don't have the stomach for it, it will make you sick." He might be on to something there. Reading, it strikes me, is like traveling: If you do not get into the habit when you are young, you will never get the hang of it.

Obviously, with few exceptions, a passion for reading is a prerequisite for my friendship. But it is not a *sine qua non*. When I was young and penniless, I read books in the hope of lifting myself out of the abyss, subscribing to the credo that knowledge is power. Knowledge is, in fact, power. But I read books for another, less noble reason: because it made me feel superior to my working-class father—a ninth-grade dropout—and everyone like him. I disliked the poor slobs I was living among back then, not realizing at the time that not all poor slobs are slobs by choice, that not everybody gets a chance to visit Baudelaire's tomb every week. When I was living in Paris at age twenty-one, I worked three days a week in a fruit market in a small town called Malakoff, directly south of Paris. Most mornings I would drag myself to work completely wasted and bleary-eyed after staying up all night drinking cheap wine and reading Molière and Balzac and Gide. It didn't take long to realize that the men I worked with in the fruit market did not read Molière and Balzac and Gide, and they most certainly did not read Sartre. But they were men whom I adored.

Reading books may make you smarter than other people. It does not make you better. I know things about the Vietnam War because I read them in books. My friend Richie, a nonreader, knows things about the Vietnam War because he went to Vietnam. The man who fixes my car has never read the essays of Montaigne, but he is one hell of a mechanic. The cops in my town have never read John Millington Synge, much less Halldór Laxness. At least, I don't think so. But they are great cops.

As a book lover, I can think of nothing more exciting than the experience of being completely surprised by another person's reading habits. I am thunderstruck when I come upon people who love books whose appeal lies outside the typical purview of their demographic group. In college I dated a girl whose father quit the post office so that he could stay home and read Plato and Boethius and Saint Thomas Aquinas. He never got very far into these books, and I'm not sure how much of the material he absorbed, but the effort was impressive. Then, when I used to write a column for *SmartMoney*, I had a thirty-one-year-old editor who had once lived in a house with a bunch of punks in Washington, before moving to Williamsburg. She may have been a punk. Whatever she was, she wasn't your typical *SmartMoney* editor. Hers was quite the alternative lifestyle. She had read and reveled in Virginia Woolf, Anne Sexton, Sylvia Plath, Stevie Smith. Beloved childhood books she still owned included *The Happiness Flower* by Eva-Lis Wuorio, Gyo Fujikawa's *Fairy Tales and Fables*, and *The Velveteen Rabbit*. She had read Milan Kundera and *The Ballad of Trenchmouth Taggart* and Marie Nimier's *La reine du silence*. All that made sense. But she had also read every last Nero Wolfe book. All seventy-three of them. Rex Stout's Nero Wolfe books are about an obese private detective who never leaves his brownstone in Manhattan's West Thirties, where he tends orchids. He has a rough-and-tumble sidekick named Archie Goodwin who does all his legwork. The books were written between 1934 and 1975, the year my friend was born. Stout's heyday was long in the past. I had never read any of them, even though I like mysteries. Neither had my older sister Ree, who has been smitten by the whodunit genre since she read Agatha Christie's *Easy to Kill* and *The Murder of Roger Ackroyd* at age twelve. I asked my friend how her Nero Wolfe fixation began, and she said that an editor at a gay men's magazine introduced her to the books, and after that she was hooked for life. Later on, after we got to know each other better, she told me that her father had been murdered when she was twelve years old and his body had never been found. It sounded like organized crime might be involved. This might explain why she read mysteries. It did not explain why she read Rex Stout.

I especially love it when I cross paths with someone who has a secret fixation on a writer on whom I also have a secret fixation. It's like being privy to the secret password, but it's also a bit like finding water in a desert. This rarely happens. People are fairly easy to size up: the *Freakonomics* reader, the Deepak Chopra reader, the woman who reads books like *The Piano Tuner*, *The Pianist*, *The Piano Lesson*, *Learning the Piano*, *The Piano Players*, or *The Piano Teacher*: anything that has something to do with the glorious old 88s. More ubiquitous still is the man who will gleefully devour any of the 1,615,000 books that have been written about Abraham Lincoln, be it *Lincoln at Peoria*, *Lincoln at Toledo*, *Lincoln About Six Miles down the Road from Dingman's Ferry, Pa.*, or *Lincoln at Lincoln*. Or *Too Ugly to Live, Too Fast to Die: The Life and Times of Honest Abe* and *Other Than That, Mrs. Lincoln, How Did You Like the Play?* Or even *Why Lincoln Still Matters to People Other Than People Who Write About Lincoln for a Living* and such newly translated overseas titles as *Lincoln, il capo di tutti cappi*; *Lincoln der Mensch*; *Sacré bleu, Monsieur Lincoln!*; and *Lincoln y la vida loca.*

The habits of such readers are fixed in stone. It does not surprise us to learn that the person who loved *The Pilot's Wife* also loves *The Time Traveler's Wife.* But it does surprise us, and it restores our faith in humanity, when a reading passion comes entirely out of the blue. This is what happened to me with my friend Tony.

Tony, just a few years older than me, is a retired Marine who flew combat missions in Vietnam, then worked for many years piloting large corporate planes, ferrying executives around the globe. I used to see him around town from time to time but only spoke with him at any length once a year, when we would both attend the annual shindig of the Tarrytown Garden Club, run by our wives. Far more interesting than most of the other husbands, Tony always had a few choice things to say about Washington, the federal deficit, *The New York Times.* He was conservative, but not rabidly so, and had a relaxed demeanor. From time to time he would send me thoughtful little e-mails after reading something irreverent I had written in *The Wall Street Journal.* I always enjoyed talking to him, though the subjects we covered never included books. This was hardly surprising, as I rarely talk about books with people I do not know well. But one winter night, around 10:15, as the garden party was winding down, Tony glanced at his watch and said, "Well, I think I'm just going to head home and curl up with my Simenon."

I wasn't sure that I had heard correctly.

"Did you say Simenon?" I asked. "*Georges* Simenon?"

"Yes," he replied, as if it were the most natural thing in the world. "I—"

"You mean the Simenon who wrote the Maigret novels?" I said, cutting him off. "The *French* Simenon?"

"He's actually from Belgium," Tony corrected me. "Liège." And we were off. Back at Manhattan College in the Bronx, after signing up for a speech course requiring the delivery of an oral report on a movie or book, Tony had gotten hooked on the Inspector Maigret novels, a good number of which had appeared in cheap English-language paperback editions in the Fifties and Sixties. There are seventy-two, all told, of which perhaps fifty have been translated at one time or another. Simenon, an author who falls into that category of Great Writers Who Are Not Actually Great—at least not in the sense that Tolstoy is great—wrote more than two hundred books. They include scores of psychological thrillers, some set in the United States, some of them quite good, some of them not. Dozens of Simenon's novels have been made into movies, some of which are also quite good. Tony did not especially care for the non-Maigret books; he found them too depressing. I had already read a hundred of Simenon's novels, most of them featuring the indefatigable Maigret. They were all about 168 pages long: terse, economical, enthralling. Simenon's work reaffirmed a conviction I had held for decades: that there is no earthly reason a mystery or thriller needs to be more than 175 pages. Agatha Christie's novels are short. Ruth Rendell's best works are short. After a mystery writer passes the 200-page mark, it's all ballast.

For almost forty years I had been reading Simenon novels in the original, not only because the books are engrossing but also because reading them is a good way of keeping up my French. Simenon is direct and easy to read. But I also love his work because it ceaselessly evokes Paris in an almost tactile fashion, in the way he describes certain neighborhoods and bars and streets and smells. He constantly repeats the same everyday French words—*le comptoir, le bistrot, le demi, la terrasse*—and even when he uses a term you have to look up, it does not prevent a native English speaker from grasping the gist of the sentence. This is utterly unlike Flaubert, who is constantly throwing up obstacles before non-French speakers with his *mot juste* fixation. For me, Maigret is not just fun; he is practice.

This is what puzzled me about Tony's Simenon *idée fixe*. He didn't speak French; he didn't seem particularly interested in the French; and aside from P. D. James, he wasn't all that interested in the mystery genre. But he loved the Maigret novels so much that he had gone all the way to Paris to visit the Quai des Orfèvres, where Maigret's police headquarters was located, and told me that he might eventually stop by the Boulevard Richard-Lenoir, the street where Maigret lived with his extremely patient, understanding wife. Hold on a second; I had lived in Paris for a year and had visited the City of Light more than twenty-five times, yet until I had that conversation with Tony I never realized that the Boulevard Richard-Lenoir, ever so slightly removed from central Paris, was a real place. So the next time I was in Paris, I visited the street where the fictional Maigret had lived for so long. Considering his dour personality, it looked about right.

Over the course of several conversations, Tony told me that he did not even think of the Maigret novels as mysteries, and that he liked the books because he identified with Maigret himself.

"He isn't a Sherlock Holmes type," he said. "He's not interested in the footprint in the garden, the thread of hair attached to the window. His books are psychological studies. He comes in and he looks at the victim's family and he asks questions. 'How long have you been married? Have you always been faithful to your wife?' He wants to find out what makes people tick."

Tony, who also thinks of Rumpole of the Bailey as his *doppelgänger*, adds: "This has been valuable to me in my own life. It has profited me to look at people the way he does. I like to analyze people the way Maigret does; it allows me to get inside of people and understand them."

My fellow Simenon enthusiast, who is trying to learn French now that he has retired from flying, says that he has encountered only one other person who shares his passion for Maigret. I have met no other soulmates. Tony and I have for all intents and purposes founded a Georges Simenon Mutual Admiration Society, Lower Hudson Valley Division. It is a members-only social club, and it is unlikely that anyone else will be joining. Now, whenever Tony spots a French-language Maigret, like *Maigret et son mort* or *Maigret au Picratt's* or *Maigret voyage*, he passes it along to me, and I keep my eyes peeled for new translations of Maigret novels, or reissues of old ones, like *Maigret at the Gai-Moulin* and *Maigret and the Headless Corpse* and *Maigret and the Strangled Stripper*. Our Simenon-based lunches are as enjoyable as anything I have experienced in five decades as a lover of books. For this, I suppose, I owe a debt of gratitude to my wife. That garden party was the beginning of a beautiful friendship.

CHAPTER EIGHT

Life Support

In 1971, Peter O'Toole made a film called *Murphy's War*. In it he played the captain of a merchant ship who survives a Nazi torpedo attack off the coast of Venezuela and is rescued by a tetchy missionary nurse and an amiable French oil engineer. The engineer was played by the incomparable French character actor Philippe Noiret, who was only just coming into his own. *Murphy's War* was directed by Peter Yates, who made several very fine films (*Bullitt, The Dresser, Breaking Away*) over the course of his long career. But *Murphy's War* wasn't one of them.

A few years ago, while riding a train from Paddington Station, immortalized by Agatha Christie in *4:50 from Paddington*, to my in-laws' home in Stroud, where *Cider with Rosie* author Laurie Lee could often be seen gadding about, I started paging through an English newspaper, when I happened upon an interview with Noiret. The interview was conducted on the set of Noiret's latest film. I recall very little that was discussed in the piece, but toward the end of the conversation, Noiret said that if the reporter should bump into O'Toole on his travels, he would be greatly in his debt if he would pass along his best wishes to the actor. The reporter asked if the two were still close friends. Noiret said that while he had thoroughly enjoyed working with O'Toole and was a great admirer of his work, they had not seen each other in the many years since they made the film. But each time he was interviewed by an English journalist, he made a point of asking after his old comrade-in-arms, and each time O'Toole was interviewed by a French journalist, he did the same. There was a bond between the men that could not be sundered by time or distance.

I loved this story as much as any I have ever heard.

One Saturday evening in the early 1980s, I was riding a north-bound New York City subway from Spring Street with my friend Clive Phillpot, the head librarian at the Museum of Modern Art. At the time I was working in a Soho art gallery, minding the store while the manager was off drumming up business that never fully materialized; my first day on the job was the morning after John Lennon died, a terrible day to be selling modern art. The gallery was managed by a woman whose father had starred in *Zulu*, Michael Caine's first movie. Sally was very striking-looking, extremely manipulative, a fabulous dresser, and had quite a tart tongue. One day two rugged-looking men, neither of them art lovers, showed up and asked why Sally didn't pay anyone to cart away her garbage. She said: I don't have any garbage. And they said: Everybody has garbage. And she said: I don't. And they said: Come on, lady. And she said: No, I will not come on. Whatever else I may or may not decide to do, I will not come on. So they went away. In all my life, I never met anyone like her. Some people give as good as they get, but she gave better.

I liked that job very much, even though we never sold anything. It was an exciting time to work in Soho, as the galleries and cafés and exotic boutiques were just opening up, replacing the foundries and sweatshops that had been there before, and there was an air of countercultural mischief in the air. It was post-Beatnik but pre-Slacker. Irony had not yet planted its flag. Soho was teeming with young people, many of them authentic eccentrics to whom one could award the very highest accolade: that one did not automatically despise them the second they opened their mouths. But within three years, corporate America would launch one of its trademark all-out blitzkriegs, and overnight the district would turn into a faux-bohemian hell, the Gotham equivalent of New Hope, Pennsylvania.

If memory serves me correctly, Clive and I were taking the subway up to my Murray Hill apartment to watch Jimmy Connors play John McEnroe in the Masters Tournament at Madison Square Garden. (We were completely blitzed that evening, so it is surprising that I remember anything.) Clive was in a jolly mood, having just returned from a book-buying expedition at the legendary Strand Bookstore, which prided itself on its 357,000 miles of used books. Clive has always been a far more eclectic reader than me—he has never read *Don Quixote*, *War and Peace*, or *Sentimental Education*—but he has read many other books that I have not. Most of them pertain to artists, often strange ones, like Ray Johnson, who once hired an airplane pilot to fly him over an avant-garde festival on Ward's Island, onto which he then dropped several pounds of frankfurters. He subsequently tried to bill his gallery for the impromptu airlift, which he characterized as performance art. The gallery declined the request.

Clive's tastes ran toward political tracts—didactic, long-winded affairs like *The Ragged Trousered Philanthropists*, a book I once owned but may have lost in a fire I started in order to avoid having to read it. He also fancied books like *A Breath of Fresh Air*, a moving account of impoverished peasant life written by the reformed communist and peasant emeritus F. C. Ball. I did not go in for this sort of material, even though I was, in the narrow technical sense of the word, an alumnus of the urban peasantry myself. That evening Clive was clutching a bag stuffed to the gills with purchases he had just made at the Strand. I remember that subway ride distinctly, because at one point a paper bag containing our two six-packs of Budweiser ripped apart and the cans began to roll all over the car. Each time we tried to retrieve them, the subway would lurch, and we would go flying, and the cans would roll just a tiny bit farther out of reach. Our fellow travelers on the subway found our maladroit salvage efforts riotously entertaining. Eventually, we threw in the towel and told everyone to go ahead and treat themselves to the King of Beers. Then we went back to discussing books.

One of the treasures he had acquired that day was *Letters from Prison* by Antonio Gramsci. I was not familiar with Gramsci at the time, but after inspecting the back cover, I learned that in the 1920s, with just the worst timing imaginable, he had founded the Italian Communist Party, which led to his being imprisoned by Mussolini. Luckless Italian Reds never did much for me, but Clive made such an animated pitch on behalf of this obscure collection of letters to family and friends, many of them deeply philosophical in nature, that I asked if I could borrow it. I took it home and set it down among other similarly provocative titles. I did not get to it that evening, nor the next evening, nor any evening after that. In fact, as I write these words, thirty-one years later, it continues to occupy the same space on the bookshelf that it has occupied since the night he gave it to me, right alongside José Ortega y Gasset's *The Revolt of the Masses*, Patrick White's *Voss*, J. P. Donleavy's *The Beastly Beatitudes of Balthazar S*, Ernest Renan's *Life of Jesus*, Tolstoy's *Hadji Murat and Other Tales*, Camilo José Cela's *La familia de Pascual Duarte*, and a few dozen other books I have never been able to part with, even though I have long suspected that I will never get around to reading them in this or any other lifetime.

Why I have never read them is a source of great mystery to me. With the exception of the impenetrable *Finnegans Wake* and *La familia de Pascual Duarte*, which is written in a language I have never learned, none of them is especially long, and with the exception of *Voss*, none of them seems like a book that conceivably could cause the human nervous system to stop functioning. But each time I pick up Antonio Gramsci's *Letters from Prison* and read on the back cover that "the book contains a useful index, as well as an informative and analytical biographical introduction, which sets into historical perspective the thoughts and life of this crucial Italian thinker," I tell myself: *No, not just yet; maybe I'll read* The Best of Roald Dahl *for the ninth time instead.*

In the years since Clive lent me the book, I have found time to read hundreds and hundreds of mysteries whose plots I have forgotten, as well as biographies of Wyatt Earp and Sonny Bono and Gina Lollobrigida and such worthy but nonessential curiosities as *Paris Sewers and Sewermen, The Toothpick, The Olive, The Pencil,* and *The Ern Malley Affair,* an absorbing account of a World War II–era literary hoax that set back the cause of Australian poetry an entire generation and possibly more. Yet in all those years I have never found time to read Antonio Gramsci's *Letters from Prison.*

I think I know why. Each time I look at that book, I hark back to that night on the subway, and the years roll away and Clive and I are young men again. A few years after that subterranean adventure, I gave up drinking forever. I do not miss getting loaded on a nightly basis, but I have no regrets about being blissfully wasted that evening. These days, when I spot a Budweiser can, I do not necessarily think of Clive or of that evening, but whenever I look at Antonio Gramsci's *Letters from Prison* standing at attention like a mournful sentinel, awaiting a relief column that he knows will never arrive, I can see those red, white, and blue beer cans merrily rolling away from us all the way down to the other end of the No. 6 train, and I can hear us laughing. So I will never part with the book, even though I will never read it. As long as my delight in reading Antonio Gramsci's *Letters from Prison* lies in the future, Clive and I will always be back there on the Lexington Avenue local.

I do not think you can have this sort of experience with a Kindle.

Twenty years ago, I bought a sweet little house on a hill high atop Tarrytown, New York, with a sumptuous view of the Hudson River. The property abutted a vast, empty field owned by the Rockefeller family, whose historic family compound—Kykuit—sat a few hundred yards down the road. Because I had grown up surrounded by cash-strapped deadbeats, the purchase was fraught with symbolism.

The house was a prim Colonial with a white picket fence, a second-story porch, and a good-sized backyard. It was really a bungalow with a chip on its shoulder, a glorified cottage that the previous owner had added on to in an inept and unsatisfying fashion to make it seem more muscular. It had a disaster-prone kitchen with a stupid, disruptive island planted right in the middle of it, an obsolete oven of an unconventional size that was impossible to replace without tearing the interior walls to pieces, and a family room with a year-round Iditarod *frisson* to it, sitting as it did directly behind a drafty garage. We lived in that house for nineteen years, never making much of an attempt to do anything about the drafts or the harebrained lighting or the comic-opera stove, because my wife would rather raise kids and tend to the needs of senior citizens and read Trollope than remodel a house, and I would rather raise kids, ignore senior citizens, and read Cervantes. At the time I bought it I was sure that I would live there forever.

You can never get tired of a Hudson River view, but even the most poignant symbolism will eventually run its course if neighbors with a different set of symbols move in next door. Seven years after we bought the house, my son ran inside one day and reported that oddly clad men armed with surveying equipment were mucking about in the fields outside. We now learned that the property had been sold *sotto voce* to a cabal of developers who had plans to build two dozen McMansions directly in back of us. This meant that our days in the house were numbered. We were less upset about the hideous McMansions than about the hideous people who would live in them. A house, no matter how large and tasteless, can only be so ugly. With human beings, the possibilities are inexhaustible.

The first set of pre-fab *châteaux malgré eux-mêmes* quickly went up at the bottom of the hill, two hundred yards from our house, in the adjacent village of Sleepy Hollow. Sleepy Hollow, as noted, is full of venal Yuppies who would have let the developer build a full-scale replica of the Circus Maximus over their mothers' graves if they thought it would broaden the tax base. Miraculously, the other half of the field—the part that was located in Tarrytown and that adjoined my house—remained empty, first because of the 2001 recession and then because of the even more severe recession that started in 2008 and never ended. Meanwhile, the village conducted a series of environmental-impact studies, staying the developer's malignant hand. One day, to our great elation, the developer went belly-up. Throughout this interregnum, there was hope that if the town could delay construction long enough, Americans might come to their senses and stop allowing builders who took most of their design cues from William Tecumseh Sherman and Genghis Khan to tear down hundreds of trees and erect single-family grain silos in their place. But while some parts of the country did eventually turn against these cretinous edifices, Tarrytown is not the kind of town that voluntarily comes to its senses: It is always emphatically behind the curve, and there is no vulgarity it will not embrace.

Eventually the property fell into the clutches of the remorseless Toll Brothers, and ground for the McMansions was broken. As the field in back of my beloved, well-appointed Colonial began to vanish under the wrecking ball, I knew that the time had finally come to prepare the house for sale. Because our children were gone, this was a good time to downsize anyway, to get rid of some things we didn't need. First I went through the LPs. Then I went through the CDs. And then it was time for the books.

This was excruciating. My books have been part of my life forever. They have been good soldiers, boon companions. Every book has survived numerous purges over the years; each book has repeatedly been called onto the carpet and asked to explain itself. I own no book that has not fought the good fight, taken on all comers, and earned the right to remain. If a book is there, it is there for a reason.

Or is it? Do I absolutely, positively have to hang on to my unread copy of *Summon's Christian Miscellany: An Amusingly Informative Collection of Unexpected Facts, Curiosities, and Trivia*? Is there no way I could be persuaded to part with *The Phillies Reader: A Rich Collection of Baseball Literature That Chronicles the Dramatic History of the Philadelphia Phillies* or *Castrated: My Eight Months in Prison*? Is there a chance in hell that I will ever get around to reading *Lust: Bisexual Erotica* by Marilyn Jaye Lewis? What are the odds that my wife will again need to consult *Understanding Pregnancy and Childbirth*? What is a fallen-away Catholic like me doing with a copy of *Unchosen: The Hidden Lives of Hasidic Rebels*? Why is *Sideshow: The Howe Street Carnival* still here? Finally, do I really need to hang on to such voluptuously vulgar items as *Va Va Voom: Bombshells, Pin-ups, Sexpots and Glamour Girls*?

Well, yes, in fact, I do. The first book was a gift from my oldest sister, the second a gift from my youngest sister; without that encyclopedic book about pregnancy, my wife might easily have given birth to simpletons. The book about Hasidic insurgents was written by a woman who played the lead in a low-budget movie I made in 1994; she survived the experience and went on to become a crusading journalist. Her book is a whole lot better than my movie. Adrian du Plessis, coauthor of *Sideshow*, a book about the notorious Vancouver Stock Exchange, helped me prepare a 1989 *Forbes* story that ultimately led to the exchange's demise. It is, as it turns out, the only stock exchange that I have ever helped destroy. *Castrated* was written by Ralph Ginzburg, a celebrity jailbird who gave me my first writing job. While in his employ I met Marilyn Jaye Lewis, whose collection of bisexual erotica moves along at a spanking pace. I have read it once and might read it again.

The final slot on the list is occupied by *Va Va Voom*, which was given to me by a close friend who died too young. When I first began to visit Los Angeles in the late Eighties, Ed was the coeditor of *Movieline*, the only entertainment magazine in American history that did not serve an explicit pimping function for the film industry. On Saturday mornings Ed would materialize at poolside, nestle his gargantuan carcass into a chair, order preposterous quantities of food at my expense, and regale me with hilarious stories about insulting James Fox on the set of *Those Magnificent Men in Their Flying Machines*, the 1965 film his father had produced.

"You don't get the girl, and you don't win the race," he one day informed Fox. Ed could not have been more than thirteen at the time. "Does the phrase 'Get me rewrite' mean anything?" Fox had the precocious little punk banned from the set. At least that was the way Ed remembered it.

I had always assumed that Ed and I would go on like this forever, he phoning me in the middle of the night to say that he was driving down to San Diego to see *The Three Faces of Eve* for the nineteenth time, I phoning him from the upper deck of Notre Dame Stadium to tearfully share the elation I was experiencing in setting eyes upon Touchdown Jesus for the first time in my life. I thought that when we were old men we would take up our customary positions by the hotel pool and he would once again tell me the story about driving a stretch limo right onto the tarmac at LAX to rescue the shell-shocked stars of *Heaven's Gate* after its catastrophic debut at the Toronto Film Festival, whisking them away to safe houses and rustic hideouts and France, where the press could not reach them. Meanwhile, I would see what he thought of my impression of John Malkovich as a geriatric Braveheart. But Ed died long before his time, succumbing to congestive heart failure at age forty-nine. Now my memories of him are forever entwined with a handful of absurd books like *Va Va Voom* and *The Bare Facts Video Guide: Where to Find Your Favorite Actors & Actresses Nude on Videotape* and *Bad Movies We Love*. In the end, I decided that the slapdash biographies of Steve McQueen and Gina Lollobrigida could go. But *Va Va Voom* was staying.

As purges go, this was not a good start, and things never really got any better. For some reason, over the course of my life, I had come into possession of three copies of *Ethan Frome*, a book I didn't even like. So two copies could go. A third book that seemed eminently expendable was a beaten-up old French translation of

Under the Volcano, the Malcolm Lowry masterpiece I had read thirty years earlier, but not in French. One night I was chatting with my college French teacher, with whom I had remained friendly for forty-three years, about my liquidation problem. He had been instrumental in getting me a scholarship to spend a year in France, the nicest thing anyone had ever done for me, the nicest thing anyone could ever do for anybody. Because of this I could never part with my battle-worn copy of *L'art de la conversation*, a drab, ugly, and not especially helpful grammar we used in my sophomore-year French-language class. I told Tom about my predicament vis-à-vis Lowry's *Au-dessous du volcan*, trying to imagine a situation in which it would ever be useful.

"I still have my French translation of Aristotle's *Nichomachean Ethics*," he said. "You never know."

The problem is, there are no books in my collection that I cannot link with a particular time and place, because I always write my name and the date and place of the purchase on the inside flap of the book. Thus, in some sense, all my books are memorabilia. A few hundred books I have kept because they are classics that I constantly reread; another hundred or so were given to me by friends I hold in high regard. The rest remind me of something. That was the case with the French-language *Under the Volcano*; someone had left it behind in a pool hall in Lourdes, and I'd nabbed it. Had they left it behind in a bar in Lille, I might have been ready to part with it. I might never have picked it up in the first place. But Lourdes? *Lourdes?* Saint Bernadette would have clawed her way out of the grave, spit out a couple mouthfuls of dirt, and pursued me to the very end of the earth. A similar situation was obtained with Patrick White's *The Cockatoos*, a short-story collection I spotted perched atop a trash can one day while I was walking down a Manhattan street with a friend I will never see again. I have always found White a handful; I started *Voss* in the summer of 1976 and am still working on it. Physically *The Cockatoos* was a ghastly aquamarine affair, and even though it is a bittersweet reminder of a friendship that is now dead, it is also a reminder of a friendship that was once very much alive. So it stays.

One day, after weeks of making these judgment calls, I decided to see just how many of my books came with a backstory. They all did. Books I bought in Chicago. Books I bought in Fort Lee. Books I bought in Providence. Books I bought in Paris. Admittedly, it was not always the literary quality of the book that accounted for its survival. I kept both *Can You Drill a Hole Through Your Head and Survive?* and Dante's *Divine Comedy* because they were Christmas presents from my daughter. I kept *Grim Legion: Edgar Allan Poe at West Point* because a good friend asked me to review it and I found it highly original and surprisingly entertaining. I kept *Andy Roddick Beat Me with a Frying Pan* because I became friendly with the author, who asked if I would compile a humorous index for the book, in which I ridiculed him for losing a golf match to his grandmother. The score was not all that close. The book is now something of a collector's item; farmed-out, freelance satirical indexes of this nature are rare.

Many books have remained in my collection for idiosyncratic or sentimental reasons. Graham Swift's *The Light of Day* was a gift from an English friend who had worked as the author's publicist. I didn't much care for him, but I certainly liked her. And the book did contain one remarkable passage: "How does it happen? How do we choose? Someone enters our life, and we can't live without them. But we lived without them before."

Road to Purgatory was inscribed by Max Allan Collins, who riveted me for two hours in a Chinese restaurant in downtown

Chicago one afternoon, filling me in on the sad, downward spiral of Eliot Ness's life after he left the Windy City and moved on to The Mistake by the Lake. I read *Radical Chic & Mau-Mauing the Flak Catchers* on the roof of a West Hollywood hotel the first night I ever slept in Los Angeles, only pausing when the hotel manager came up to say that people on the lower floors were complaining about my loud, incessant laughter. So I handed him the book and said, "Okay, you try." *Girl with a Pearl Earring* I bought at Heathrow Airport after appearing on a radio program with Tracy Chevalier; people who have been on radio or TV shows together form a bond that can never be ruptured, having pooled their resources and worked together to survive a potentially disastrous experience. James Crumley's *Dancing Bear* and *The Wrong Case* I picked up in a Charlottesville bookstore where my son was briefly employed. Both books are here for the duration.

For similar reasons, I will never be able to part with *Mister Blue, Op Oloop, Days of the Endless Corvette, Work Shirts for Madmen, So Long, See You Tomorrow*, or even *The Lamentations of Julius Marantz*, all of them gifts from a friend who one day abruptly vanished from my life. Arnold Bennett's mirthless *The Grim Smile of the Five Towns, Jimmy Stewart: Bomber Pilot*, and Gerhard Dohrn-van Rossum's majestic *History of the Hour: Clocks and Modern Temporal Orders* were all books given to me by friends, ex-friends, colleagues, relatives, or my wife; *Creative Insomnia, The Joys of Jargon, The Wizard of Lies, Fools' Names, Fools' Faces*, and *Crazy U* were all written by friends. These are all excellent books, but most people could have parted with them after a single reading. Not me. The same holds true for Oakley Hall's *Ambrose Bierce and the Trey of Pearls*, which I purchased in south Jersey the last time I took my dying mother to her favorite casino, the Claridge. The last time I took her to Resorts International, I bought *Shipwreck* by Louis Begley. I recently read what I had written inside *Ship-wreck* that day:

> *Joe Queenan*
> *January 18, 2005*
> *Atlantic City, of all places*

And so, the two south Jersey acquisitions are staying.

It soon became apparent that Operation Winnow wasn't going anywhere. The whole thing was a farce. One morning, perhaps halfway through my fruitless purge, I looked out the back window and saw that the first micro-colossus was going up at the end of the road. *El momento de la verdad* had finally arrived: The scum were moving in; soon it would be time for us to move out. But as usual I could not decide when we should go or what specific outrage would constitute the last straw. Should we stay one more year, just so we could say that we had spent a full two decades in the house? Why bother? Should we wait until the developers had finished building one of their Halicarnassus-scale eyesores right next to us? Should we wait until all twenty-four ersatz-Alhambras were built and then bail out, profiting from the halo effect, the situation in which people who cannot afford to purchase a house built for *nouveaux riches parvenus* instead buy a house right next door and then bask forever in its porcitectural penumbra? It was all a puzzle to me. Meanwhile, my wife, a practical sort, said that we should leave when we felt that it was time to leave. Well, thanks. That helped.

Predictably, I devised a book-related solution to the problem. I decided that I would not leave until I had finished reading every book in my house that I had not already read. This was a way of putting a time limit on things—say, two years. But I immediately sabotaged the operation by going back and rereading books like *The End of the Affair* and *Beau Geste* and *The Plague* and *Persuasion*, all of which I had read many times before. I then modified the original plan and decided that I would not sell my house until I had read every book that had made me happy while I was living in it. This, of course, would take years. Then I decided that I would read every one of the books that my children had left behind, including *From the Mixed-Up Files of Mrs. Basil E. Frankweiler* and *The Polar Express* and, yes, even *Dune*. This also would take years, none of them pleasant. I continued to devise these jury-rigged templates for implausible reading programs until even I had to admit that things were getting out of hand. When, I asked myself, was I finally going to get around to reading *Jacques le fataliste*? When would the moment be propitious to tackle H. G. Wells's *The Outline of History*? Whom did I think I was kidding in suggesting that a moment in my life would arrive when I would be in the mood to read both volumes of *Titian: His Life and Times*, given that I only owned volume one, or *Livingston's River: A History of the Zambezi Expedition, 1858–1864*? As I devised one fatuous schedule after another, it dawned on me that this was the role books had always played in my life, that I had always used them not only as a diversion and as a way of raising my spirits but as a way of putting off difficult decisions. Now, as ever, I was using books to avoid confronting reality.

Can an obsession with reading prove detrimental to one's well-being? Yes, I think it can. Reading books has not always been a positive experience for me. It has encouraged me to develop a skewed, fun-house vision of the world. Devoting so many hours to reading is the reason I never tore up the revolting carpeting on the steps leading to the second floor in my house, or had the cracked wall in the dining room replastered, or replaced our lunkheaded stove, two of whose gas jets have not worked for years. An exquisite diptych languished on my office floor for four years; I could never free up fifteen minutes to hang it properly, because I was too busy reading Proust. The faucet in one of my sinks dripped nonstop for two years while I worked my way through Tacitus. Bills did not get paid, invoices did not get submitted, calls did not get returned because of my fixation on books. One day I realized that I had not had the picture window in my office washed for the past twelve years. Worse, I had not had the windows in my house washed since the first Clinton administration. All those years, I simply let the rain take care of things while I reread Proust. Sometimes Tolstoy. This was no way to run a railroad.

One day, fed up with not owning a high-definition television set or a Blu-ray player or a garage door you could actually open, I decided to get serious. For the next month I would not read a single page of a book. My only reading would consist of newspapers. I had tried this sort of thing once before, with middling results, but this time, for once in my life, I stuck to the program. Bookless but determined, I managed to buy a 3-D TV, set up the Blu-ray player, clean out the closets, hang the diptych, reorganize my compact discs, replace my blown speakers, purchase a laptop, buy a smartphone, install a new printer, get the three-year-old roll of film from my first and only trip to Rome developed, return seventy-five phone calls, and pay all my bills. I also spent time with my family. Then I went back to reading Proust. To this day, the windows, both home and office, remain immaculately unwashed.

Recently I read a mean-spirited review of a new book about video games. Its thesis was that video games were more exciting and rewarding than real life, so it was no surprise that young people preferred them to what most of us would refer to as "reality." The reviewer thought this was horrible, as did I: What about sunsets and love affairs and long walks along the Schuylkill? But the more I thought about it, the more I realized that my own relationship with books mirrored the relationship so many young people have with video games. I started reading at a frenzied pace when I was a little kid living in a housing project under the thumb of a dipsomaniacal father who was literally robbing me and my sisters of our childhood. Clearly, I read to escape. But so did my sisters. And so did my father. Some of my favorite books—*Treasure Island*, *Kidnapped*, *A Tale of Two Cities*, *Around the World in Eighty Days*, *A Study in Scarlet*—were his favorite books, too. He didn't like being cold, hungry, and miserable any more than we did. If video games had been around at the time, he might have given them a shot, too.

The way I see it, a person develops early in life a pattern of behavior or a set of compensatory skills to deal with a particular problem, but then, long after the problem has been resolved, he does not automatically abandon or at least modify the behavior. Decades after my bitter housing project days were over, I continued to read feverishly, almost desperately, at all hours of the day and night, because reality—even my new, vastly improved reality—was never as sublime as the reality to be found in books. Thus, much like teenagers who get raked over the coals for the years they waste on video games, I could easily be taken to task for the ridiculous amounts of time I have devoted to reading when other, more pressing matters demanded my attention. Christianity took root because it offered the poor an uplifting alternative to life on this planet. Reading does the same. And once you are hooked—on books or religion—you are hooked. Throughout my life, I have let important projects wither on the vine because I was too busy reading. I refused to make any headway on my career until I was in my mid-thirties because I was too busy reading. I refused to cultivate the kinds of contacts that would be useful in my line of work because I was too busy reading. Well, that and the fact that the people were appalling. Yet the long and the short of it is: If I had to do it all over again, I'd do it the same way. If it ain't broke, don't fix it, is my attitude. In fact, even if it is broke, don't fix it.

That said, I now accept that I must stop using my books as a delaying mechanism and sell a house I expected to die in. Otherwise, I will find myself ten years down the line despising the neighbors who live right next door in Babylonian splendor, with their seven-car garage and cathedral windows and swimming pool the size of Latvia, while I myself remain paralyzed into inactivity because I have not yet finished *Middlemarch*. Accordingly, I have decided to pack up our belongings, sell our house, and move somewhere else where I can install lots and lots of bookcases and blow off the next twenty years of my life getting caught up on my reading. Everyone has to grow up sometime, the old saying goes. It's the single worst thing about life on this planet.

There are many sad and beautiful stories about books. After being banished to a backwater on the edge of the Black Sea, Ovid wrote a eulogy in honor of his nemesis Augustus Caesar in the language of the barbarians that inhabited the region. Both the eulogy and the language have disappeared. Homer wrote a comic epic that has vanished without a trace. Fifteen hundred of Lope de Vega's plays are no longer with us. Almost all of Aeschylus's work went up in flames when cultural pyromaniacs burned down the library of Alexandria in A.D. 640. Aeschylus, it turns out, wrote eighty plays. The Egyptians had the only copy of his complete works; it was out on loan from the Greeks. Only seven plays have survived.

Electronic books will ensure that these tragedies—described in Stuart Kelly's *The Book of Lost Books*, a personal favorite that someone has filched from my personal library—never reoccur. That's wonderful, but I'd still rather have the books. For me and for all those like me, books are sacred vessels. Postcards and photos and concert programs and theater tickets and train schedules are souvenirs; books are connective tissue. Books possess alchemical powers, imbued with the ability to turn ennui into ecstasy, a drab, predictable life behind the Iron Curtain into something stealthily euphoric. Or so book lovers believe. The tangible reality of books defines us, in the same way the handwritten scrolls of the Middle Ages defined the monks who concealed them from barbarians. We believe that the objects themselves have magical powers.

People who prefer e-books may find this baffling or silly. They think that books merely take up space. This is true, but so do your children and Prague and the Sistine Chapel. I recently read an article in which a noted scientific writer argued that the physical copy of a book was not important, that it was nothing more than a fetish. He said that books were "like the coffin at a funeral." Despite such comments, I am not all that worried about the future of books. If books survived the Huns, the Vandals, the Nazis, and the Moors, they can surely survive noted scientific writers. Some people will continue to read and treasure books; some won't. One friend says that in the future "books will be beautifully produced, with thick paper, and ribbons, and proper bindings." People who treasure books will expect them to look like treasures. And so they will have ribbons. Another says: "People still paint a century and a half after the invention of the photograph, but the relationship of painting to life is different. I suspect a similar journey for the book." A third says: "Books will survive. Books are in our DNA." "Paper is still a great technology," says a fourth. And a fifth says, wistfully, that books will survive "as a niche, a bit like taking a carriage ride in Central Park. But more than that."

One can only hope.

The reading life I have described has been thrilling for me, but I am willing to concede that people like me are as mad as hatters. Perhaps madder. We have invented a way of dealing with the world that works for us, but it will not work for everyone. The presence of books in my hands, my home, my pockets, my life will never cease to be essential to my happiness. I will never own an e-reader. I have no use for them. A dimly remembered girlfriend's handwriting will never take me by surprise in a Nook. A faded ticket to the Eiffel Tower will never fall out of a Kindle. I am a Luddite, and proud of it.

I was once told a story about a man who fell in love with a woman who lived far, far away. They rarely saw each other, but they regularly sent each other gifts. She would send him books; he would send her music. She did not select the books haphazardly; each one of them meant something. Often written by obscure writers, they were nothing like the books he would have chosen himself, but almost without exception they were poignant and inspiring. The books, mostly novels, introduced him to a world he had never known. There were books by Japanese writers, Belgian writers, Argentine writers, Vietnamese writers. They were exotic, strange, wonderful. During their friendship she sent him forty-seven books, all told, all but one of which he read. When the books arrived, he would take his time with them, not wanting to rush things. When he was done, he would place the books on a shelf and look at them and caress them several times a day, because every time he touched one of the books, he felt her presence in the room. The books were the chronicle of their love affair. They were *prima facie* evidence that two people once loved each other enormously.

Life intervened, and the romance faded. They lived too far away from each other, emotional fatigue set in, they had other commitments, the flame had gone out. They sometimes spoke on the phone but both hated it, because the things they said on the phone were the idle, mechanical chitchat of friends, while the things they said when they were together were spoken in the secret language of lovers. One day the woman wrote and said that she did not wish to see him anymore, that their love affair was over. She would not call him; she would never let the word "goodbye" pass through her lips, because "goodbye" is the worst word in the English language. She vanished from his life. He would never see her again. She would never send him any more books.

He was angry and disappointed, and his heart was broken. He felt betrayed. He took all of the books she had given him and stuffed them into boxes and hid them in the basement. For a moment he came close to giving them away, perhaps even destroying them. But he relented. That would have been inconceivable.

Time passed. He never heard from the woman again, but his anger slowly subsided. It was better to have loved and lost than never to have loved at all. He had read that somewhere in a book. One day he went down to the basement and carried the boxes upstairs and put all the books back on the shelf. He arranged them in the exact order in which he had received them over the years of the love affair. And then he began rereading them in the order in which they had come into his possession. He reread the book about the samurai and the book about the doomed ship. He reread the book about the chess players and the book about the angel of mercy and the book about the tormented explorer and the book about silkworms. He loved these books now as he had loved them then. He would read and reread these books until the day he died. He knew that he would never see the woman again, but the books would keep her in his heart forever.

Only the very last book she sent to him, a novel about a man pursuing a mysterious and elusive woman, he would never finish reading. He had started this book just before the romance ended and was not more than ten pages from the end when the fateful missive arrived. He closed the book that day and would leave it closed forever. For until he had read the final page of the very last book the love of his life had sent him, she would never cease to be the love of his life. As long as he did not finish this book, there would always be one more gift awaiting him. It would arrive like a gift from the future. It would arrive like a gift from the past.

This story does not work on a Kindle.

Jacqueline Calvet, mother of one of my oldest and closest friends, spent the last six years of her life in a Berlin apartment with her daughter and her German son-in-law. She was sickly and frail and the only thing that still excited her was the occasional visit to the public library. In those last six years, as her heart gradually failed her, Jacqueline read two thousand books. *Two thousand*. She was literally using books as a form of life support. She was reading for her life.

My father was cut from a similar cloth. My father and I were not close, but we shared a passion for books. The day he was buried, I visited his tiny apartment one last time. All of his possessions could fit into three plastic trash bags, a metaphor for his monastic lifestyle. He did not own much, and he did not leave much behind. When I entered his apartment, I noticed that he had no food in the refrigerator, no artwork hanging on the walls, a tape player that worked only when it felt like it, and no television. But there were books all over the place. There were books about holy men and books about cowboys and books about the Romans and a book about the Hound of the Baskervilles. There were lots of books about the day somebody died: Abraham Lincoln, John Fitzgerald Kennedy, Wild Bill Hickok, Jesus Christ. As his life wound down, as death closed in, he had shed all the trifles that one does not need in this world. There was nothing on television that could possibly mean anything to him at this point. There was nothing he could hang on the walls that would make any difference now—not a photograph, not a painting, not even a crucifix. But his books still mattered to him, just as they had mattered when he was young and full of hope, before alcohol got its hooks into him. His books still held out the hope of doing a far, far better thing than he had ever done, of going to a far, far better rest than any he had ever known. His books allowed him to cling to dreams that would never materialize. Books had not enabled him to succeed. But they had mitigated the pain of failure.

Reading is the way mankind delays the inevitable. Reading is the way we shake our fist at the sky. As long as we have these epic, improbable reading projects arrayed before us, we cannot breathe our last: Tell the Angel of Death to come back later; I haven't quite finished *Villette*. This is, I believe, the greatest gift that books give to mankind. Every life, even the best ones, ends in sadness. People we adore pass on; voices we love to hear are stilled forever. Books hold out hope that things may end otherwise. Jane will marry Rochester. Eliza will foil Simon. Valjean will outlast Javert. Pip will wed Estella. The wicked will be overthrown, and the righteous shall prosper. As long as there are beautiful books waiting for us out there, there is still a chance that we can turn the ship around and find a safe harbor. There is still hope, in the words of Faulkner, that we shall not only survive; we shall prevail. There is still hope that we shall all live happily ever after.

Acknowledgments

The author wishes to thank Rick Kot, Laura Tisdel, Kyle Davis, Francesca Belanger, and especially Kate Crane. The author is also deeply indebted to his wife, Francesca Spinner. Portions of this book appeared in different form in *The New York Times*, *The Wall Street Journal*, the *Los Angeles Times*, *GQ*, *New York* magazine, *The Weekly Standard*, and the Toronto *Globe and Mail*.